Tuscany

TUSCANY

A History

ALISTAIR MOFFAT

BIRLINN

First published in 2009 by
Birlinn Limited
West Newington House
10 Newington Road
Edinburgh
EH9 1QS

www.birlinn.co.uk

ISBN: 978 1 84158 831 5

British Library Cataloguing-in-Publication Data
A catalogue record for this book is available from the British Library

Endpaper photograph: The Palio, Siena (© Simeone Huber)
reproduced by permission of Getty Images

Typeset by Hewer Text UK Ltd, Edinbugh
Printed and bound by MPG Books Ltd, Bodmin

For Tom Pow

Contents

List of Illustrations

Massive defences kept Lucca independent for many centuries.

Now glazed and decorated, this gateway is one of four guarding access to Lucca.

The portcullis still survives.

The magnificent town hall, the Palazzo Pubblico, of Siena in the Campo.

The Palio, the great annual horse race, is run around the perimeter of the Campo.

A bronze sculpture in Siena of Romulus and Remus being suckled by the She-wolf.

The gorgeously decorated façade of Siena Cathedral.

A elaborate portal to an inner courtyard off one of Siena's narrow streets.

The famous medieval towers of San Gimignano.

The Florentine skyline. Above the line of the Arno, the Palazzo Vecchio and the cathedral.

The Franciscan church of Santa Croce in Florence.

Brunelleschi's dome for Florence Cathedral.

Rich decoration on the façade of Florence Cathedral.

Florence Cathedral and its bell tower, designed by Giotto.

A view looking down the Arno as it flows west through Florence.

Some vestiges of Florence's massive defences remain.

Michelangelo's *David*, the copy in the Piazza della Signoria.

The Ponte Vecchio with the windows of the Corridoio Vasariano on the 1st floor.

The town hall at Montepulciano.

The medieval streets of Montepulciano.

The villa of La Foce, the wartime home of Iris Origo and her family.

The lush produce of Tuscan farmland and market gardens.

The butcher shop in Pitigliano run by the Polidori family.

Four views of the intensively cultivated and stunningly beautiful countryside of Tuscany.

Acknowledgements

In the late summer of 1971 I found myself in Rome's main line station very early in the morning looking for the platform for trains to Florence, or Firenze, as I discovered just in time. Almost forty years ago, in what seems like another life, I was an undergraduate at St Andrews University. Astonishing now to relate in these days of student debts and huge tuition fees, the Scottish Education Department paid for everything, all fees and a maintenance grant of £300 a year. And even more astonishing to relate, St Andrews University were about to pay for my trip to Florence, or Firenze, and give me a further grant for six weeks so that I could learn Italian and look at the great buildings, paintings and sculpture of Tuscany. My travel, bed and breakfast were all paid for, there was an immersion course in Italian every weekday morning and I was to receive 1,500 lire a day for subsistence.

Astonishing, but in 1971 education was still going on in Britain – and Italy, for anyone who could pass the exams, and all of that was considered to be not a privilege but an essential part of studying the Italian Renaissance – the ability to go and see its great achievements for yourself, whoever you were. For a young man who had been raised on a council estate, with no money past what could be earned from part-time jobs, it was the only way I could ever have beheld the marvels I discovered that summer long ago. In the Scotland of the 1960s and '70s I was lucky to receive an education for free and it is nothing less than a tragedy that very few from my background can now afford to see what I saw in the galleries, churches and streets of the great cities of Tuscany.

I had company in 1971. My oldest and dearest friend, Tom Pow, was with me and we forged a bond then which has never wavered. This book is dedicated to Tommie with much love and in memory of all the splendours we first saw together in the Tuscan sunshine. The Italian classes were a waste of time for T.P., but the Masaccios made an indelible impression.

When I left St Andrews I was extremely fortunate to be given a place as a postgraduate at London University's Warburg Institute. Its focus was the study of the Italian Renaissance and I had the privilege of listening to and sometimes working with very great scholars such as Michael Baxandall and Frances Yates. But most of all my tutor, Sir Ernst Gombrich, taught me how to look at works of art and not to fuss too much. 'Simplify, Mr Moffat, you must always seek to simplify.' All the time I was writing this book, I could hear his quiet voice. I hope I listened.

Other voices require ready acknowledgement. The *Insight Guide to Tuscany* edited by Barbara Balletto is excellent, even enclyclopaedic, and I leaned heavily not only on the information in it but also on the keen observations. Dame Iris Origo wrote two very different accounts of Tuscan lives, *The Merchant of Prato*, about the fourteenth-century Francesco Datini, and her account of the Second World War as it swirled around her house and estate. *War in the Val d'Orcia* is a superb piece of reporting and I am grateful to Allison & Busby for permission to quote from it extensively. I acknowledge substantial debts to all the authors listed in the bibliography and recommend all the books to those interested in reading further.

My agent, David Godwin, has been steadfast and sensible as ever, and he managed to persuade my publisher, Birlinn, to do something different by taking on this project. Hugh Andrew, Jan Rutherford, Andrew Simmons and Nancy Norman have all been wonderfully helpful and supportive. Visits to West Newington House are always a pleasure. Liz Hanson has once again adorned one of my books with beautiful photographs and Jim Hutcheson has conjured an atmospheric cover. Many thanks to all.

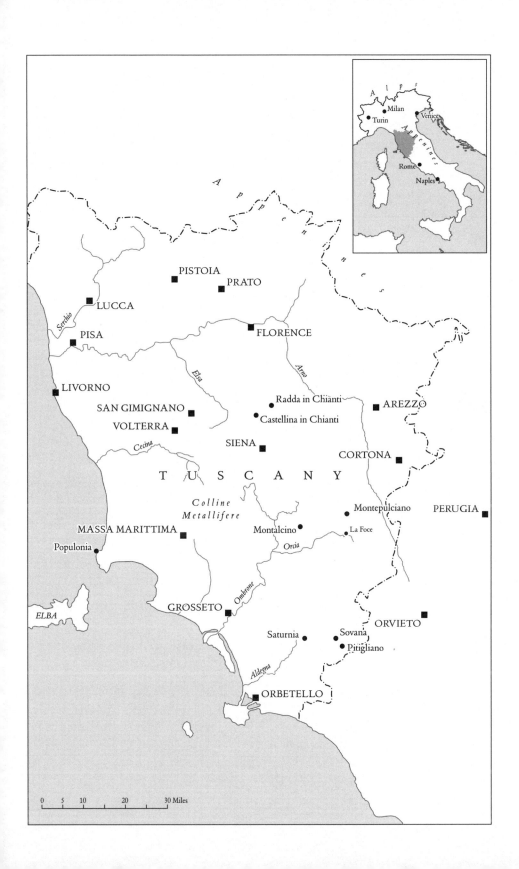

The Dream of Tuscany

In the seventeenth and eighteenth centuries the British began to fall in love with Tuscany, its faded glories and half-forgotten heroes. At first a few pilgrims and artists bound for Rome lingered in Lucca, Florence or Siena, cities which lay on the Via Francigena, the old north road to the holy places and the shrine of St Peter. The famously reluctant traveller, Dr Samuel Johnson, was moved to remark that 'a man who has not been to Italy is always conscious of inferiority'.

By the early nineteenth century the romance had begun to blossom. So many came that by the 1830s *inglesi* had become a generic term for all foreigners. A hotel porter in Livorno might tell a maid that 'some inglesi have arrived this morning but I can't tell if they are French or Russian'. Byron, Shelley, Dickens, Dostoevsky, Goethe, Stendhal, the Brownings, D.H. Lawrence, Virginia Woolf and E.M. Forster all spent time in Tuscany. After he had seen the Giotto fresco cycle of the life of St Francis in Florence, Lord Byron declared himself dazzled, drunk with beauty. Other pleasures beckoned and his torrid affair with the Contessa Teresa Guiccioli led him into aristocratic Tuscan society so that he moved 'amongst all classes, from the *conti* to the *contadini*'. No-one can be absolutely sure how much of a play on words the hot-blooded lord intended.

Much later, Dylan Thomas was also dazzled: 'The pine hills are endless, the cypresses at the hilltop tell one all about the length of death, and the woods are deep as love.' But like Byron and most of the others he spent his time in a miasma of indulgence: strawberries and mascarpone, asparagus and olive oil and Chianti at 20 lire a glass. Few writers managed to do much work in Tuscany as they bathed in its warmth and sensuality, strolling around the great churches and galleries and dozing, sated, in the long afternoons.

What was and remains the hypnotic attraction? The art, the sheer antiquity, the food and drink, the fact that the climate and the landscape appear to be so perfectly in harmony – sunshine over a green and undulating landscape. Lying between the sheltering Apennines to the north and east and bounded by the shimmer of the Mediterranean to the west, Tuscany seems magical. And it looks old, and very beautiful, and very detailed. Punctuated by tall cypress trees, patterned by fields, olive groves and vineyards of every shape and size, crossed by dusty, winding roads and tracks, the landscape bears the marks of the men and women who have worked every corner of it for millennia. Perhaps more intensively than anywhere else in Europe, it has been cultivated and cared for. Between the rows of vines leading the eye into the distance, lavender is often planted, subtle purple beside pale green in the brick-dust soil. Ancient rose bushes sometimes flower at the end of the rows, climbing up the iron endposts. And yet, in the hazy sun the green, pillowy hills seem drowsy under the press of an immense past, even now closely resembling the still landscapes which peep out from behind the blue mantle of a Florentine Madonna or a martyred saint. But of course they are alive, made vivid with the memory of uncountable generations of *contadini*, the farm-workers who made them, the landowners who fought over them and the fire and smoke of war as armies and history rumbled across Tuscany.

The hilltop towns and riverside cities also seem old. Despite the suburban sprawl of shiny factories and freight depots, their hearts have often remained unchanged since the Middle Ages or the Renaissance. Parasol-shaded piazzas show off the enclosing and imposing palazzos, and down narrow streets and lanes, 21st-century shopfronts are crammed into crumbling façades once used by apothecaries or cobblers. Often these warm, comfortable and human-scale townscapes are no more than the result of conservation by default. Many Tuscan cities, including Florence, Siena, Arezzo and Pisa, slid into obscurity after the Renaissance, surviving only as torpid backwaters while Europe's attention wandered elsewhere. But then the British began to come and to fall in love with it all, even if they did not clearly understand why. Amongst the dusty roads, the shaded groves and the narrow streets, a dream of Tuscany grew.

In E.M. Forster's A *Room With a View*, the heroine, Lucy Honeychurch, visits the great Franciscan church in Florence, Santa

Croce, but having forgotten to bring her guidebook, begins to panic. She would become lost, not understand anything of the frescoes, the strange, frozen episodes in the story of the Franciscans and their great saint. And then, 'the pernicious charm of Italy worked on her, and, instead of acquiring information, she began to be happy'.

1

Pitigliano

The town is asleep, fast asleep under the dark blanket of the night. It is long past midnight and in the Piazza Petruccioli only a handful of yellow streetlights twinkle. No-one is about and the silence seems deepened by the fluttering of umbrellas outside the shuttered cafés. Over the parapet by the arched entrance to the town, the ravines plunge down into fathomless blackness. And the high ramparts of the massive bastion disappear into the night sky. On the gentle breeze the warmth of the day still lingers, and there is no need to hurry, head down, through the silent streets. History waits in the shadows of Pitigliano, the story of Tuscany waits to whisper its secrets.

Many of them are to be found in Pitigliano, a spectacular hill-town built on a tongue of rock with sheer cliffs on three sides. In the southernmost quarter of Tuscany, only 140 kilometres north of Rome, it is one of the oldest continuously occupied settlements anywhere in Italy. The cliffs of tufa, a soft volcanic rock, make Pitigliano easy to defend and the fertile countryside around it has nourished its people for a thousand generations and more. The stones of its streets and houses are steeped in Tuscany's history, and on dark, silent nights the ghosts of an immense past murmur in the gloaming.

Through the arch under the bastion is the Piazza Garibaldi and the Municipio, the Town Hall. They cower below the brutal mass of the Orsini Fortress, its hundred-foot walls pierced only by a scatter of tiny windows. The citadel sits astride the eastern approach to Pitigliano, the only one not guarded by the sheer tufa cliffs. Recognising its ancient strength, a division of the Wehrmacht set up its headquarters in the fortress in 1944. Part of the Gothic Line, the brilliant fighting retreat which slowed the Allied advance up through Italy, Pitigliano became a key centre of operations. The grey uniforms of German grenadiers were seen patrolling the ramparts, their binoculars searching the horizon for enemy movement, and below them armoured cars rumbled through the archway under the bastion, past the Medici aqueduct and into the Piazza della Repubblica. Blood-red banners bearing the black swastika were tumbled out of the high windows above the gateway to the fortress, and Pitigliano waited for the attack that would surely come.

On the morning of 7 June 1944 the townspeople heard the fighters before anyone saw them. Screaming out of the cloudless sky, they strafed the walls of the fortress and the buildings close by. Circled stars on their wings, American bombers droned over the summer countryside, the engine noise growing ever louder, and they scored direct and devastating hits on Pitigliano. They completely missed the Orsini Fortress and the German headquarters but destroyed most of the houses on the western side of the Piazza della Repubblica. Eighty-eight were killed, many of them women and children. Even in the darkness and silence after midnight, the only modern buildings in the town loom up across the deserted piazza like new tombstones in an old graveyard.

Piercing them like a sunken road, the Via Roma burrows into the maze of medieval lanes, narrow and shadowy, winding its way back into the past. Stray cats sidle warily along the street – and suddenly swim under the ancient oak doorways of storehouses and stairways. On each side dark alleyways open, running away downhill towards the houses which perch on Pitigliano's cliffs. Five hundred years ago all of Tuscany's towns were like this. In Florence, Pisa, Lucca and Siena people lived piled on top of each other, densely packed, constantly in contact. Gossip, news, argument and laughter left only the wealthy and the pious with anything like privacy or quiet. And unobserved under the cover of the night conspirators met and muttered behind their hands.

Just as the canyon of the Via Roma seems to crowd in overhead, it suddenly opens upon an apparition. The ghostly white marble façade of a cathedral rears up, and an ancient medieval bell-tower soars away into the night above it. St Peter and St Paul look down from their niches, the pillars of Holy Mother Church, its rock and its founding theologian. But the telling dedication, what explains this startling building, is to be found on a discreet street sign. Beyond the shadows of the Via Roma is the Piazza San Gregorio VII and it commemorates the greatest of medieval popes. Born into the Aldobrandeschi family, the lords of Pitigliano, and known as Ildebrando before he was crowned with the tiara, Gregory VII achieved political miracles.

Elected in 1073 by the College of Cardinals, he promulgated a remarkable document, the *Dictatus Papae*, the 'Supremacy of the Pope'. For the first time it elevated the doctrines of papal infallibility, of the right of popes to nominate all bishops and established that God's Vicar on Earth was supreme over all other rulers. And despite the fact that Gregory had no army to back his huge claims, he forced their adoption.

After Charlemagne had been crowned Emperor of the Romans on Christmas Day 800, and had revived and reinvented the Holy Roman Empire, the ancient title had been held by a succession of powerful German kings. When the challenge of Gregory VII's *Dictatus Papae* became clear, the Emperor Henry IV threatened war, mustered armies and planned an invasion of Italy. The impertinent pope would be deposed. But what became known as the Investiture Contest eventually degenerated into a humiliating defeat for the German emperor.

When Gregory VII excommunicated him, casting Henry and his family out of the Church, denying them the sacraments and condemning them to eternal damnation, the emperor's authority began to crumble. The winter of 1077 was more severe than anyone could remember, but Henry and a small imperial party were forced to make a dangerous journey across the Alps. At the end of January they reached the castle at Canossa in the mountains on the northern borders of Tuscany. There Pope Gregory was under the protection of the powerful Countess Matilda, and when news of the Holy Roman Emperor's journey to Italy became known, an attack on the fortress was expected. But behind its walls the Holy Father would be safe.

To the astonishment of Gregory and his supporters, no attack came and instead an extraordinary sequence of events took place. Without attendants, having put aside his royal robes, Henry IV walked barefoot through the snow, and below the gates of Canossa he begged the pope for forgiveness. For three days, dressed in rags, the greatest prince in Europe stood alone and pleaded to be taken back into the arms of Holy Mother Church. And on the fourth day, triumphant, Gregory relented. Absolving the emperor of his sins, accepting his penitence, he received Henry once more into communion with the Church. The amazing story of Canossa spread like wildfire. The papacy was now a European power, able to humiliate emperors and bend them to its will and the will of God.

The cathedral at Pitigliano is an unexpected monument to the events of the winter of 1077, almost buried amongst the jumble of medieval houses and winding lanes, but it is no more unexpected than Ildebrando's invention of the modern papacy. In a gloriously Italian version of respect, his name is often seen in the trattorias of the town, on the labels of an excellent local white wine.

Beyond the Piazza San Gregorio VII runs the street named after his family, the Via Aldobrandeschi. It descends to the oldest part of Pitigliano, the Capisotto, which lies at the very tip of the tongue of tufa rock. The lanes on either side are wider and tumbling out of terracotta pots and tin pails, small flower gardens line the walls and in the balmy summer night their scents float in the soft air. Below the steps up to the church of San Rocco, a spout spills ice-cold water into an ancient cistern. At the end of the street is an open space, the Piazza Becherini, but it is no larger than a courtyard. In the darkness the drop below its parapet can only be guessed at.

The sheer cliffs conceal more secrets. They are hollow with tunnels, old passageways chiselled out of the soft tufa rock which honeycomb under the streets. Sometimes entered from the base of the cliffs, often from openings under Pitigliano's houses, this cool subterranean maze is now used to store wine, cheeses and hams. But once it had another, darker purpose. Some of the oldest tunnels were originally sepulchres, the last resting-places of a mysterious people.

Two thousand years ago the brilliant civilisation of the Etruscans was slowly flickering to a close. For seven or eight centuries this rich and gorgeous society had extended all over Tuscany. It gave the place its name. *Etruschi* is derived from *Tusci* and it is cognate to the Latin *turris,* and it seems that the Etruscans were first known as the tower-builders. Versions of them still stand. Famously in San Gimignano, in Florence, soaring in Siena, in Volterra and most appropriately at Tuscania and Tarquinia, not far north of Rome, the towers of the old cities punctuate the horizon. And on the Capisotto, at the western tip of Pitigliano, there was an Etruscan citadel. Built from massive blocks of tufa, it serves as the foundations of the medieval houses and some of its lower walls still stand at the foot of the cliffs below the parapet at the Piazza Becherini.

Around Pitigliano and the nearby village of Sovana many Etruscan tombs, temples and sunken ceremonial roads have been found. Eighty kilometres to the north-west, near the Tuscan coast, a discovery was made which brought history full circle. Etruscan tombs can be fatally obvious in the landscape. Around the sleepy town of Vetulonia, north of Grosseto, the largest grave-mounds were robbed out very early, in the fourth century BC, when Rome began to gain mastery over the Italian peninsula. Other tombs remained hidden from sight. In secluded, wooded groves, large sepulchres were easily cut out of the tufa, and their small entrances blocked and quickly overgrown.

Close to the centre of Vetulonia one such forgotten tomb accidentally came to light in the 1980s. Gold grave-goods, beautiful miniature sculptures of chariots and horses dating to the sixth century BC and gorgeous ceramics were found. Amongst the floor debris, one of the excavators picked up a small, double-headed axe, too small to be practical. Beside it lay a bundle of bronze rods. At first appearing insignificant, it turned out to be the most remarkable of all the finds. This was the fasces, the quintessential symbol of Roman power, the means to punish and execute – also the symbol of Mussolini and his vile regime. Soon afterwards another example, another bundle of whipping rods and axe, was recognised on a piece of Etruscan tomb sculpture. Fascism, it turned out, had one of its poisonous roots in the Tuscan soil.

When dawn breaks over Pitigliano and the warmth of the butter-coloured sun washes down the houses on the tufa cliffs, the town wakes and quickly begins to bustle. The sharp twang of two-stroke engines rents the stillness and the bars at the Piazza della Repubblica fill with coffee-drinkers who grab a pastry in a paper napkin. No-one sits or stays longer than a few minutes. Metal shutters rattle up as shops and offices open at eight or sometimes earlier and the medieval streets and lanes clatter with footsteps. The occasional car noses impatiently along the narrow Via Roma.

Pitigliano is no museum, but a working town where people live and die. But not in ignorance. Tuscans are everywhere aware of their past, and in countless otherwise inconsequential cultural habits and many colourful public festivals, they celebrate its ancient glories. And the past is not something apart, categorised as history, something separated from the everyday business of living and making a future. It is an indivisible part of life. This seamlessness is very attractive – and immediate. For those who come to Tuscany simply for its beauty, to the place where everyone in the world would like to live, according to one writer, this book is intended as a way of understanding something of that seamlessness, of how it all came about.

2

Before History

In the deepest glades of the forest, where not even the brilliant midsummer sun can break through the canopy, the only tracks to be wary of are made by the wild boar. Their coarse, dark coats half-camouflaged in the shade of the great oaks and the undergrowth, they can be very dangerous if startled, erupting into a charge, their razor-sharp tusks able to rip huge gashes. An enraged sow, protecting her young, has been known to kill, propelling her massive bodyweight over short distances to devastating effect.

The hunters were always wary, carrying their weapons and ready to use them, moving quietly through the temperate jungle. When he gathered his men, the chief would give clear and simple instructions. Those most experienced would form small hunting parties and would follow the boar tracks in the heart of the great forest. The chief huntsman would know where the prey had made their dens and how wide their territory was. The day before he would have looked for signs, their fresh droppings, where they had been rooting the forest floor, and new tracks. At places where he had heard and sometimes even seen the boar, at stream crossings, at the foot of the cliffs, where paths met, the old man would command his hunting parties to take up their positions. There they would use the wildwood as cover, making no sound, waiting. And on no account were they to move.

A second, much larger, group would take their pack of hounds and begin to sweep through the woods, making as much noise as possible, shouting, whistling, clacking primitive wooden rattles. They and their dogs were to drive the boar before them, towards where the hunters lay in wait. With luck, and if the gods smiled, they might kill two or three. And the rich meat would keep.

When the chief huntsman hears rifle shots crack in the still morning air, he knows that the beaters have flushed an animal. And as the yelp and howl of the dogs becomes audible down at the lodge, and seems to be moving across the hillside in the direction he set them, the man known as the *capocaccia* relaxes. Boar hunting is tightly regulated in Tuscany. Each hunt, or *caccia*, involves paperwork, for all those with guns must register, and when the *capocaccia* tells each party where to go, they must do exactly as he says. Gunfire in dense woodland can be dangerous to more than the wild boar, the *cinghiale*, and if hunting parties moved around, not only potentially fatal chaos would follow but nothing would be caught.

The Tuscan boar hunt is ancient, a long echo from prehistory, certainly 8,000 years old, probably more. The only change made in the modern era is in weaponry. Long before rifles, a boar spear was carried by the most experienced – and bravest. To deliver a killing thrust, a hunter needed to get close to a large charging animal with its head down and leading with the points of its tusks. Others fired arrows. These in themselves were rarely fatal but they slowed a fleeing animal and the dogs could track its blood trail as it grew weak.

Hunting wild boar by chasing it, in the way that pink-jacketed horse-riders used to go after foxes in Britain, was not only dangerous but likely to be a waste of effort and time. The use of the drive and sett is also ancient and much more efficient. As the beaters swept the tangled wildwood of prehistoric Tuscany, they put up many other frightened animals, and at the sett, the hunters waited with nets. In 4000 BC there was no sport involved, only survival.

Now, the *capocaccia* must report what his men have killed and if they register to go after *cinghiali*, they cannot touch anything else – no birds, no hares, no deer. If boar are brought down, then more immensely old traditions come back sharply into focus. Each animal is butchered at the lodge and divided amongst the huntsmen. The haunch is most valued because it can be salted and hung up to be air-dried to preserve it. *Prosciutto crudo* means 'raw ham' and while most of it now comes from domesticated pigs, boar meat is widely available. And some of it is hunted in the wildwood.

After the end of the last ice age Italy was quickly carpeted with dense forest, a temperate green jungle stretching away far into the distance to every horizon. As the ice melted in the north, the level of the Mediterranean rose and the western coastline shrank back close to its present line. And as the Adriatic refilled, it crept north to Trieste and

Venice. The Apennine spine of Italy had been very cold during the ice age, what prehistorians call 'park tundra'. In the low temperatures and the chill of the near-constant wind, no trees grew except in the shelter of ravines, and the thin soil of the lower slopes supported only a brief flush of vegetation at the height of summer. But when the ice-sheets of the Alpine range began to groan and crack and the weather improved after 10 000 BC, the tree-line climbed slowly up the mountain sides. Pine, oak, chestnut and beech began to spread their wide canopy over the land and drop their seeds. Watered by the rains of a thousand winters and warmed by summer temperatures close to modern norms, the Tuscan wildwood grew lush and filled with life.

Animals of many kinds browsed the young spring shoots and in the autumn rooted for ripe nuts on the forest floor. In natural clearings red deer grazed, always listening, always alert for the tread of a stalking predator. The famous Tuscan lion is long extinct, and was in any case probably a jaguar. But the memory of this impressive beast was persistent and it lived on in sculpture and medieval heraldry. Perched on a column by the entrance to the Orsini fortress in Pitigliano, a melancholy-looking lion gazes out over the Piazza della Repubblica.

The giant prehistoric cattle known as the aurochs thrashed through the wildwood, almost certainly unafraid of any predator, wolf, lion or jaguar. With a hornspread of up to 2 metres and as big as a rhinoceros, these great grey-coloured juggernauts were kings of the wildwood. Pine martens, polecats and squirrels scuttled through the canopy, beavers felled trees and dammed the streams, bears fished, ate berries and sought out the nests of wild bees, and a host of smaller animals rustled the leaves as they searched and snuffled for food. Several varieties of succulent wild fruit and berries tempted many species of birds, and as the land began to rise towards the Apennines in the east, eagles hunted, flying high and turning their stern gaze on the wildwood below.

The great birds live for many years; captive eagles have been recorded as surviving to the age of 100 and beyond. When they spread their wings and glide in the warm updrafts by the mountains, they can see the shimmer of the sea far to the west. Bounded by the Mediterranean, Tuscany is almost encircled on the landward side by the sheltering Apennines. Near the dazzling white gashes made by the marble quarries at Carrara, on the northern borders, the mountains edge close to the sea. Then they swing away to the east before turning south-east towards the Adriatic coast. These are the natural limits of Tuscany, and only in the south was there a need for an artifical line. In the twenty-first century it follows the low hills north of Lago di Bolsena before reaching the Mediterranean near Capalbio.

During the last ice age the Tuscan coast and the lower-lying land west of the Apennines was cold but habitable. There appears to have been no break in human settlement, and the earliest remains, found mostly in coastal caves or shelters by the lake shores, are half a million years old. But these early people were not like us, not like modern Tuscans.

At several sites archaeologists have found the bones of the descendants of these first Europeans, the Neanderthal men and women. They had long, low and large ape-like crania, massive brow-ridges and a chinless jaw. To protect their brains from shock, Neanderthal noses were broad and long enough to warm up cold air as they breathed it in. Their skeletons suggest long bodies, short legs and tremendous musculature. Detailed examination has discovered evidence of healed fractures, and one scholar has conjectured convincingly that Neanderthal hunting parties attacked their prey at close quarters. Using short, stabbing spears to bring down deer, wild horses, even aurochs and bison, they may have suffered severe injury. It was a bruising, dangerous way of life. Despite the pejorative use of the name, there is no evidence to suggest that Neanderthals were stupid or brutish. It may be that they simply failed to adapt to a changing climate and a changing world.

Between 40 000 BC and 35 000 BC the Neanderthals who hunted the European wildwood disappeared. Their extinction seems to be related to the arrival of new people from the east and south, *Homo sapiens*, the ancestors of modern Europeans. They too were hunter-gatherer-fishers, and archaeologists have found gossamer traces of their lives along the Tuscan coast, especially at river-mouths. These were places where families could over-winter, finding year-round supplies of food on the sea-shore; shellfish, crabs, lobster and edible seaweed. They could fish the estuaries and the inshore waters, and drawing on stores of preserved food from the summer wildwood it was possible to survive. The dried funghi known as *porcini*, dried figs, and roasted nuts, often mashed into a paste, can still be bought in Tuscan grocers' shops. *Pinoli*, 'pine-nuts', are now seen as a delicacy, but for the hunter-gatherer-fisher families of prehistory, they were a necessity.

The early peoples seem to have flitted through the wildwood, passing like evening shadows, leaving little more than soil-stains where they lit fires and pitched their shelters. But the presence of *pinoli* and *porcini* and other fruits of the wild harvest are more than a pleasing tradition. They are emblems of continuity, of a real and living link across 300 generations with the hunter-gatherer-fishers of prehistory.

In his brilliant *The Mediterranean and the Mediterranean World in the Age of Philip II*, the French historian Fernand Braudel developed a thesis out of these fragments of continuity. In what is called the *longue durée*, he argues that climate and landscape, and 'the liquid plains of the sea', have exerted similarly determinant influences over millennia. For the hunters, the fishermen, the shepherds and the ploughmen of the Mediterranean life has certainly changed, but some of its essentials provide clear and unequivocal links with our ancestors. And so by understanding more modern, better recorded lives we may see into the darkness of the past and know something of all that lost experience. Prehistory is alive and it often unconsciously inhabits the lives of country people all around the Mediterranean. And nowhere more so than in Tuscany.

Perhaps one of the most striking examples of the *longue durée* is tree-bread, *castagnaccia*. Chestnut trees live for up to 500 years and each can drop many hundreds of nuts at the end of summer. For thousands of years Tuscans have depended on this wild harvest to make bread. On a griddle over the embers of a fire, ripe chestnuts are roasted and carefully raked off before becoming burned and inedible. Once cool, they are shelled and ground into a brown, faintly sweet-tasting flour. Sometimes it is mixed with the dried grains of wild grasses or cultivated cereals before being baked into flat, tough, unleavened bread. Roman legionaries are recorded carrying cakes of *castagnaccia*, and until the early twentieth century it was a countryside staple. Now chestnut flour is used to make a sweet cake known as *baldino di castagna,* and often it is mixed with chocolate, orange peel and nuts. Few bake the ancient tree-bread any longer; perhaps it is still too reminiscent of hard times, the poor peasant life of scratching a living, gathering food in the wildwood.

A mixed woodland of chestnut trees and pines was not only a source of two sorts of nuts, and of firewood, it was also believed to be the most likely place to find funghi. Much more than just mushrooms, funghi have been hunted for millennia in the woods of Tuscany, and all over Europe. Some are poisonous but there are 230 edible varieties, and fifteen of these are common. White truffles are the most sought after and expensive, but these notions of value will have counted for nothing in prehistory. In addition to nutrition, what mattered particularly to the early communities of hunter-gatherer-fishers was that funghi were easy to preserve. Once dried in the sun, they would keep through the hungry months of winter and early spring. And when they are soaked and softened in water, most varieties taste almost as good as when they are picked fresh.

Usually on September weekends, especially if there has been a period of heavy rain followed by days of sunshine, Tuscans most resemble their prehistoric ancestors. Armed with baskets or plastic bags and a stick to root around with (and deal with snakes), they search the wildwood for food, and a flavour of their long past.

Not far beyond the northern borders of Tuscany, at Arene Candide, archaeologists have found the remains of a hunter-gatherer-fisher settlement which has preserved evidence of what they hunted. Dating to around 6000 BC, the large bones of wild boar mark the documented beginning of an ancient tradition. But other finds suggest something quite different, perhaps the most profound change in human history.

Farming began in Mesopotamia, the fertile crescent between the rivers Tigris and Euphrates, some time before 7000 BC. Animals such as goats, sheep and cattle were domesticated and edible plants grown from seed. Almost immediately, small fields were fenced to keep these animals from browsing young and succulent shoots, and what might be easily recognised as farming communities established themselves. No more than a set of ideas and techniques, farming was gradually transmitted westwards and around the Mediterranean shore. By 5000 BC, the hunter-gatherer-fishers at the settlement of Arene Candide had also become shepherds.

As well as the bones of wild boar, archaeologists found the remains of many young lambs, too young to have been weaned. They had been killed not only for their tender meat, but also for their mothers' milk. Even at that early stage ewes' milk was almost certainly being made into the cheese now known as pecorino. By an unknowable accidental sequence, shepherds and their families discovered how to use rennet to curdle the milk, either taking it from the gut of animals or using the stamens of certain plants, and even funghi. In the cool of a hillside cave cheese would keep for a long time and become another precious winter staple.

Rennet may have been discovered when young lambs were killed and butchered. An observant shepherd will have noticed that their mothers' milk had curdled in their gut, cut it out and experimented with fresh ewes' milk to see if it had the same effect. Some Tuscan farmers' wives still make pecorino at home. As they heat the rich milk in a copper, rennet is added, and when the mixture curdles, the cheese-maker pulls out the curds, squeezing out as much whey as possible. After the pecorino is patted down into moulds, or forms, and then turned frequently for several days, it is ready to be eaten. And it will keep for many months, its wonderful flavour intensifying all the time.

Wasting nothing, the farmer's wife uses the whey to make the soft white cheese known as ricotta. In Italian it simply means 're-cooked'. A copper of whey is boiled up and the white curds lifted out with a slotted spoon. Ricotta does not keep so well as the full-fat pecorino and is best eaten soon after it is made. Farmhouse cheese is much prized in Italy – and it has been made for a very long time.

Drainage helped form the pattern of settlement and cultivation in early Tuscany. River valleys flooded easily, spates tearing down from the encircling mountains in *torrente*, and in the summer they became infested with mosquitoes and malaria. The flat coastal plain known as the Maremma was also largely uninhabitable. Much later, malaria claimed famous and powerful victims. It killed Tuscany's greatest poet, Dante Alighieri, and two popes, Alexander VI in 1503 and Leo X in 1521, were both fatally bitten while out hunting.

Although by no means every valley was intolerable in the summer, many of the early farming communities preferred the upcountry. Much of Tuscany is hilly and wooded, and for the first shepherds, with only very small flocks to tend, no vast tracts of pasture were needed. In any case, the ancient cycle of transhumance appears to have begun very early. In spring shepherds began to drive their sheep, goats and cattle to higher pasture, to new and more nourishing grass, shoots and leaves. Down at their winter quarters, the land needed to recover, and where crops were planted, the absence of hungry animals was an advantage.

The annual journey to the upcountry has been made for millennia. By the early Middle Ages the shepherd-roads in Italy were called *tratturi,* and many can still be made out. Transhumance affected the way in which land was both owned and managed. Low-country villages usually claimed customary rights to high pasture, and often medieval parishes looped up into the hills to include it. The *tratturi* led to clearly defined areas where encroachment by neighbours was not tolerated. In the Chianti hills and elsewhere walkers are often surprised to find walls and ditches marking off what appears to be wild land.

Some of the first farmers in Tuscany may have been immigrants from the south. Around 5000 BC the new techniques spread very rapidly, moving from Greece to Portugal in less than 500 years. What is known as enclave colonisation may well have been the means of transmission. Small pioneering groups, probably a younger generation, split off from established communities and, travelling by sea, went in search of new territory. Domesticated animals and bags of seed travelled with them as the new ideas leap-frogged up the Italian coast to Tuscany.

Where the first farmers settled, they began a profound cultural shift – but also laid down traditions which have remained virtually unchanged over 6,000 years. These reinforce powerfully the sense of continuity over immense periods of time, the *longue durée.*

Farmers have been extremely conservative. Throughout the world there are 148 species of large animals and yet only fourteen of these have been domesticated as farm animals, grown for meat, milk or wool, or all three, or used to supply muscle-power to pull carts, ploughs or carry people. And with plant species the proportion which has been cultivated is even smaller. From 200,000 higher plant species, only 100 or so are grown for food. And almost all of these were first tended or cultivated in the fourth millennium BC in Europe.

Farming also changed the face of the land. Hunting, gathering and fishing did of course continue (up until the present day), but the way in which land was used and the customary rights to it developed in a new direction. It seems likely that hunters exercised rights of some kind in the wildwood, and will certainly have attempted to exclude others from their ranges. A supply of firewood was of crucial importance, and hunter-gatherer-fisher bands will sometimes have been forced to move on when it ran out. But the resources of the wildwood were probably nurtured and areas of it allowed to recover.

When farming was adopted and great labour invested in the cultivation of crops, land became much more securely owned. And defended. Field systems were hacked out of the forest, the process of clearing scrub and trees, and especially their roots, required a tremendous and sustained effort. Those who did the hard work will have developed a very emphatic sense of ownership. Some idea of what these early fields looked like can still sometimes be glimpsed in Tuscany, especially in the uplands.

They were small, more like large patches of garden, and unlike modern fields tended to include several different crops. A primitive type known as emmer wheat and six-row barley were common, but in the *cultura mista,* vegetables such as beans were also planted in the same patches, and around the edges of fields were olive trees, fig trees and others, like oak, grown for timber, for shade and as a windbreak. In the more remote upland areas of Tuscany it is still possible to see the outline of these ancient fields, often with later terracing stepping up the slopes behind. Sometimes the old broadleaved trees, the beeches and the oaks, have been pollarded and not allowed to grow too high, a sign that they were once used for growing vines.

As the techniques of farming moved rapidly westwards across the Mediterranean, the ability to cultivate grapes and make wine appears to have marched in step. Archaeologists believe that wine-making began in Georgia and northern Persia some time between 6000 BC and 5000 BC. These surprising origins are occasionally recalled in language, most notably the popular red wine style known as shiraz. It is a Persian place-name, one of the largest cities in modern Iran, and its association with wine is very significant. Outside its walls several large clay pots were found and they contained the oldest samples of wine ever found. It dated to around 5000 BC, and it was a dark red colour.

Wild grapes grew in the prehistoric Tuscan forests and around the shores of the Mediterranean, but it is likely that these were small and bitter. A helpful analogy might be a comparison between crab apples and cultivated apples. As the new technology spread and reached the coast of what is now Lebanon and Syria, the land of the ancient Phoenicians, it boarded their merchant ships and was quickly passed on westwards. Wine was an eminently tradable item and evidence of its production is found in Greece around 4500 BC, and at the same time its consumption was recorded on inscriptions and paintings in Egypt.

It was almost certainly either the Greeks or the Phoenicians who first brought wine and grape seeds to Tuscany, and by the time of the glittering civilisation of the Etruscans, in the first millennium BC, it features in the many wall paintings which show banquets and celebrations. The Romans and their imperial provinces established almost every wine-producing region in western Europe, and also developed different grape varieties and methods of cultivation.

The pollarded trees still visible on Tuscan hillsides are a relic of the Roman method known as *arbustum*. The vines were supported by the trees, and a *compluvium*, or trellis, was usually slung between two or along a row. This allowed farmers to train the growing tendrils in a variant of the espalier technique. Roman wine-making is particularly remembered in Tuscany, where Sangiovese is the dominant grape-type used to make Chianti. The name comes from *sanguis Iovis*, the 'blood of Jupiter'. Venus, the Roman goddess of beauty and sensual pleasure, was the daughter of Jupiter, and etymologists insist that her name and the Latin word *vinum* for wine are closely cognate. After a glass or two of Chianti, who would argue?

Not long before the early wine makers of northern Greece began to harvest their cultivated grapes, more innovation was sparking into life only a few hundred miles away, on the other side of the Balkans. Near Nova Zagora in north-western Bulgaria Europe's first metals were being dug out of the ground. From long and deep trenches, miners were excavating copper ore. Around 5100 BC smiths were refining it and making axeheads and chisels out of the new, shiny metal. Based on stone or flint models, the new copper objects appear to have been used, at first, not for any practical purpose but rather served as tokens of prestige, as gifts or as talismans with some spiritual significance. There must have been something magical and mysterious about the process of smelting, how apparently solid rock liquified and then cooled into something different. It seems likely that the first smiths enjoyed great prestige. Gold was also used for display (it still is) and large quantities were found in the form of grave goods in a prehistoric cemetery at Varna on the Black Sea. One man had 990 gold objects arranged round his corpse, including a penis sheath.

Magical metal, highly polished, lustrous, made into beautiful objects and worked by increasingly skilled smiths, began to stimulate trade and cultural contact all over the Mediterranean. It conferred names. Cyprus means 'Copper Island'. Those who controlled or could exploit areas rich in minerals became more powerful, and in the rich deposits of copper and tin mined in the Colline Metallifere, the 'Ore Mountains', Tuscany would in time be able to develop a rare advantage. Meanwhile, the eastern Mediterranean was dominated by the vivid civilisations of Crete, and on mainland Greece, Mycenae. Their ships almost certainly sailed as far west as the Tyrrhenian Sea to trade for metal and other desirables.

While copper was attractive to look at and malleable, it was also soft and easily bent out of shape. Smiths had at first used arsenic to make a harder alloy but, understandably, had been highly motivated to experiment and discover safer admixtures. Between 2200 BC and 2000 BC significant quantities of bronze began to be produced in Britain and Ireland. Nine parts copper to one part tin combined into a rich, gold-like alloy which could be polished to a dazzling sheen. But crucially it was also hard; bronze weapons in particular could deliver devastating blows, and bronze armour could deflect them. Immense prestige was attached to war-gear made from this tough and beautiful metal. Here is Homer's description of the arming of Patroclus in *The Iliad*:

> Patroclus put on the shimmering bronze. He began by tying round his legs the splendid greaves, which were fitted with silver clips for the ankles. Next he put on his breast Achilles' beautiful cuirass, scintillating like the stars. Over his shoulders he slung the bronze sword, with its silver-studded hilt, and then the great thick shield. On his sturdy head he set the well-made helmet. It had a horsehair crest, and the plume nodded grimly from on top. Last he picked up two powerful spears which suited his grip.

The central difficulty with the development of bronze production was that tin is rare in Europe and occurs in only a few localities, Tuscany among them. Cornwall and southern Ireland had workable deposits and British and Irish bronze-making technology spread eastwards, and when it reached the Mediterranean, trade accelerated once more. Sails were hoisted for the first time on sea-going ships, journey times shortened and the world began to shrink. Elites became more powerful as their reach extended and their wealth increased. The beautiful palaces at Knossos and Mycenae speak of great kings, and archaeology was beginning to turn into history.

Except when underwater archaeologists occasionally come across their shipwrecked cargo, merchants rarely leave much of a mark. What they trade is consumed or passed on. War is what scribes and chroniclers remember, and quite suddenly, around 1250 BC, war burst over the eastern Mediterranean. The navies of the mysterious Sea Peoples sailed out of the northern mists, scattering the merchant ships, destroying the royal palaces at Mycenae and on Crete and attacking the great empire of the pharaohs in Egypt. The armies of Rameses III succeeded in repulsing the warrior fleets, but not before much damage had been done and territory lost. One insurgent group was almost certainly the Philistines and they took over the biblical land of Canaan.

Inscriptions on the walls of the Egyptian temple at Medinet Habu recorded other names of the Sea Peoples; the Shardana, the Shekelesh and the Teresh. After a generation of destruction and chaos, the Sea Peoples seemed to disappear as suddenly as they had arrived. Historians have argued convincingly that the Shardana colonised and named Sardinia, the Shekelesh, also called the Sikels, gave Sicily its name and, less certainly, the Teresh made landfall on the Tuscan coast.

Very recent and statistically significant DNA studies have supplied remarkable corroboration of the legends of the Sea Peoples and their migration to Tuscany. Samples taken from hundreds of modern inhabitants of the cities and towns of Arezzo, Chiusi, Pitigliano, Tarquinia and elsewhere show very clearly that the genetic make-up of Tuscans is very different from their neighbours and the rest of Italy. Moreover, it also shows conclusively where they came from. There are unmistakable affinities with the peoples of Anatolia in central Turkey, the supposed homeland of the Sea Peoples. This new evidence speaks eloquently and loudly of an ancient migration, the arrival of an exotic new civilisation on the shores of Italy, people who spoke a different language and who brought a vivid new culture. As warrior élites with the confidence and prestige of great deeds in the east, where empires were humbled, they may have been able to establish themselves towards the end of the second millennium BC.

They chose to colonise a maritime economy which had tremendous potential.

Almost enclosed by Sicily in the south and Corsica and Sardinia in the west, the Tyrrhenian Sea had developed as a distinct trading network. And between 1350 BC and 1000 BC Tuscany was growing, perhaps stimulated by ambitious incomers. Almost wholly agricultural in nature at the beginning of this period, the population appears to have been evenly spread, with small hilltop villages of only one or two hundred at most. The Tuscan climate was temperate, the land productive, the harvests predictable. But under the tranquil surface, change was simmering.

By the beginning of the first millennium BC powerful kings had emerged and begun to create very large towns, especially in southern Tuscany. Several eventually occupied sites of between 250 and 500 acres, and most were built on easily defensible heights. Orvieto is perhaps the most spectacular, perched on its singular outcrop of tufa above the Val di Chiana. Other early towns have survived into modern times at Tarquinia, Cerveteri and Veio.

Not only could Tuscan agriculture support these large concentrations of population, their geographical location encouraged even more growth. Close to the sea and the Tyrrhenian network, Tarquinia, Cerveteri and the others also linked with the northern passes through the Apennines. Manufactured metal goods, amber and weapons all came down to the Tuscan merchant cities and were shipped out to markets around the Mediterranean. Long traditions began to establish themselves as riches were amassed and as kings became more powerful. The high summer of Etruscan civilisation was about to blaze into life.

3

The Tower-Builders

In November 2007 a myth drifted out of the mists of antiquity and became history. A team of archaeologists had been working on the Palatine Hill in Rome amongst the ruins of its imperial palaces. Augustus, the first emperor, had lived in a modest house overlooking the Forum, but those who followed him onto the throne had built ever more elaborate structures which eventually covered the whole summit of the hill with halls, antechambers, bedchambers, guardrooms and servants' quarters. The Palatine grew so grand that it is the origin of the English word 'palace'. In digging down through the strata Professor Giorgio Croci hoped to build up a clear picture of the sprawling buildings which stood at the heart of the Roman Empire. But he found much more than he bargained for.

On the morning of 7 November 2007 excavators working near the edge of the Palatine plateau suddenly stopped digging. They had come across a large void directly below. After all their gear had been carefully removed, with as little ground disturbance as possible, a specialist team was able to insert an endoscope through the roof of what seemed like a buried structure of some kind. Lit by a miniature searchlight, a camera probe revealed something entirely unexpected and entirely astonishing. On their small monitor the archaeologists saw that it was not a building but a cave. Richly decorated with sea-shells, mosaics and beautifully veined marble, it seemed to be a shrine of some kind, and when the camera panned around, it revealed a small sculpture standing in the centre. It was a white eagle, the eagle of Rome.

Professor Croci was astounded. He knew exactly what his team had discovered, but was almost unable to believe the pictures transmitted by the tiny camera. Sixteen metres below a previously unexplored area of the Palatine, under the house of the great Emperor Augustus, he had found the Lupercale, the most revered shrine in all the empire, the very essence of the Eternal City, the place where Rome had been founded.

The Lupercale had been thought of as the unlikely location of a myth, part of the origin legend of Rome, and no serious scholar or archaeologist believed that anything tangible would ever come to light. But it had. Buried under millennia of rubble a half-forgotten story began to whisper.

The Lupercale is named for the she-wolf, the *lupa*, who rescued the twins, Romulus and Remus, abandoned in a basket amongst the reed-beds of the River Tiber. Having taken the baby boys up to her cave on the Palatine Hill, she suckled them, saving their lives and beginning the long story of an empire and a culture which lasted for more than 2,000 years. In many Italian cities there stand sculptures of the unlikely but powerful image of a wild animal standing protectively over two human babies as they greedily drink her milk.

A canny, capable and utterly ruthless politician acutely conscious of his place in history and mindful of how precarious that might become, Augustus wanted to forge a powerful link between himself, his dynasty and the founders of Rome, Romulus and Remus. When he built his deliberately unostentatious villa above the Lupercale on the Palatine, it looked as though destiny was at work, as though Augustus was the rightful and legitimate heir to all that the divine twins had set in train. An unbreakable symbolic, even mystical, bond was made between the first emperor and the babies in the cave below his house. But the story of the foundation of the city of Rome is also a profoundly Etruscan story, the best documented and detailed account of how and why cities were established. According to Marcus Terentius Varro, writing at the beginning of the first century BC and the first really rigorous scholar of Latin literature and antiquities, the rituals and mysteries which swirled around the foundation of Rome were almost all borrowed from the elaborate practices first played out in Etruria. For in the eighth century BC, when the she-wolf found Romulus and Remus amongst the rushes, Rome lay on the southern edge of Etruria as it moved into a golden age. And when the facts are winnowed out of the myth, a powerful sense of the beginnings of Etruscan civic society can be clearly discerned.

In 1988 archaeologists had made an earlier fascinating but much less sensational discovery on the northern slopes of the Palatine Hill.

The Wall of Romulus, little more than a stratified discolouration, was dated to the eighth century BC, very close to the traditional date of 753 BC for the founding of Rome. Ancient chroniclers were even more precise and they confidently asserted that Romulus and his men began to dig a ditch around the Palatine on 21 April, 753 BC, or in their own reckoning, Year One AUC, *Ab Urbe Condita*, 'from the founding of the city'. Agreeing with the chroniclers, the great Italian scholar, Andrea Carandini, believes that the Wall of Romulus in fact buttresses Rome's origin legend and its traditional date with solid archaeological evidence.

The ditch and its wall were the outcome of a dispute, the cause of a fratricide and a revealing element in any clear understanding of how the Etruscans saw their cities. Although thousands of texts have been found in the Etruscan language, most are very short, often little more than lists and sometimes difficult to understand; there are very few which might be seen as useful historical documents. No contemporary history has yet been found and any coherent sense of an Etruscan view needs to be compiled from fragments or by analogy. Rome lay within the orbit of Etruscan politics and culture, and by contrast is rich in documents and history. The early period may sometimes be held up as a mirror, or at least an analogy, for lives of the peoples who lived north of the Tiber.

Having resolved to found their own city, Romulus and Remus promptly disagreed over the precise site. Romulus wanted to build on the Palatine Hill while his brother insisted on its more easily defensible neighbour, the Aventine. Eventually a means of divine judgement was settled on. Each brother would sit on his hilltop and await a sign from the gods. Flights of birds were thought to be highly significant, and when Remus searched the sky he saw six vultures pass overhead. But it was not enough. Romulus claimed to have seen twelve, and that his choice of the Palatine ought to prevail. In an unseemly squabble Remus insisted that he had seen his birds first, and that even if his brother was telling the truth, his twelve vultures didn't count. So there. Bad blood simmered.

When Romulus decided to ignore his brother and his men began to dig a ditch around their hill, it was not only for defence; they were creating a sacred precinct. All over western Europe the peoples of the first millennium BC were using ditches and banks to mark off holy ground, many of them at the tops of hills. It may be that the location of the Lupercale had been agreed at that early stage, but more likely the victorious brother was following Etruscan custom and preparing an area inside which a shrine of some kind would be built. There were of course gateways to allow access for mere mortals, but the ditch and the bank created by its upcast were holy, invested with great significance and probably the repository of sacrifice. North-west of Rome, the Etruscan city of Tarquinia still stands on a wide plateau with commanding views over the Mediterranean and the coast roads. Under the walls of its ancient sanctuary the remains of a newborn baby have been discovered and dated to the first quarter of the seventh century BC. Nearby, even earlier burials of three newborns and an epileptic boy (his skull was so malformed as to have caused fits) and the skeletons of pigs, sheep and cows as well as pottery, metalwork and weapons. It is as though the ground on which the city and its walls were built was literally being invested with sanctity, with gifts to the gods, perhaps even human sacrifice amongst them. It is not difficult to imagine a belief that an epileptic boy had been touched by the divine.

Not long after Romulus and his men had begun to dig Rome's sacred ditch, Remus arrived and began to mock the work, even obstruct it. And bad blood boiled over into fatal bloodshed when Remus committed the sacrilege of jumping over the ditch. Romulus in great anger slew him, wrote the Roman historian, Livy, and in a menacing way, added these words, 'So perish whoever else shall leap over my walls.' If it was not a grievous sacrilege; it is difficult to understand why Romulus killed his brother for jumping over a wall. The quote was later thought to be a premonition of Rome's coming greatness and invincibility, but it was really a punishment for offence against the gods – and also a brutal means of gaining undisputed power for Romulus. Perhaps Remus' death was a foundation sacrifice. One of the early sources confirmed that he was buried immediately, maybe under the upcast from the sacred ditch.

Rome was built in the Etruscan position, that is, on the top of an accessible hill and with ready access to water. But these practical considerations were always less important than the spiritual. In fact the early peoples of Etruria would have made no such distinction. All aspects of life were governed by the gods and the need to appease them and understand their wishes. Nothing of the modern habit of compartmentalisation, the division between secular and

religious, existed. The sites of Etruscan cities appear always to have
included shrines and sanctuaries around them. The most spectacular
of these holy cities, the great tufa rock topped by Orvieto, was
the central shrine for all Etruria, the Fanum Voltumnae. Visible
from every side, from the Val di Chiana and the hills around it,
were many shining temples built on its flat summit, and when the
Roman general, M. Fulvius Flaccus, overran the city in 264 BC, he
plundered more than 2,000 statues. The shrines and the priests who
cared for them were of central importance to the Etruscans, and
in ruthless Roman fashion the entire population was expelled and
the Temple to Voltumna removed to Rome. Known as Volsinii, the
cleared and empty site was renamed the Old City, *Urbs Vetus*, now
rendered as Orvieto.

Although Rome was founded in a firmly Etruscan atmosphere, later
writers recognised how the two cultures grew apart. Livy thought the
Etruscans 'a nation devoted beyond all others to religious rites (and
all the more because it excelled in the art of observing them)' and that
Etruria was the 'begetter and mother of superstitions'. Seneca held a
more nuanced view:

> This is the difference between us and the Etruscans, who have
> consummate skill in interpreting lightning: we think that because
> clouds collide, lightning is emitted; they believe that clouds collide in
> order that lightning may be emitted. Since they attribute everything
> to divine agency, they are of the opinion that things do not reveal
> the future because they have occurred, but that they occur because
> they are meant to reveal the future.

Trade in Etruria was governed by sacred precepts. To modern
sensibilities few areas of human activity might seem more secular,
but it should be borne in mind that this is a recent view and that
many markets are still held on saints' days and that the religious
calendar often regulates trade, especially as Christmas approaches.
The Etruscans conducted business in and around shrines probably
because commerce often involved making promises which needed to
be sanctified to render them binding, and because deceit was less
likely when the gods were watching. A bronze and lead weight found
in an Etruscan tomb at Cerveteri named its owner and has inscribed
on it the name of the sanctuary at which it was dedicated.

When Greek merchant ships began to appear in the Tyrrhenian Sea and trade with Etruria in the eighth century BC, more sophisticated commercial practices were gradually introduced. Inscribed tablets recorded loans and personal guarantees. Marriages were sometimes contracted as part of a business deal, particularly where trust was more than usually important, and these relationships needed priestly blessing. Often sea voyages of some length and danger were involved, and at a shrine sacrifice could be made in a necessary attempt to persuade the gods to smile on the enterprise. As Roman writers noticed, Etruscan priests (called *haruspices*) were especially adept at divination, the ability to interpret natural phenomena as signs from the gods and a way to see into the future. The entrails of animals were examined after sacrifice, particularly their livers and a remarkable life-size bronze model of a sheep's liver has been found near Piacenza. An unusually valuable written document, it carries the names of many Etruscan gods inscribed into marked-off sections of the liver. There are sixteen and they are thought to mirror the areas of the heavens controlled by each god. Of the four compass directions, only the west, where the sun sinks, was thought to be unfavourable. How the *haruspices* read the sheep's liver is unclear, but in the planning and layout of cities, the east was believed to be the most auspicious location for a shrine and the influences of certain gods were more prevalent in the north than the south. It must be significant that at Orvieto all but one of the Christian churches have been built in the eastern or southern quarters and that the Etruscan Tempio del Belvedere survives on the more easterly spur of the great rock. Before the merchant ships of the first millennium BC hoisted their sails, a priest will have slaughtered a sheep, a pig or a cow and examined its bloody liver very carefully.

When Phoenicians from the coasts of Syria and Lebanon and Greek traders came west, they established themselves in enclaves in or near Etruria. These were not autonomous colonies, as were set up elsewhere, and it must be a reflection of Etruscan military strength that none was attempted. At Pyrgi, not far to the north-west of Rome and at Gravisca, the port for Tarquinia, there is strong evidence that both groups established sanctuaries (presumably with rights of asylum) and these acted as cultural entry points. The distinctly oriental cast of much Etruscan art may have originated with Phoenician contact, and the pantheon of Greek gods certainly infiltrated through commerce, and through artefacts in particular. The greatest merchant, according to Herodotus, was Sostratus, from the island of Aegina. He was certainly at Gravisca *c*. 510 BC and through the port vast quantities of Greek pottery flooded into Etruria. Politically displaced aristocrats sometimes led mercantile adventures out of Greek ports and Demaratus of Corinth established himself so well that his son, Tarquinius Priscus, became an early king of Rome.

The transmission of religious belief from Greece to Rome was not direct. The names of many of the gods passed through the Etruscan language before finding expression in Latin. Athene became Menrva before she was Minerva, Ares became Maris, then Mars, and Persephone was Phersipnai, then Proserpine. Many gods and cults appear to have been unique to the Etruscans, and they died with the ultimate eclipse of their culture. Perhaps the most attractive was Voltumna, whose shrine was on the rock at Orvieto. He or she was the god of Etruria itself and was also seen as the god of all that grew out of its soil; in other words, of the way the land looked in all its seasons.

By the early eighth century BC the Etruscans were a power in the western Mediterranean. Their rich mineral resources had attracted both Phoenician and Greek merchants, and their sense of enterprise had persuaded the Etruscans themselves to sail west along the northern coasts of the Mediterranean in search of markets for their own goods. Shards of their unique black *bucchero* pottery have been found in several places and particularly at St Blaise in the Rhône delta, where they appear to have founded a trading colony. Made only in Etruria, finds of *bucchero* accurately track activity along the coasts of the Golfe du Lion.

Fine wine and the techniques of making it probably arrived in Etruria when the Greeks sailed into the Tyrrhenian Sea. Viticulture quickly established itself, no doubt blessed by Voltumna, and a surplus was soon produced for export. Celtic Europe, the lands to the north of the Mediterranean shore, developed a lucrative thirst for Tuscan wine and trade began to flourish. Its spread can be traced by finds of the ceramic kit sold with the amphorae, the great pear-shaped containers which allowed export in manageable bulk. Cups and mixing bowls were a necessary accessory for the high status Celtic aristocrats who consumed the new luxury drink. Beer could still be sloshed into beakers but fine wine all the way from Italy was too upmarket to be slurped out of a locally produced mug.

The most vivid records of the lives of wealthy Etruscans are to be seen on the walls of their tombs. Many reliefs and frescoes show banquets and wine-drinking parties. At Viterbo a moulded clay relief was found which depicts Etruscan social life in full swing; a flautist and a harpist entertain an animated group of men and women who are drinking from encouragingly large cups. While they lounge on couches, a slave stands to one side mixing wine in an even larger bowl, known by its Greek name as a *krater*. Other tomb paintings also depict the *krater*, some of them extremely large, and drinkers are occasionally entertained by dancers. Even though these are almost certainly all funeral banquets, the painters often accurately catch the mood of a party lubricated by wine and all its rituals.

The Mediterranean peoples rarely drank their wine neat. It was mixed and diluted with water, sometimes sea-water, to enliven a wine's smoothness according to the Roman writer, Pliny the Elder. Occasionally honey was added to concoct a drink called *mulsum* and it seems that sweet wines were the most sought after. Aged for long periods and growing darker in colour, they were sometimes stored in warm places to encourage the flavours and sugars to concentrate more quickly. Roman commentators sniffed when they wrote of the consumption of huge quantities of wine by the Celts of the north. They drank it neat, without water, and were consequently famous for their uncouth drunkenness.

There exists rich archaeological evidence for the expansion of the wine trade out of the port at Gravisca, and it seems that its diffusion around the Mediterranean shore was more than the runaway success of a new drink. The amphorae also contained a clear set of cultural precepts which took root wherever they made landfall and wherever the climate allowed. After vine growing and olive oil production were well established in Italy, they spread to southern France and to Spain.

The funeral banquets show more than the Mediterranean fondness for long suppers, good talk and good wine. In many frescoes, reliefs and free-standing ceramic sculptures, women are prominently featured. Not merely decorative, or prostitutes or dancers, they are full participants in conversation and in general social interaction. On the walls of a tomb found at Cerveteri, it has been possible to make out inscriptions painted on wine vessels. One reads 'I am the bowl of Papaia Karkana', presumably one of the women depicted at the banquet. And in another tomb nearby a similar bowl carries 'I am the bowl of Squria'. Their presence at parties, it seems certain, was not a special occasion but a regular occurrence.

The high social status of Etruscan women was nothing new. In the burials of the Villanovan culture which flourished in Tuscany at the beginning of the first millennium BC, archaeologists have discovered that women have grave goods beside them every bit as prestigious as those found with men. After the eighth century BC women are depicted as spectators at games, as participants in religious ceremonies and as actors in drama. In later Etruscan sculpture, usually on the lids of sarcophagi, couples are shown in what seem to be genuinely affectionate poses, the husband's arm often protectively around his wife's shoulders.

Etruscan women appear to have been unique. In no other contemporary Mediterranean culture has evidence of such high, perhaps even equal, status yet come to light. The starchy Romans did not allow women to drink, far less invite them to take part in banquets, and commentators considered the Etruscans' treatment of their wives and daughters as no more than evidence of their general degeneracy and effeminacy.

As Etruscan trade reached west along the Mediterranean shore and they increasingly exploited their great mineral resources on the island of Elba and in the Colline Metallifere, the cities grew prosperous and ever larger. Even though they formed themselves into an alliance, the League of the Twelve Peoples (sometimes rising to fifteen), it was only a loose federation with a religious focus on the central shrine, the Fanum Voltumnae at Orvieto. The most important cities along the coast were Cerveteri, Tarquinia, Vulci, Roselle, Vetulonia and Populonia, and inland, Veio, Orvieto, Chiusi, Perugia, Cortona, Arezzo, Fiesole, Volterra and Pisa.

While the Romans referred to the federation as the Etrusci or the Tusci, and the Greeks knew them as the Tyrhennoi or the Tyrsenoi (the latter perhaps an echo of one of the Sea Peoples, the Teresh), the Fifteen Peoples called themselves the Rasenna, probably a commemoration of a divine ancestor. It is a measure of the influence of Etruscan names that the seas on both sides of Italy were named after them, the Tyrrhenian Sea and the Adriatic. Adria was one of their northern colonies on the far side of the Apennines, and it lies about 50 kilometres south of Venice.

In the early part of the first millennium BC most of the cities of the federation were ruled by kings or kingly priests and a great deal of their paraphernalia found its way into Roman tradition. Like them, Romulus was said to have surrounded himself with a bodyguard of twelve lictors who carried the fasces, the double-headed axe wrapped inside a bundle of whipping rods. Also borrowed from the Etruscans were the curule chair, a kind of throne sat on by magistrates, the purple-bordered toga, a sceptre and a ceremonial chariot.

By the seventh century the subjects of kings and kingly priests knew each other by a different way of naming, a cultural shift which arose as a consequence of the growth of the great Etruscan cities. An agrarian and tribal society generally used a system of patronymics, or *in extremis*, matronymics. It survived longest in Britain in the Scottish Highlands where Iain macDomnhaill, or John son of Donald, or John Macdonald is an everyday example. But very early in Etruria, by the eighth century at least, fathers' names were replaced by family names. A first, or given, name such as Arath or Larth was followed by the name of the gens, or family, usually that of an ancestor. People began to signify that they belonged to family groups because there were social and economic advantages in doing so, and historians have seen this trend as echoing the rise of a wealthy middle class in the productive commercial milieu of the Etruscan cities. When the incidence of double names increased dramatically in the second half of the seventh century, that class was clearly expanding. And in many of the cities of the federation, kings and priests were eventually supplanted by an oligarchy, aristocrats and upper middle-class merchants grown rich on the proceeds of trade. It was the beginning of a long, persistent tradition in Tuscan history.

When families widened into several branches, a third name eventually became necessary in order to avoid confusion. By the third century BC many urban Etruscans had a first name, a family name and a name to identify a particular branch of that family. Roman society adopted this system wholesale with the praenomen, nomen and cognomen.

The Greek city-states of the mainland and the Aegean coast of Asia Minor were also expanding rapidly from the eighth century onwards, too rapidly for their infrastructure to keep pace. Problems of food and water supplies and the wildfire spread of deadly diseases forced large contingents of citizens to emigrate. Whereas Greek merchants had previously been content to set up trading posts in the western Mediterranean, what they called *emporia*, after *c.* 800 BC they began

to found permanent colonies. Tentative at first, anxious not to
threaten their stable markets in Etruria, a group of settlers from the
Greek island of Euboea established themselves on Ischia – a small
island off the coast of the Bay of Naples. A few years later another
group founded a colony on the mainland opposite, at Cumae. Further
south the surplus populations of other Greek cities had built towns
at Syracuse on Sicily and at many other places around the coasts of
Calabria, Campania, Basilicata and Puglia. The area became known
as Magna Graecia, Greater Greece.

Around 600 BC Greek colonists grew more aggressive, offering a
direct threat to Etruscan commercial interests. Merchant adventurers
from the town of Phocaea on the coast of Asia Minor sailed into the
Tyrrhenian Sea in warships. Known as penteconters, these 50-oared
galleys were much larger and faster than merchantmen. By 600 BC
the Phocaeans had built a colony and a harbour at Massalia (which
later became Marseilles), and in so doing cut off Etruscan trade to the
west. No more is heard of the trading enclave at St Blaise in the Rhône
delta. Fifty years later the ambitious Persian kings began to press hard
on the Greek cities of Asia Minor and in 544 BC the entire population
of Phocaea fled into the west. Their fleet sailed to Corsica and a large
colony was established at Alalia, where a small group of Phocaeans
had settled twenty years before. Directly opposite the Etruscan coast,
in the heart of the Tyrrhenian trading system, the Greek settlement
presented a powerful threat. And when the penteconters began to
raid commercial shipping, the Phocaean presence became intolerable.
Several individual Etruscan cities (the League of the Twelve Peoples
rarely acted in concert) formed an alliance with the Carthaginians,
an immensely wealthy and influential Phoenician colony based in
North Africa, where Tunisia is now and which controlled much of
the coast of the Southern Mediterranean. The combined fleet sailed
to war with the Phocaeans. They sighted each other off the Corsican
coast, near Alalia. There were sixty ships on each side and at least
eighty were sunk in a ferocious battle. Even though the great Greek
penteconters are believed to have prevailed, it was a close-run thing
and the Phocaeans decided to decamp to Elea on the Italian mainland,
in Magna Graecia.

Naval warfare was even more chancy and haphazard in ancient
times. Winds and currents could prevent proper engagement, ships
were very expensive to build and maintain, and when a sea battle

was fought, many skilled and valuable sailors could drown – as happened at Alalia. Tactics were limited and very direct. Using the muscle-power of their banks of oarsmen, ships' captains, known as trierarchs, attempted to ram opposing vessels. If they could gather enough speed over a short distance, it was best to ram an enemy amidships, splintering oars and holing the hull below the waterline. Platoons of marines threw out grappling hooks as archers tried to pick out targets or at least force the enemy to keep their heads down. Once ships were tied together and engaged, fierce hand-to-hand fighting took place on the swaying and slippery decks.

Several pieces of Etruscan pottery show sea battles and small groups of warriors waiting in their ships to fight. They look very like Greek hoplites, the heavy infantry which fought with such extraordinary determination and success against the might of ancient Persia and which also followed Alexander the Great across half the known world. Illustrations of Etruscan hoplites begin to appear around 650 BC as the cities were growing and falling under the control of oligarchies. It is likely that these soldiers were part of a citizen army (there were also cavalry, archers and certainly charioteers) composed of free men with a military obligation, enough wealth to own their own gear and weapons, and enough time to have had some training in warfare. The armies of the Etruscan cities were small, probably drawing their manpower as widely as possible, from teenagers to grizzled old veterans of sixty. Life expectancy was much shorter and there will have been few of the latter in the ranks.

Hoplite kit would not have been uniform, since each man supplied his own, but it did consist of some basic items. A bronze helmet with wraparound cheek-pieces and a T-shaped opening for the eyes, nose and mouth cut down on both vision and hearing. Most men attached a horsehair plume on top. It made them look taller and more menacing to an approaching enemy. Body armour and greaves protected as much as possible without restricting movement more than was necessary, and each man carried a thrusting spear, a sword (as a secondary weapon) and a large shield. Made from wood and faced with sheets of bronze or leather, these were usually round or sometimes in a figure-of-eight shape. It was all very heavy, hot and tiring to wear and carry. Battles did not last long, and it was often the fitter rather than the more ferocious who emerged victorious.

The Etruscans adopted the model of the hoplite and their particular method of fighting some time in the seventh century BC, and when men were summoned to fight, a battle generally followed a familiar pattern, something most men had trained for. When enemies sighted each other (battles were often fought at agreed sites, near road-meetings or river-fords), they tended to stop and stand to. An animal sacrifice was made and the liver and entrails examined by the *haruspices*. Then the generals made their speeches, something which indicates how small armies usually were – in that everyone could hear. Once the advance had begun, men sang the paean of their city, an anthem designed to remind them why they were fighting. War cries were roared and then armies clashed, and hacked at each other, trying to kill and stay alive at the same time.

There are no surviving records of Etruscan battles, but it seems very likely that the armies of the cities fought in a formation known as the phalanx. Hoplite armour and weapons were designed for it. Men were drawn up tightly together, with a front rank keeping close order, their shields locked and their spears out-thrust, bristling and hard to penetrate. Behind stood several ranks of soldiers ready to push at the backs of the men in front. Forward momentum was almost always absolutely decisive and the phalanx aimed to drive over the top of the enemy, get them to the ground and butcher them with sword and spear thrusts.

Phalanxes were made up of men who knew each other, who were often relatives and who depended on a collective courage to survive. Wise commanders usually set the older men in front. They knew what to expect, and if they were beside brothers, cousins and nephews, then their courage stiffened even more. Few fought more fiercely than family groups, and the older men would have reassured their womenfolk that they would be sure to look after their boys.

When battle was joined on the summer plains of Etruria, it would have been a hot, dusty and bloody business. Only those in the front ranks will have had a clear view of what was happening. Behind, their comrades had their heads down, pushing hard, dripping with sweat, grunting with effort. Over the din of war cries, the screams of the dying and wounded and the shouting of commanders, few will have heard anyone except the men on either side. And the stink of human excrement will have been gagging as men involuntarily soiled themselves with fear, and the unmistakable stench of blood will have filled the air. Though few had any accurate appreciation of the ebb and flow of the fighting, it was said that a phalanx was instinctively sensitive. Even those compressed in the middle ranks knew if they were about to move backwards or were threatened from the rear or in the flanks. Blinded by kicked-up dust and sweat, exhausted by heavy armour and weapons and deafened by the clamour, all of the men in a phalanx prayed that their fight would be short and victorious.

The Romans adopted and adapted the gear of the hoplite and the tactics of the phalanx as they developed their armies of legions. But battles continued to be fought in similar ways. When the great Carthaginian general, Hannibal, invaded Italy at the end of the third century BC, he defeated the legions at the battle at Cannae in southern Italy. It lasted for many hours, well beyond the ordinary endurance of heavily armed soldiers, and was only settled when the opposing front lines disengaged several times to recover, and then charged again into bursts of ferocious close-quarter fighting. Rome lost on that terrible day, but in the future an empire would be won as their soldiers became professional, well trained and fitter than their amateur opponents.

After the foundation of the Greek colony at Massalia around 600 BC and the sea wars of the sixth century, the Etruscan cities were forced to find new directions and new markets. They turned north. Over the Apennines, in the broad valley of the River Po, colonies were founded at Felsina (Bologna), Spina and Adria. Merchants ventured further north and lucrative contacts were made with the Celtic kings of the Hallstatt culture on the northern flanks of the Alps. The Etruscans' pack animals climbed up through the summer passes to reach them. Archaeologists have shown that the most favoured route was via Lake Como. There is good evidence that Etruscan traders or their agents may have reached the Baltic. In Pomerania archaeologists have found cremation urns very similar in style to those used in the Po valley and Etruscan artefacts have been discovered in several locations. Amber was what the merchants wanted. Very valuable, small and light, it was an ideal cargo for the return journey through the high alpine passes. The inland cities of Pisa, Volterra, Fiesole and Arezzo were well placed to exploit the new northern markets. Unlike the fast and capacious merchant shipping of the Mediterranean, overland trade was expensive, slow and small-scale, but cargoes like amber and silver from north of the Alps were worth the long haul.

Etruria also extended its reach southwards. Tradition, now supported by archaeology, insists that the fourth king of Rome after Romulus was an Etruscan. Tarquinius Priscus' accession coincided with the development of what was a minor settlement into a city – and engineering took a determinant hand.

All over southern Etruria productive farmland had been created or enhanced by ingenious drainage systems. Channels cut out of soft tufa rock had diverted watercourses for irrigation and also drained boggy, malarial areas. At Veio in the fifth century BC a tunnel was driven through the rock to alter the course of the Cremera river and use its old channel as a drainage fall. In Rome, bold Etruscan engineering transformed the face of the city. The marshy area between the foot of the Palatine Hill and the Tiber was drained when the first course of the Cloaca Maxima was dug and lined, and the Roman Forum laid out over it.

It was probably during this period that Rome borrowed even more from the Etruscans. Linguistic maps of ancient Italy show that all of the early dialects of the peninsula, Faliscan, Latin, Osco-Umbrian, Venetic and the Greek spoken in the south were all Indo-European in origin. The exception was Etruscan. Unrelated to its neighbours, it may have been introduced by a far-travelled immigrant elite, perhaps the Sea People, the Teresh. Conquerors – such as the English – often impose their language, even if they are in a small minority. The Etruscans adapted the Greek alphabet to write down their strange language and the process of transfer can be seen clearly in a fascinating inscription. The Etruscan language has not survived on perishable paper or vellum but on objects, most of them ceramic containers of one kind or another. On a pottery bottle found in southern Tuscany *mi larthaia telicles lechtumuza* is inscribed. Each word is eloquent. *Mi*, I am, gives the impression that the bottle is speaking, is also precious and possibly magical. *Larthaia* is the genitive of a common Etruscan name. *Larth* appears in the historical record as the first part of the name of a king of Chiusi, an actor in the early history of Rome. Joined with Telikles, a Greek name, the bottle talks of someone who was either a Greek immigrant or the child of a Greek and Etruscan marriage. And he was the owner, or perhaps the maker, of the object. *Lechtumuza* is an adaptation of the Greek word for flask expressed in an Etruscan idiom.

Literacy was almost certainly the prerogative of the aristocracy. Ivory-handled styluses have been found in the tombs of the wealthy and a wax tablet found which had been clearly inscribed around its edges with the Greek alphabet so that it could be easily copied by someone learning to write. Greek letters evolved to represent the sounds made by speakers of the language and its dialects, but they needed to be adapted to cope with Etruscan. The differences were radical and suggest a very different vocabulary and syntax.

What makes Etruscan awkward to read and understand was the ancient habit of writing without punctuation or any spaces between words. And disconcertingly, short inscriptions need to be read backwards, from right to left. Longer pieces are organised in what is known as boustrophedon, that is, reading alternately from right to left and then in a continuous loop from left to right, right to left, and so on.

The earliest Etruscan inscriptions date from around 700 BC, and after two centuries of evolution it is possible to detect changes in pronunciation, to hear the development of an ancient language. In a process known as syncope, the first syllable of names begins to be so heavily accented as to cause subsequent syllables to fall out of use or become truncated. The name the Etruscans used for themselves, Rasenna, was gradually shortened to Rasna.

In a crucial cultural transfer, it was the Etruscans who taught their subject-neighbours, the Romans, how to read and write and therefore began the development of the alphabet we use in the twenty-first century. This almost certainly happened in the century after the takeover of the Tarquin dynasty, when Tarquinius Priscus became king of Rome in 616 BC. The Lapis Niger inscription, the earliest Latin text, was found under the stones of the Forum and it dates from the early seventh to the late sixth centuries.

In 510 BC, according to legend and romance, a hero stood forth to free Rome from the Etruscan yoke. The last king, Tarquinius Superbus, Tarquin the Proud, was expelled by an aristocratic coup d'état and the republic founded. When Tarquin and his ally, King Lars Porsenna of Chiusi, appeared with an army outside Rome, there was momentary panic. It looked as though they would breach the defences by taking the Sublician Bridge, the only bridge across the Tiber into the city.

Then out spake Brave Horatius,
The Captain of the gate:
'To every man upon this earth
Death cometh soon or late.
And how can man die better
Than facing fearful odds,
For the ashes of his fathers
And the temples of his Gods.'

Known as Horatius Cocles, or 'One-eyed Horatius', he was joined on the narrow bridge by Spurius Lartius and Titus Herminius, and the 'Dauntless Three' held off the Etruscan hordes long enough for the timbers behind them to be cast down. All successfully broke off from fighting, gained the Roman bank and the city was saved. Four years later republican Rome welded together an alliance of the other Latin-speaking cities and won a measure of independence with victory over the Etruscan hoplites at Aricia in 508 BC.

When they turned their gaze seaward, the coastal cities of Etruria were forced to trade in the increasingly congested Tyrrhenian. Their colonies south of Rome, in Campania, were being pressed hard by the merchant cities of Magna Graecia and frustration flared into conflict off the coast of Cumae in 474 BC. An Etruscan fleet was badly beaten by an allied Greek naval force led by the warships of Syracuse, the Corinthian colony established in the late eighth century in Sicily. Syracuse had grown into a huge, powerful and very wealthy city, and at Cumae it flexed its military muscle.

Defeat drove the Etruscans out of the southern Tyrrhenian Sea, and several of their coastal cities went into decline. The Celtic kingdoms beyond the Alps appeared to be expanding as populations grew and demand for trade goods increased accordingly. But these demographic shifts would ultimately prove dangerous and destabilising for Etruria. Within only three generations of the disaster at Cumae, dark clouds were gathering in the north.

Some time around 450 BC large bands of people were seen climbing up through the Alpine passes. Led by warriors, they were refugees, women and children trudging behind carts carrying all their possessions. Whole tribes were moving from the Hallstatt kingdoms across the mountains to seek new lands in the fertile northern plains of Italy. Pliny the Elder believed that having had a taste of the luxuries produced in Italy, the Celts came south for more. But the mass migration was really the result of over-population and the pressure on agriculture. Livy held this view, and reckoned that the Celtic kings brought 300,000 tribesmen, women and children over the mountains. Roman and Greek historians used the term Gaul as well as Celt, and the Po Valley became known as Gallia Cisalpina, or 'Gaul on this side of the Alps'.

At first the immigrant tribes settled in the southern foothills, around the great lakes at Como, Maggiore and Garda, but as more and more came down from the passes and pushed southwards, they came into hostile contact with the Etruscans. At Bologna (Felsina) a relief sculpture showing a battle scene has been found with clearly identifiable Etruscan and Celtic warriors, and archaeology at the nearby town of Marzabotto suggests a phase of destruction at the time of the invasions from the north. One of the last tribes to find their way into the Po valley was the Senones. No Etruscan record survives, but the Romans thought them a fearsome, barbaric force of nature, their warriors obsessed with the bloody rituals of decapitation.

> They cut off the heads of enemies slain in battle and attach them to the necks of their horses. The bloodstained spoils they hand over to their attendants and carry off as booty, while striking up a paean and singing a song of victory; and they nail up these first fruits on their houses ... They embalm in cedar oil the heads of the most distinguished enemies, and preserve them carefully in a chest and display them with pride to strangers, saying that for this head one of their ancestors, or his father, or the man himself, refused the offer of a large sum of money. They say that some of them boast that they refused the weight of the head in gold.

At the same time as their colonies north of the Apennines were being overrun by the Senones and other Celtic tribes, the Etruscans faced aggression from the south. It was to prove a fatal pincer movement. By 396 BC the Romans had seized the cities of Veio and Civita Castellana, and all the land as far as the place they called the Ciminian Forest. It was a feared and trackless wilderness in which few dared tread. Forming the southern boundary of Etruria proper, this primeval mirkwood ran from the Cimini hills, a spur of the Apennines which turned towards the sea north-west of Rome to Lake Bracciano, and it was a source of particular terror. When the legions later defeated an Etruscan army in 310 BC, their general and consul, Fabius Maximus Rullianus, was specifically forbidden from entering the Ciminian Forest in pursuit of fugitives. When he ignored the Senate's orders, all Rome feared for the fate of the army. Throughout their otherwise glorious military history, the Romans remained terrified of the dangers that lay in the deep, dark woods.

Just as the southern cities were beginning to fall to Rome, Etruria's northern boundaries were breached. Having been temporarily halted by the wall of the Apennines, Celtic warbands suddenly broke through in 391 BC. They may have been a new wave of invaders who had only recently crossed the Alps. Having attacked and pillaged several of the inland cities, the warbands rode back through the Apennine passes at the onset of winter. But it was only a seasonal respite.

The following spring their kings once more roared their war cries and led their hard-riding Celtic cavalry into battle. Blazing through Etruria, they plunged into the Ciminian Forest, and at the River Allia were confronted by the shield-walls of the Roman legions. It was a rout; the furious Celtic charge swept aside the infantry and the warbands rode hard for Rome. The sparsely defended city was quickly overrun – except for a small garrison which doggedly held out on the Capitoline Hill for several months. Once it finally fell and the Celts had plundered all the booty they could carry and taken as many captives as they could drive before them, they withdrew back over the Apennine mountains. The sack of Rome was a disgrace and a defeat which the city never forgot. New walls were built, a circuit of six miles known as the Servian Walls, and the long and slow process of expansion – and revenge on the Celts – began.

Disunity made Etruria weak and fatally open to conquest. After the Romans had re-established control of Veio and Civita Castellana, they took the towns of Sutri and Nepi. Livy described them as the barriers and gateways of Etruria. Some of the cities, especially those closer to Rome, attempted a policy of appeasement, but, as often, it failed and became little more than a prelude to absorption. Cerveteri offered itself as a Roman ally and was awarded the status of *civitas sine suffragio*, in essence, a non-voting colony. Tarquinia was more aggressive in its defence, Civita Castellana broke away and both forced Cerveteri to join a growing alliance of Etruscan cities against Rome.

As the threat of invasion and colonisation grew, more and more cities began to rouse themselves and more diplomatic activity eventually put a powerful army in the field. Etruscan hoplites were strengthened by mercenary squadrons of Celtic cavalry and soldiers from the Italic-speaking cities of the east. But at Sentinum in 295 BC, the discipline and determination of the legions scattered the allies and immediately afterwards the city of Perugia fell into Roman hands.

To consolidate their conquests in the north, the consuls ordered their engineers into the front line. Four great roads were built through Etruria to maintain Rome's grip. Along the Tyrrhenian coast the Via Aurelia ultimately led right up to Pisa and the River Arno, and all of the once powerful merchant cities lay within its reach. Paved and wide enough to take cart traffic and guarantee dry and solid marching conditions, this vital piece of military infrastructure allowed the legions to reach trouble quickly or to supply garrisons where they were needed to discourage or prevent it. The Via Cassia was cut through the centre of Etruria, snaking through the Chianti hills to the banks of the Arno, and the Via Flaminia struck almost due north of Rome, close to the valley of the Tiber and eventually reaching the Adriatic at Fano.

The shortest of the four great arteries linked Rome with Saturnia. Unlike the others, the Via Clodia has not been overlaid by modern roads and beside the fields and hedgerows to the south of the modern town, its arrow-straight line can be clearly seen. Even some of the paving and drainage ditches survive. Saturnia was founded as a colony from Rome. Veteran soldiers and others were granted land, often estates forfeited by formerly hostile Etruscan aristocrats, and this habit of planting loyal and trustworthy communities, connected by a road, lasted throughout the long drive for empire.

Rome reorganised the political and economic geography of Etruria radically. Its impact can be seen clearly into modern times. Whereas the old road system had run from the inland cities to the ports on the coast, in a north-east to south-west direction, the new Roman roads ran at a 90-degree angle, completely altering the axis of communication and trade. This in turn had the effect of making the sites of some of the old Etruscan cities obsolete, badly placed to take part in commerce and the movement of peoples and goods. The new colonies were designed to cause further displacement. The most obvious example lies at the north end of the Via Cassia. On a convenient ford over the Arno, the Romans established Florence (the grid plan of the central streets and the Piazza della Signoria still sit on a Roman pattern) in direct competition with the nearby Etruscan city of Fiesole, which eventually shrank into a satellite settlement.

In Etruria there is also a sense of a culture in decline. What prompted the Romans to intervene at Orvieto, the most sacred shrine, in 285 BC, was a process of political evolution which had run out of control. The Orvietan aristocracy had gradually emancipated many slaves, using them as soldiers, administrators and magistrates. Marriage to aristocratic women allowed some former slaves to enter the equivalent of the senate at Orvieto. According to a Roman version of events, M. Fulvius Flaccus was invited to restore the old order. What the idle aristocrats may not have anticipated was that the Romans would clear them off their highly defensible site on top of the tufa rock and move them all to the shores of Lake Bolsena, which were flat. The old name for Orvieto survives there: Bolsena is only slightly changed from Volsinii.

In the civil wars of the first century BC several of the Etruscan cities sided with Marius, the great general and moderniser of the Roman army. But when his rival, Sulla, emerged triumphant, terrible revenge was taken. Between 82 and 80 BC Sulla's troops besieged the old city of Volterra, starved it into submission and slaughtered thousands of its citizens. There were bloody battles at Talamone, Populonia, Arezzo and Chiusi and much of the common land in Etruria was grabbed by Roman aristocrats. Huge estates were compiled, villas built and the fields worked by slaves. Many of those who were dispossessed simply abandoned Etruria to seek a better life elsewhere in the empire. Near Tunis in North Africa three inscriptions in the Etruscan language have been found.

By 89 BC almost all of the peoples of Italy had been granted Roman citizenship and absorbed into the growing empire as full participants. Sixty years later Etruria had ceased formally to exist. In what became known as the seventh region of Italy, Latin was introduced and insisted upon as the language of government and business. Contemporary historians noticed that as early as the first century AD the Etruscan language was disappearing.

Some cultural attitudes survived though. The wonderfully named Urgulania was descended from an aristocratic family from Cerveteri, and she had had the good fortune to find herself well connected in early imperial Rome. Augustus' wife, Livia, was a close friend, but when Urgulania became involved in litigation it all became very embarrassing. When summoned to appear in court, the sniffy old Etruscan aristocrat refused, saying that such things were beneath her dignity, and the future emperor, Tiberius, was sent off to plead for her. And on another occasion, Urgulania disdained to attend the Senate as a witness in a trial and a praetor was sent to her house to take a statement. Fascinating incidents – an aristocratic old lady insisting on the ancient dignities of a civilisation which had outshone and predated the new glories of Rome. There existed a great cultural debt owed by the world's greatest empire to the glittering cities of the north which had lit the first millennium BC, and perhaps the indulgences granted to Urgulania reflected that.

4

God's Empire

At Koblenz the Rhine becomes a truly mighty river. Joined by the Moselle and released from the confines of its gorge, it widens dramatically and is deep enough to allow large ships to dock in the heart of the city. Winter often brings flooding as the snows of the Alps and the Vosges melt into torrents. But in the winter of AD 406, the snow froze everywhere, even on the banks of the mighty river, and fingers of ice began to reach into its stately flow.

On the west bank, the *limitanei* kept watch, forces of Roman frontier guards posted along the fraying edge of the empire. They were sparse but experienced, and the Rhine was their greatest ally, a broad, deep and dangerous natural barrier. There were no bridges and no fords. On the far bank, stretching away to the east, the soldiers could see the smoke of several clusters of campfires. In such bitter weather, the barbarians who huddled around them must surely move on soon. Firewood and food would be close to exhausted. The kings of the Suebi, the Alans and the Vandals were all in the habit of sending scouting parties to gather intelligence, to look for weakness in the frontier garrison, to question those who lived on the east bank about what they might have seen.

In Trier, the principal city of northern Gaul, and even as far away as Italy, the threat of barbarian incursion was taken very seriously. The young emperor, Honorius, had moved his capital from Milan to Ravenna, a safe haven near the Adriatic with ready access to the sea and on the landward side surrounded by trackless and treacherous marshland.

By the middle of December 406, the weather had worsened, and for the first time in living memory it looked as though the ice-sheets would reach right across the Rhine. As temperatures dropped, the *limitanei* could see that warbands were mustering on the far bank.

By midwinter the ice would bear weight, and at first light they came.

Streaming across the frozen Rhine, their ponies slithering, fighting to get purchase, the warriors of the Suebi, the Alans and the Vandals attacked the Roman frontier defences. And when they had burst through, tens and then hundreds of thousands poured into the empire. After sacking the city of Trier, they fanned out over the province of Gaul, killing, plundering and burning. It was the dramatic opening of the last act in the fall of the Western Empire.

The first, and ultimately fatal, thrust had come thirty years before, when the Goths crossed the Danube and defeated a Roman army, killing the Emperor Valens at Adrianople, not far from Constantinople. Under their charismatic leader, Alaric, the Visigoths, or Western Goths, then went on to raid Greece and attack Athens. Various accommodations were made and treaties agreed. But by 401, they were moving again. Having ridden north through the Balkans, Alaric led his warbands across the Alpine passes and down into Italy. Rome lay at their mercy. On their way south, the Gothic army, or at least part of it, appears to have climbed through the Apennines and descended on Tuscany. Florence was besieged – but the walled town withstood the assault.

The late Roman Empire had managed to absorb many barbarians, settling them under treaty inside the frontiers, or buying them off, or both. Many of their kings had no wish to destroy the empire, seeing it as a destination and a career rather than a prize. For more than a century barbarian warbands, and many men, had been recruited into the imperial army. Some of their leaders had risen high. After the death of the Emperor Theodosius in AD 395, a man known as Stilicho the Vandal became regent on behalf of his successor, the young Honorius. Skilled at negotiation as well as strategy, he managed first to stall Alaric's invasion in two indecisive engagements in the Po valley, and then agreed a truce with the Goths which involved their leaving Italy.

By AD 405 a barbarian army was once again seen on the Arno. This time it was the Ostrogoths, the Eastern Goths, led by Radagaisus, and they were confronted by Stilicho at the old Etruscan city of Fiesole, just to the north of Florence. Roman only in name, the imperial army included warbands of Huns, Alans and Goths. The battle at Fiesole seems to have been some sort of negotiated victory for Stilicho.

Twelve thousand of Radagaisus' Ostrogoths were induced to stop fighting the Roman army and join it. Despite the threat from the hordes which had crossed the frozen Rhine in the last days of AD 406, Italy seemed to be stabilising.

The young and ill-advised Honorius would quickly change that. After Fiesole, Stilicho's stock had risen dangerously high. Whispering grew into plotting and a palace official at the imperial court at Ravenna put it about that the Vandal general was about to impose his son on the eastern throne at Constantinople. The commander of Rome's Gothic forces, Sarus, had Stilicho's bodyguard of Huns massacred and Honorius had him arrested. On 22 August 408, the great commander was beheaded, and 30,000 of his soldiers immediately defected to Alaric. In less than two years the Goths had blazed down through Italy and Rome was taken. The Eternal City was sacked.

The shock waves rippled to the furthest corners of the empire. Even though the imperial capital had moved to Milan and thence to Ravenna, Rome's symbolic significance was immense. Not for 800 years, since the Gauls had sacked the city in 390 BC, had an enemy breached the walls. Honorius cowered behind the marshland at Ravenna and Alaric led his men further south to plunder and kill. There was no Stilicho to stop him.

The storm gathering over Italy in the fifth century and the fecklessness of the emperor would have greatly dismayed his predecessors. When Augustus looked out from his modest house on the Palatine Hill, he saw a city which ruled over all the land around the Mediterranean, and much of western Europe besides. For advice on the great affairs of state he often turned to an Etruscan nobleman. Maecenas came from Arezzo and had been with Augustus from the beginning, from the earliest days of growing ambition, from the alliance with Mark Antony and Lepidus and the civil war which followed. With Marcus Agrippa, Maecenas and Augustus formed the tight inner circle which drove hard for empire and ran it with iron control. In contrast to all that famous ruthlessness, the cultivated Etruscan was an important patron of the arts, supporting the poets Virgil and Horace. But amongst the toxic tangle of jealousies swirling around the Palatine Hill, one of the most adhesive was Maecenas' Etruscan heritage. Louche, corrupt, effeminate and somehow mysterious were adjectives used by his enemies which stuck fast and survived into the historical record, and they say much about how the more austere

Roman aristocrats saw their ancient neighbours to the north. And when Augustus needed to see into the future, or at least to be seen to enquire, he turned to more Etruscans.

After it had become part of the empire, a particular aspect of Etruria was seen as part of history, as part of the mosaic of Rome's past – and part of how it thought about what lay in store. The Emperor Claudius wrote a vast, sprawling, 24-book chronicle of the origins and beliefs of the Etruscans. It is almost all lost, and only tiny fragments quoted by other authors survive:

> It frequently happened that when the state fell on evil days, the Etruscan soothsayers were summoned to Rome and ceremonies were revived and thereafter faithfully observed. The leading citizens of Etruria were the depositories of this religious learning and, either of their own accord or at the request of the Roman Senate, passed it on to their descendants.

Cicero reckoned that the Etruscan skill in divination had suitably mysterious origins. A strange, child-like sage, called Tages, appeared to a ploughman in the fields near Tarquinia and began to talk of many things. A crowd gathered and they collected and wrote down all he said. And what he in fact spoke of was the science of divination from the entrails of animals. In the second century AD Cornelius Labeo brought together all the Etruscans' religious skills and practices into a fifteen-volume history. But it too has been lost.

During the high summer of empire, when the future seemed assured, Tuscany appears to have dozed contentedly and only a few events of significance took place within her borders. When St Peter suffered martyrdom in Rome in AD 64, his followers scattered. Paulinus made his way north and found sanctuary in the town of Lucca, between Florence and Pisa. Having gathered around him a group of converts, his *familia*, he founded what was likely the first Christian church in Tuscany. Its precise location has been effaced, and in any case it was probably no more than a small, informal room or chapel. Paulinus was called bishop, but all that the early use of the title implied was that there was more than one priest at Lucca.

By the third century Christianity was only one of several flourishing cults imported from the Near East. Alongside Mithraism, the worship of the Sol Invicta (the 'Unconquered Sun') and the blood-soaked followers of Cybele, the teachings of Christ and St Paul attracted many devotees. The empire had long tolerated a profusion of beliefs, but loyalty to the state was not negotiable. And since it was required to be expressed through sacrifices to the old gods of Rome, which the monotheistic Christians refused to make, they became conspicuous and deeply suspect. When the Emperor Decius issued an edict in AD 250 compelling sacrifice to the traditional gods, the refusal of the Christians triggered widespread persecution. As in modern times, women were particularly devout, and in his history of the Church, Eusebius recorded how powerfully they clung to their faith:

> Ammonarion, a most respectable young woman, in spite of the savage and prolonged torture ... kept true to her promise and was led away. The others were Mercuria, a very dignified lady, and Dionysia, the mother of a large family but just as devoted to her Lord. The Governor was ashamed to go on torturing without results and to be defeated by women, so they died by the sword without being put to any further test by torture.

In Lucca, and the other early Christian communities in Tuscany at Chiusi, Pisa and probably Siena, believers began to meet and worship in secret. Some famous iconography recalls the years of persecution. In order to recognise each other, Christians used the *Chi Rho* symbol. The Greek versions of the first two letters of 'Christ', a title meaning 'anointed', were combined; the 'Ch' is written like a Latin 'X' and the 'R' like a 'P'. One was superimposed on the other with the vertical stroke of the P bisecting the X. Some scholars believe that the *Chi/ Rho* was the origin of the round-headed Celtic cross. Another famous secret sign to survive is the *ichthus*, the Greek word for a fish. Often represented by a stylised drawing, like a flattened version of the Greek letter alpha, the word is an acronym for *Iasos Christos Theou Hwios Sowtare*. In English, 'Jesus Christ, the Son of God, the Saviour'.

Early Christian communities all over the Western Empire tended to nucleate in towns and cities. It was certainly easier for small, clandestine groups to meet without arousing suspicion than it might have been in the countryside. But this tendency gave rise to an interesting and persistent dichotomy. The Latin word for a country dweller is *paganus* and in the Italian language it mutated in two connected directions. *Paesano* means a 'countryman' and *pagano* means a 'pagan', someone who is not a Christian.

After the persecutions in the reign of Decius, Italy began to decline economically. The Emperor was defeated and killed in battle against the Goths in AD 251, and in 259, 268 and 271 large Germanic warbands broke into Italy itself and attacked several cities. All were eventually repulsed by the legions but defensive walls were built around Rome, Verona and probably Florence and Fiesole as well as many other cities. Trade contracted and inflation began to erode the value of the imperial currency. A downward cycle was beginning to spin, and the focus of the empire drifted eastwards. By the end of the fourth century Bishop Ambrosius of Milan wrote despairing notes on the once thriving Bologna, Modena, Piacenza and other towns along the line of the Via Aemilia in the Po valley. He saw little more than 'the corpses of half-destroyed cities'. Tuscany is unlikely to have fared any better.

After the sack of Rome in AD 410, it suffered more humiliation in 455 when the Vandal King Gaiseric and his army pillaged what had survived. Emperors with exotic names enjoyed short and shaky reigns, often little more than the puppets of barbarian leaders. The last emperor in the West carried the ironic name of Romulus Augustus. Only a boy, the bearer of the fabled name of the first king and the first emperor almost certainly had no idea that he was to be the last.

In 476 Odovacer deposed Augustulus, the disrespectful diminutive by which he was known, and 'on account of his youth and beauty' did not kill him but sent him into a comfortable retirement on an estate in Campania with a pension of 6,000 gold *solidi*. The boy was never heard from again.

Meanwhile Odovacer, a general commanding an army of mixed Germanic warbands, called himself, not emperor, but King of the Nations, presumably a reference to his multicultural power-base. And it is only the fact that he did not arrogate to himself the imperial title which signalled to later historians that the Western Empire had ceased formally to exist. Contemporaries barely remarked on the change.

It was no more than a recognition of political reality. Barbarian successor-states had been established in most of the old Roman provinces/dioceses in Iberia, North Africa and Gaul – and now in Italy. But the Emperor in the East did not recognise them. And having in any case seen Romulus Augustus as a usurper, he took the same view of Odovacer. The Emperor Zeno then did what most of his successors were forced to do. In order to deal with barbarian usurpers, he enlisted the service of more barbarians. Theodoric, an Ostrogothic prince, had spent his boyhood in Constantinople as a hostage for the good behaviour of his people. He understood something both of imperial politics and of the ambitions of the Ostrogoths. Zeno's ministers began negotiations.

Originating from Scandinavia (where their name survives in Västergötland and Östergötland, and is remembered in the modern city of Gothenburg), the Ostrogoths had been settled in the empire in what is now Bulgaria. Some time after Odovacer seized power in Italy, Zeno gave Theodoric a commission. If he would lead the Ostrogoths west and depose this illegitimate king, he would rule the old Roman province as a viceroy. As the tribe began to move through the Balkans, the emperor enshrined his promise in a treaty: 'after the defeat of Odovacer, Theodoric, in return for his efforts, was to rule Italy for the emperor until he arrived in person'.

It took three ferocious battles to subdue the usurper-king, and even then it was only possible to extract a promise to rule Italy jointly with Theodoric. At Ravenna the formalities of a peace treaty were to be enacted between the two sides. When two Ostrogothic noblemen grasped each of Odovacer's hands in supplication and held them fast, Theodoric drew his sword and cleaved the king from collar-bone to hip, distractedly remarking that the old man's body seemed strangely boneless.

There were, however, to be no deceptions in dealings with the Emperor Zeno, and Theodoric took only the title *magister militum*, 'master of the soldiers'. Cities such as Milan submitted to him, but only because he was the formal representative of Constantinople. Consuls were appointed from the Roman Senate and Ravenna was rebuilt as a capital city. Over the rest of Italy, Ostrogothic noblemen took over a third of estates and property, no more than Odovacer's henchmen. In Tuscany, a rich and probably less war-torn province, Theodoric's cousin by marriage, Theodahad, was installed as governor.

The Ostrogothic king is sometimes described as Theodoric the Great. While the adjective may have been handy in distinguishing him from other Theodorics, he does seem to have ruled sensibly and with an eye to the future of his dynasty. The vast majority of his subjects were Italians who spoke Latin and were Catholic Christians under the spiritual care of a developing papacy. By contrast the Goths were Arians – Christians who believed that God the Son was not co-eternal with God the Father but created by Him out of nothing. This distinction may raise little more than a shrug in this secular age, but fifteen centuries ago such doctrinal differences were highly combustible. Theodoric understood that and kept Italians and Goths separate, both legally and culturally.

The other, more secular, distinction was between civil and military. Well understanding the source of his elevation and power, and never forgetting that his people were a small minority, Theodoric permitted only Goths to have any military function. On the other hand, he was very ready to use Italian expertise and experience in administration, and ultimately he appointed a fascinating figure as his *magister officiorum*, his prime minister.

Anicius Manlius Severinus Boethius was called 'the last of the Romans' by Lorenzo Valla, the great Renaissance philosopher and lexicographer. His distinguished lineage included emperors as well as popes, Boethius' family having been converted to Christianity at the end of the fourth century AD. Born somewhere on the borders of southern Tuscany, he was orphaned, taken in and raised by Symmachus, a Roman senator, thereby becoming part of the late imperial patrician class which, against considerable odds, survived in Italy for several generations after the fall of the West.

Boethius' life and legacy speak of parallel universes, of a sophisticated yet tenacious way of life, making its skills useful to waves of incoming barbarians, their kings and ferocious warbands. In reality, it may well be that the Roman heritage was less precious and fragile than it appears, and that the invaders were more knowing and educated. Boethius' story supplies evidence for both interpretations.

Born around AD 480, he may have studied in the Greek-speaking eastern Empire, at Athens and possibly Alexandria. With a huge population of around half a million at its zenith, in the third century AD, and its fabled library, Alexandria was also an important Christian centre. Traditionally the see of St Mark the Evangelist, its important role in the development of the early church and early Christian philosophers like Boethius, is sometimes overlooked. Some time around 470 Flavius Manlius Boethius, the father of Anicius Manlius, was involved in running a school in the city and family connections may have persisted.

After receiving an education in the relative peace of the eastern Mediterranean, the younger Boethius returned to the turmoil that was late fifth-century Italy. Through the influence of his adopted family and alongside Symmachus himself, he began to work at the court of the Ostrogothic king, Theodoric, as a member of what seems to have been a civil service. Some clear sense of the Gothic king's motives and attitudes can be found in a message he had written to King Gundobad of Burgundy, ruler of a barbarian successor-state carved out of eastern Gaul and centred on the Rhône and Soane valleys. It accompanied a water-clock and a sundial designed by Boethius: 'Possess in your native country what you once saw in the city of Rome ... Through you, Burgundy lays aside its tribal life, and, in its regard for the wisdom of its king, it properly covets the achievements of the sages.' The sages, by which he meant the ancient philosophers, became a passionate interest at Theodoric's court, which developed into an attempt to preserve the great canon of classical knowledge and thought. Boethius began to organise the translation of all the works of Plato and Aristotle from Greek into Latin. And he himself completed a great deal of work, translating and commenting on Euclid, Ptolemy and Porphyry, and some of his own original thoughts on the classification of music have survived. This was such a comprehensive and conspicuous project, such a vast labour undertaken and overseen (Boethius cannot have worked as a senior court official and been personally responsible for all the translations ascribed to him) by someone in his employ that King Theodoric must have known and approved. If he truly wished to lay aside the tribal life, then he and his people needed to make a decisive cultural shift and try to understand something of the ideas and philosophies which had been left behind by the Greeks and the Romans. And it was a vital legacy. Until the twelfth century most of the classical texts to survive in western Europe had passed through Boethius' hands.

By 520 Theodoric had made Boethius the most powerful Roman in Italy by appointing him *magister officiorum*, and to do him honour had also made his two sons consuls. But the power and the glory were short-lived. In 523 palace rumour and treachery had persuaded Theodoric that Boethius was no longer trustworthy. The king had his first minister arrested, stripped of all his wealth and privileges, condemned to death and thrown in prison in Padua to await execution. The charge was conspiracy. Perhaps suspected of reviving old eastern contacts, reverting to past loyalties, Boethius was accused of plotting with agents of the Byzantine Emperor to bring down Theodoric. It was a dismal and cruel end to a stellar career, a late and crucial flowering of classical scholarship, but the year in prison did produce something of enduring value.

While he awaited his certain death, Boethius composed a famous work, *The Consolation of Philosophy*. Taking the form of a dialogue between himself and the spirit of philosophy, it opens, not surprisingly, on a note of despair and bitterness. But as he develops his theme of philosophical detachment and Christian stoicism in the face of adversity, Boethius' great learning and talent transform *The Consolation of Philosophy* into an outstanding memorial. Adapting an old metaphor, he talks of the Wheel of Fortune, of how it spins between good and bad luck, between success and downfall.

Boethius' last work had immense influence in the Middle Ages, and as Lorenzo Valla noted, nothing comparable was produced in Italy until the fifteenth century. The Catholic Church canonised Boethius and in 2007 Pope Benedict XVI reminded believers of the continuing value of *The Consolation of Philosophy*.

The contrast between the sophistication of Boethius' intellect and the cruel manner of his death could not have been sharper. When his executioners came for him in 524, they had instructions to garotte him. But not quickly. As the cord was gradually tightened around his neck, they beat him with clubs.

Two years after this episode of barbarism, its instigator died. Theodoric was eventually succeeded as King of Italy by Theodahad of Tuscany. A Gothic chieftain said to be much less interested in the classical tradition, he occupied the throne for less than two years before the Roman past came back to haunt and hunt him.

In 536 the brilliant Byzantine general, Belisarius, invaded Italy with only 7,500 crack troops and swept north towards Rome. The emperor in the East, the long-lived Justinian, saw himself as a man of destiny who would return Rome to her ancient glories and become the restorer of the West. Having agreed an advantageous peace with the Persians which produced a rich annual tribute, he turned his gaze to the provinces once ruled by his predecessors. The Western Empire of Augustus, Trajan and Hadrian would once again be Roman.

Belisarius had mustered a mainly mercenary army and set sail from Byzantium at midsummer. There were many barbarian warriors in the expeditionary force, most of them Hunnish cavalry renowned for their ferocity, their accuracy with the bow and their horsemanship. They were also renowned for their unpredictability and indiscipline. Before the fleet had left the Sea of Marmara Belisarius was forced to put ashore and hang two Huns who had committed a drunken murder. Control was established early and it rarely wavered afterwards.

Behind its walls, Naples defied the Byzantine army for three weeks. Just as supplies were beginning to run low for the besiegers, a barbarian warrior stumbled on a way into the city. He had found an entrance to an old water pipe which ran under the walls. Wide enough for a man to crawl along, it turned out to be the key to Naples. After 400 chosen men had squeezed through, the city fell in a matter of hours. Byzantium's barbarians went on a rampage, killing, raping, looting. The pagan Huns surprised and terrified the population with their disregard for the sanctity of churches as they unhesitatingly slaughtered all who sought sanctuary inside them. Belisarius made a show of restraint, but he knew that a bloody example made of Naples would slacken the Gothic will to resist. Theodahad was deposed and Vitiges, the new king, retreated behind the marshes around Ravenna. The road to Rome lay open.

In December 536 Belisarius marched his small army up the Via Appia and they entered the great city by the Porta Asinaria. At the same time the Gothic garrison was leaving by the Porta Flaminia in the north. Rome was returned to the Roman Empire without a blow being struck. But the citizens were not necessarily happy to see the Goths go. Theodoric's tradition of tolerance and peaceful co-existence might have seemed preferable to the barbarian horde who rode into the city in the name of the empire and Justinian. What had happened in Naples had no doubt sent a shiver up the spine of Italy.

Having dispatched scouting parties of skirmishers north into Tuscany and Umbria, Belisarius knew that when it regrouped, Gothic resistance would be stiff and sustained. He prepared Rome for a long siege. In the middle of March 537, King Vitiges appeared at the head of a large army below the walls. And as the Roman Empire attempted to hold on to Rome, the city suffered as never before. To cut off supplies of clean water, the Goths cast down all the aqueducts and the defenders were forced to rely on the Tiber. It would be more than a thousand years before Rome's water supply was restored. And as the Goths assaulted the long circuit of the Aurelian walls, only makeshift defence was possible. Since its peak of around a million inhabitants in the first century AD, the city had shrunk inside its elaborate defences, and as Byzantine soldiers raced towards a point of attack, they used whatever came to hand. It is thought that thousands of pieces of sculpture were broken up and hurled down from the ramparts as missiles.

With the arrival of substantial reinforcements from the east, Belisarius was able to send sorties out of the city and one force of 2,000 cavalry captured Rimini on the Adriatic. Vitiges began to feel very vulnerable and a year after his army arrived outside Rome, he lifted the siege and retreated. Within months most of Italy south of Ravenna had fallen to the Byzantines. The only significant city still to resist was Fiesole, on a highly defensible site in the hills above Florence. And despite the intervention of a Frankish army, it too capitulated to Rome.

Belisarius was recalled to Byzantium in 540 and within a short time all of his extraordinary achievements began to unravel. A new Gothic king, Totila, defeated an imperial army in the Mugello, an upland district north of the Arno, and although Florence's walls held fast, most of Italy was lost.

The empire did strike back but when he returned, Belisarius' forces were insufficient to recover his earlier gains. After a generation of warfare, the cities and countryside had suffered terribly. Worse was to come, much worse. In 552 an unlikely Byzantine general arrived on the scene. Narses was an eighty-year-old eunuch with little military experience, but Justinian trusted him and sent a much larger expeditionary force under his command. At Scheggia, on the eastern borders of Umbria, Narses met Totila's army, killed the king and inflicted a crushing defeat on the Goths. It seemed that a measure of stability might at last be possible, but if there was optimism, then it was fleeting.

Fifteen years after Narses' victory over the Goths, another barbarian nation arrived in the north. Led by their king, Alboin, the Lombards had migrated over the Alps. Perhaps as many as 150,000 had trekked through the mountains, and amongst them were 70,000 or so warriors. It was another episode in the age of what German historians call the *Völkerwanderung*, the 'folk wanderings'. The

Lombard name has survived down to modern times and it originally meant 'the Longbeards', and they appeared to be an alliance of several different Germanic groups, certainly including a large contingent of Saxon warriors in their army. As they streamed down out of the mountain passes, they so terrified the inhabitants of the old Roman town of Aquileia that they fled to an archipelago of small islands in a northern lagoon of the Adriatic. The new and safer settlement eventually grew into the great city of Venice.

Italy had been so enfeebled by the Byzantine expeditions that the Lombards quickly secured the Po valley, and in 567 King Alboin was sending raiding parties across the Apennines into Tuscany. A year later the province became part of the new Lombard kingdom and a duke based himself at Lucca in the Arno valley and another at the old Etruscan city of Chiusi. Pisa was quickly isolated by land and only able to maintain maritime links with Rome. All that was left of the Byzantine conquests in northern and central Italy was the area around Ravenna which became known as the Exarchate. Linked by the Via Flaminia, it had a common frontier with the area near Rome controlled by the papacy. To the south, the Lombards carved out dukedoms based on Benevento and Spoleto, the latter causing the line of the old Roman road to move westwards out of its reach. The new road between Rome and Ravenna was called the Via Amerina and it divided Italy until the nineteenth century. It took the romantic heroism of Garibaldi and the Italian patriots of the Risorgimento to resolve the political patchwork first created by the Lombard and Byzantine wars.

Revival lay far in the future. Across the face of post-Roman Italy the dominant theme was decay. Even during the relatively enlightened reign of Theodoric, the great cities were sliding into ruin and disuse. Once buildings had lost their roofs and rain penetrated, they quickly degenerated after frost had cracked the plaster and the soaking floors caved in. Stone and tile robbers inflicted more damage but the most corrosive of all the elements was war. Pillaging armies destroyed trade, made markets impossible and often – as in the Gothic siege of Rome – actually physically destroyed the fabric of cities. In an age before explosives or bombs, substantial buildings were not easy to bring down, but much ancient stonework was reused as defensive walling. When war burst over them, the inhabitants of cities fled before it to the relative safety of the countryside, and if they returned, they found that more and more of the infrastructure needed to sustain even small populations had broken down.

Promulgated around 500, the collection of laws known as the *Codex Theodosianus*, the 'Decrees of Theodoric', talked of how great public buildings which had not tumbled down were occupied by squatters and those that had fallen had become little more than quarries for building materials. In many of the cities of post-Roman Italy and elsewhere in the empire, those who stayed on tended to live in the simplest sort of domestic buildings which had survived more or less intact. Many opted to live in the suburbs, where there was space to make vegetable gardens.

A century later, after the tremendously destructive Byzantine invasions, urban conditions had grown even more dismal. Some cities had declined dramatically. According to the contemporary historian Procopius, Rome had only 500 souls rattling around inside the vast circuit of the Aurelian walls. The actual number is more likely to have run into several thousands, but in an ancient and monumental city which had been home to a million people, the effect must have been haunting. The abandoned grandeur of the Colosseum, the Circus Maximus and the half-ruined, empty palaces on the Palatine Hill must have moved the hearts of those who came and walked its weed-encrusted streets – or at least stirred their curiosity.

Popes, their priests and the modest ceremonial at St John's Lateran were little more than a memory of empire, and many were acutely aware of its withering heritage. Gregory the Great reigned between 590 and 604 and left an elegiac record of what had happened in his lifetime: 'Now the cities have been depopulated, fortresses razed, churches burned down, monasteries and nunneries destroyed, the fields abandoned by mankind, and destitute of any cultivator the land lies empty and solitary. No landholder lives on it; wild beasts occupy places once held by a multitude of men.'

Archaeologists support Pope Gregory's gloom. Between *c.* 600 and *c.* 750 the countryside of central and northern Italy appears to have been all but deserted. Roman villas were entirely abandoned, no trace of occupation can be found, and the great *latifundia*, the estates around them, lay fallow and fragmented. Those few who lived off the land could manage no more than subsistence agriculture of the most primitive sort. Procopius wrote of plague and famine emptying the dying landscape. And more prosaically, a certain indicator of commercial breakdown was the complete cessation of large-scale pottery manufacture. No demand for containers meant negligible agricultural production and little more than highly localised trade. The amphorae out of which the wine of Italian vineyards had flowed were no longer needed. In his attempt to bring Italy back into the imperial fold, Justinian had all but destroyed it.

By around 700 Tuscany, or Tuscia, had been established as a Lombard dukedom. Alongside the new dukes were set up men known as gastalds, royal appointees who acted as judges in disputes. They tended to base themselves in the old cities while dukes built strongholds in the countryside. As the eighth century wore on, both tended to grow more and more independent of the royal court at Padua.

Lucca emerged as Tuscia's pre-eminent town. Perhaps it had survived the long years of war better, safe behind its Roman walls. Around *c.* 700 several new churches had been consecrated and their location offers some idea of how the settlement functioned. The ancient basilica of San Vincenzo was built to the north of the town, outside the walls, and the name of another very early foundation remembers its origins in the suburbs. Santa Maria Forisportam means 'St Mary's Outside the Gate'. But town life may have been reviving amongst the rubble of the centre of Lucca. As early as 715 there exist records of the cathedral, SS Giovanni e Reparata, built near the old Roman forum.

In the suburbs archaeologists have uncovered some evidence of commercial activity. Craftsmen such as goldsmiths and moneyers had set up workshops in their houses around the fringes of Lucca. And what they made is a further encouraging indication of a reviving economy, at least around the centre of the Lombard dukedom. Towards the end of the eighth century, the inhabitants began to build houses into the fabric of the Roman amphitheatre. Its basic oval shape can still be clearly seen in the Piazza Anfiteatro.

Lucca's early importance as a centre of the Christian Church had surprising origins. After the Rhine froze in 406 and the Western Empire was gradually dismembered by pagan and heretical barbarian kings, organised Christianity had retreated westwards. Only in Ireland, it seemed, did a light continue to shine and the religious communities survive and prosper. In the sixth and seventh centuries missionaries were sent to re-convert Britain and Europe. As late as the ninth century, they were still preaching the word of God and an exasperated French chronicler noted: 'Almost all of Ireland, despising the sea, is migrating to our shores with a herd of philosophers.'

At Lucca the old church of San Vincenzo was rededicated to the memory of an Irish monk who came to revive the worship of God. His name is lost but must somehow have resembled the Italianised San Frediano, the new name of his church. Not far to the east, at Fiesole, another Irish scholar, more formally known as Donato, was elected as bishop and reigned there for fifty years. The conversion of the Lombards is by no means an exclusively Irish achievement, but these wisps and scraps of names and traditions appear to point to significant involvement.

In November 753 shepherds in the high alpine Val d'Aosta saw something unexpected. Even though it was dangerously late in the year, a large party of aristocratic travellers was making its way up to the Great St Bernard Pass. Stephen II, the Patriarch of Rome, the Pope, was accompanied by many priests and escorted by Duke Aitchar, a Frankish nobleman, and his soldiers. Bands of brigands were a constant threat.

Pope Stephen had been forced into the winter mountains by politics. Aistulf, an aggressive and ambitious Lombard king, had attacked and captured the Byzantine exarchate of Ravenna, and his agents were demanding that the Roman pope pay annual tribute for the lands he held around the city. In effect, Aistulf was attempting to make him subject to the Lombard kings. The freedoms of the Church were clearly under threat.

Despite a visit to Aistulf in Padua and many tearful appeals to the king's Christian nature, and messages to Byzantium begging for the support of the emperor, no relief and no help were forthcoming. But Stephen was astute. Two years before his election, Pope Zacharias had granted his blessing to the new kings of Francia, a vast successor-state occupying most of Gaul and reaching far to the east, into Germany. When he deposed the moribund King Childeric, Peppin, the mayor of the palace and, in essence, a usurper, sent a question to Rome as to whether it was just for one to reign and another to rule. On receiving the right answer, Peppin III found himself obliged to the papacy, and Stephen II was climbing through the alpine snows to ask a favour in return.

In spite of centuries of neglect, the old paved Roman road through the mountains was still passable and the papal party arrived at the court of Peppin in Ponthion, almost 100 miles east of Paris, on 6th January 754. And a political bargain was struck, an arrangement which would profoundly shape the history of medieval Europe, and the history of Tuscany in particular.

In return for renewed confirmation of the legitimacy of Peppin's claim to the throne of Francia, the king promised to invade Italy and remove the Lombard monarchy. In the event, Stephen's new protector did more. Having defeated Aistulf, Peppin transferred the captured exarchate of Ravenna into papal hands. From the Adriatic to the Tyrrhenian Sea, the area that became the Papal States was forming and Tuscany would find itself on the frontier between the temporal domains of the Frankish empire and the Lands of St Peter.

At the same time as the Franks were campaigning in Italy, scribes in the papal chancery were carefully constructing a legal and historical framework to underpin their diplomatic success. Pope Stephen was party to a remarkably durable forgery. Some time in the early 750s a document which became known as the 'Donation of Constantine' mysteriously came to light, at just the right time. With the ink barely dry and using anachronistic Latin (words like *feodum* for 'fief'), it was represented as proof positive that the Emperor Constantine had given huge tracts of land to the Church 400 years before. Grateful to Pope Sylvester I for baptising him and curing him of leprosy, the emperor had bestowed lands all over the empire, from Judaea to Africa, and especially in Italy, certainly the area around Ravenna, and definitely the city of Rome. All very convenient. And not until Lorenzo Valla proved the text to be false in 1518 was the Donation seriously challenged.

In 773 a great king led his army into Italy. Charlemagne had succeeded his father, Peppin III, and in a long reign compiled a huge empire stretching from the Pyrenees to the Danube. In more than fifty campaigns, and a lifetime in the saddle, he recreated much of the Western Roman Empire.

Desiderius, Duke of Tuscia, had taken the crown of Lombardy by force and once again threatened the papacy, marching an army to the gates of Rome in 772. But when Charlemagne crossed the Alps, Desiderius quickly discovered discretion, surrendered and promptly went into exile somewhere in his old dukedom, perhaps a congenial castle in the Chianti hills. The new kingdom of the Franks, the renewed empire of Rome, now reached down to the southern borders of Tuscany.

On Christmas Day 800 Charlemagne knelt before St Peter's Tomb in Rome as Pope Leo III celebrated mass. When the formalities concluded and the great king rose, he became an emperor in name as well as in fact. Placing the imperial crown on his head, the pope led the congregation in hailing a new emperor in the West, acclaiming him Caesar Augustus, the heir of Rome. It was a highly significant moment, signalling a break with the Byzantine Empire, and also asserting the independence of the papacy from the Greek Patriarch in the East. On Christmas Day 800 Latin Christendom was born.

Charlemagne's formidable civil service, run by learned and worldly clerics such as Alcuin of Northumbria and the arch-chaplain, Fulrad, began to organise and systematise his immense domain. A common coinage appeared (whose multiples lasted more than a millennium) with 240 pennies to the pound and 12 to the shilling, and the new empire was divided into a network of more than 300 counties, each run by an imperial appointee. Tuscany became one such and over time its counts and countesses grew powerful.

When the great king conquered northern Italy in 773, he found himself riding amongst the ruins of a fast fading empire. It must have fascinated him. And if he was truly to revive it, then he needed to understand how it had understood itself, its thoughts and its history. At Pisa there lived a man known simply as Peter the Grammarian. Charlemagne insisted he accompany the army back over the Alps and teach the great king the language of the Romans. This minor cameo not only speaks of the ambition and aspiration of a new and young monarch, it also makes clear that pockets of learning did survive amongst the debris of Italy.

The new empire barely survived the death of its first emperor. After 814 Charlemagne's sons and grandsons repeatedly divided and redivided their sprawling inheritance. Italy became the southern part of the Middle Kingdom alongside Burgundy and Provence, and in reality its counts and bishops began to act independently.

With the disintegration of the Carolingian Empire, the ninth century saw Italy fall prey to more waves of aggression, this time by sea. The sails of Viking longships were seen in the Tyrrhenian and they attacked coastal settlements in Liguria. But even more serious and sustained were the ambitions of the Muslim conquerors of most of the Iberian peninsula. Their fleets had captured Sardinia and Corsica, and in 813 they mounted a savage raid on Civitavecchia on the Tuscan coast. Sicily and the far south of Italy were next, and for thirty years, until 871, there existed an emirate based at the city of Bari. Four years later the Byzantines returned and they held significant territory in the south for 200 years.

In the midst of all this instability pilgrims began to appear in the north of Italy. Usually banded together for safety and sometimes protected by mercenary soldiers, they made their way to Rome on the Via Francigena. By 800 this route had become established and was serviced by local monasteries and hospitals where pilgrims could sleep out of the elements and protected from brigands. The tomb and relics of St Peter were the major attraction, but along the way were shrines to lesser figures. Still very obvious in places and waymarked, the old pilgrim road crosses the Alps by the same route as Pope Stephen, through the Great St Bernard Pass and down into the Val d'Aosta. After it reaches Lucca, it aims for Siena and enters the Eternal City from the north. Many northern kings travelled the Via Francigena to pray at St Peter's tomb for forgiveness for their many sins and in 1040 Macbeth of Scotland was in Rome, where 'he scattered money like seed'.

The volatile politics of the western Mediterranean certainly inhibited trade, but the need for warships allowed one Tuscan city in particular to assert itself early. In 828 a fleet from Pisa attacked Muslim pirates and harried the coast of North Africa, and forty years later assisted the Lombard dukes of Benevento in defending their port of Salerno against more Muslim raiders. As its navy grew in size, Pisa gained control of the Tyrrhenian Sea with the seizure of Sardinia in alliance with Genoa, another developing maritime power. Two great admirals navigated Pisa to the zenith of its power. In 1051–52 Jacopo Cuirini conquered Corsica, and when Giovanni Orlando took the Sicilian town of Palermo from Muslim pirates, he won a huge treasure. There was enough gold for Pisa to begin building work on the great Piazza dei Miracoli, the 'Square of Miracles', now the site of its cathedral, baptistry and the famous leaning bell-tower.

The cathedral, Il Duomo, was begun in 1063, built to a design by a master-mason/architect known as Buscheto. It is a quintessentially Mediterranean building, its influences showing the reach of Pisa's sailors and merchants. On the façade Muslim-style arches can be seen and the mosaics of the interior have an unmistakable Byzantine feel.

The Piazza dei Miracoli was conceived on a grand scale by an ambitious and aggressive city. Beside the Duomo there was to be a baptistry and a bell-tower to summon the faithful. Both were begun in the second half of the twelfth century and the bell-tower quickly became famous – but for all the wrong reasons. It started to lean noticeably soon after building work began in 1173. Not only were the foundations for such a tall and heavy building too shallow, at 3 metres, the subsoil in which they were dug was also prone to subsidence. When the marble blocks of the third storey were first hoisted into place, the masons were horrified to see the structure lurch to one side, leaning about five degrees out of true. If any more storeys had been added the bell-tower would certainly have collapsed. But war intervened, and as Pisa fought against its great maritime rival of Genoa, resources were diverted, money dried up and the project was abandoned.

As the summers and winters of a century passed and Pisa's fortunes waxed and waned, the tower appeared to stabilise, the foundations settling and the marble coursing stayed in place. No-one appears to have suggested that the building be dismantled: a bell tower had to be adjacent to its cathedral. When scaffolding was erected once again in 1272, under the direction of Giovanni di Simone, the masons tried to build the walls back into a safe alignment. Their solution was simple. By using trapezoidal stones (cut at different thicknesses, with no two sides parallel and exactly to fit), they built up the storeys with one side slightly taller than the other. It worked. The north stairway has two fewer steps than the one in the south, the general direction of the lean. But the effect is curious. The tower looks both lopsided and curved, like a wind-bent tree trying to straighten up to reach the sun.

War halted construction several times, allowing the building to settle, and the top floor was not completed until 1319, with the bell-chamber being finally added in 1372. Almost 500 years after masons laid its inadequate foundations, the tower was complete, the last and largest bell being hung in 1655. But all was not well. For the following 250 years the tower continued, very slowly, to lean to the south-west. By 1990 the angle had become dangerous and it was believed that there was an imminent possibility of collapse. Cables were attached and anchored on the northern side, and as they held the

14,000-tonne structure, concrete was injected into the foundations. The work was delicate and painstaking. For twelve years visitors were not allowed to enter the building or even approach too closely as engineers began to pull it towards the vertical and the founds were filled and strengthened. By May 2008, the chief engineer, Professor Michele Jamiolkowski, reported to the world's press that the lean had been corrected by 15 inches from the dangerous angle of 1990 and was now roughly as it was in 1700.

Almost a millennium before Professor Jamiolkowski's team rescued Pisa's greatest monument, the city was establishing foundations of a different kind. The city began to flex its muscles against its Tuscan neighbours. In 1003 a long tradition of inter-city warfare was established when Pisa attacked Lucca to secure its immediate hinterland in the valley of the Arno, and in 1060 it soundly defeated Genoa in a naval engagement.

Powerful enough to exclude the counts of Tuscany from any meaningful involvement in the government of the city, the Pisans sought to formalise their de facto independence in law. In 1077 Pope Gregory VII recognised the *Consuetudini di Mare*, the 'Laws and Customs of the Sea', as the basis for the self-government of the city. And Henry IV, the Holy Roman Emperor, as Charlemagne's title was styled in the eleventh century, followed suit in 1081, promising no interference. Pisa chose a Roman model for the governance of its new republic and elected a Council of Elders, or a Senate, and each year two consuls had executive power.

These were turning moments in the story of Tuscany. Military clout had won Pisa independence but political geography would also prove useful. The city was formally part of the Holy Roman Empire but remote from the German princes who held the title, and it was not part of the Papal States, but it was handily close to Rome. As the events of the eleventh century unfolded, Tuscany's cities began to awaken and assert themselves. What became known as the Age of the Communes was dawning.

5

The Communes

Ringing through the medieval streets, ancient songs of celebration are sung by hundreds of men and women. More like martial anthems, they announce that the past has come back to vivid life. Around a corner the choir appears with banners flying, all wearing the same bright, heraldic colours. Prancing sideways in front of them, wild-eyed, sweat-flecked and terrified, a horse is led in a halter. Tied around its neck is the silk flag of a parish, one of the seventeen *contrade* of the city. When they reach their parish church, the supporters fan out into the small piazza in front and, linking arms, they sway as they sing. Then, on an unseen signal, the horse is led clattering and unwilling up the marble steps, its shoes striking sparks, and taken through the doors of the church. Inside, a packed congregation roars approval. Horses have been known to rear at this and at least four strong men hold hard on its lead-ropes and halter. Once at the high altar, a smiling priest blesses the bewildered animal (often it splatters diarrhoea on the marble pavement – but that is always seen as a sign of good fortune to come) with the words 'Go, little horse, and return here a winner.'

This is the afternoon of the Palio, the great horse race run around the Campo, the huge public space at the heart of the Tuscan city of Siena. And this is the moment when its past comes racing across the centuries to create spectacular, intense and very real drama. All that differs from the thirteenth century are the clothes and the haircuts of the vast crowds assembling in the Campo to watch.

Days before, the city works department has been busy. Each year, around the fan-shaped piazza, they build a race-track of rammed earth and border it with brightly painted barriers. Because the Campo is canted at an appreciable angle, the horses are forced to race downhill on one side and then make a sharp right-angled turn in front of the

Palazzo Pubblico. Mattresses are tied to the pillars of its arcaded entrance. The jockeys ride bareback, without saddles or stirrups, and with only rudimentary bridles, and when they attempt the dangerous turn, some go flying, skidding across the rammed earth and crashing into the barriers. No jockey has ever been killed in the Palio, it is claimed, but fallen horses can be trampled to death by pursuers unable to avoid them. Animal rights organisations make justifiable protests, but they are always ignored. This is an emphatically medieval event and medieval values govern it. No-one cares much if a jockey is unseated or breaks a leg. A riderless horse can win the Palio and winning is all that matters to the 10,000 packed into the Campo. The race is not a tourist attraction, not something revived to amuse the charabanc trade. There is no commentary or explanation of its arcane rules and no Sienese would ever consider changing it. The Palio is what sets the city's heart racing, an ancient and dangerous set of traditions which animates modern Siena. And it is incidentally the best sort of history lesson, an occasion which accurately recreates the civic life of the medieval communes of Tuscany for the length of a summer's day.

In fact there are two Palii each year, one in early July and a second in mid-August. Each follows the same ritual. After ten horses of roughly equal ability have been found in local stable yards, they are brought into the city and paraded on the track in front of the Palazzo Pubblico. Thousands come to watch as each competing *contrada* is awarded a horse by lot. Three days of *prove*, trial races, are then run to allow the horses and the riders to become accustomed to the setting. When the day comes, and the horse has been blessed in the afternoon, the bells of the Palazzo Pubblico ring out over the rooftops.

A stunning pageant begins to process. Called the Corteo Storico, it features equerries, ensigns, pages and drummers, all dressed in medieval costumes made in the colours of the *contrade* and the black and white of the city. Accompanied by thunderous bass drumming, the *alfieri* appear with their banners. Casting them above their heads, behind their backs and flinging them high in the air in the synchronised flourishes known as *sbandierate*, their nonchalant grace draws gasps and applause. And tears. The Sienese are passionate about their *contrade* and when their colours fly in the air on the day of a Palio, the tears always come.

Behind them march the bearers of the ancient offices of the commune and the medieval republic, and at their head is not the flag of the city but the standard-bearer of the small town of Montalcino which lies 30 kilometres to the south. It is a place of pride, and of memory. When in 1557 Siena suffered the humiliation of being bought by its blood-rival, Florence, from the Spanish emperor, Charles V, 2,000 exiles fled to the little town near the Via Cassia. There they defiantly set up the Republic of Siena at Montalcino. It survived for four years.

Behind the *alfieri* and the drummers trundles the Palio itself. It is a banner, a pall, which carries the image of the Virgin Mary, and it will be presented to the winning *contrada*. Installed in a wagon, pulled by two white oxen, it is cheered as it passes. The wagon is the *carroccio*, the war chariot of the city, the only one that survives in Tuscany. Wherever a battle took place, and there were plenty in the Middle Ages, the *carroccio* was pulled onto the field and the banners of the city planted in it. A rallying point in the melee, it was something to be defended to the death.

The *contrade* of the city were originally military organisations, each one bound to provide contingents of men for the armies of Siena. Once there were sixty of these wards, and the seventeen which survive are unique in Italy. Most are named after the heraldic devices of their banners: the Eagle, the Caterpillar, the Snail, the Tower, the Shell and the She-Wolf, and around the city each different neighbourhood is identified by plaques set high on the street corners. Now as social and dining clubs, as religious confraternities focused on the parish church, they maintain a mutual assistance fund and initiate neighbourhood improvement schemes. When a child of the *contrada* is born, he or she is baptised twice, once in the parish church and again in the parish fountain. At weddings and funerals a herald decked in the colours is always sent. Crime and drug use in modern Siena is negligible. Nothing to do with the police force; it is the power of the officials of the *contrada* which keeps the old city peaceful and makes its streets safe. Everyone knows everyone else's business, and before anything gets out of hand offenders are taken aside and a quiet word is spoken.

The only time violence, bribery or intimidation are tolerated is in the week of a Palio. The *contrade* are not quaint and kindly archaisms in July and August but coiled springs wound up for victory. Fighting between rivals sometimes breaks out, and as a means of letting off steam it appears to work well. Siena has a long tradition of short bursts of public violence. When the Palio used to be run through the streets, the Campo was given up to the Gioco del Pugno, literally, the 'Game of the Fist'. Huge gangs from the *contrade*, 300 or more a side, fought each other in the piazza as crowds bayed and jeered. The only rule appears to have forbidden weapons, but otherwise the young men had licence to beat each other senseless with their fists. Compared to this so-called sport, the occasional modern skirmish between *contrade* rates as little more than a disturbance.

Bribery is the most common and effective means of making a win in the Palio more likely. Jockeys are often approached and if thick wads of notes are not sufficiently persuasive, they are sometimes accompanied by offers no-one could refuse. It is surely no accident that after the race is run, jockeys keep galloping, heading straight out of the piazza, dismounting and departing as quickly as possible before disappointment catches up with them.

So ferocious is the rivalry that grudges are held over centuries, nursed through the winters to keep them warm and refreshed each summer. The Eagle, based just to the south of the Campo, hates the Panther *contrada* for long-forgotten reasons and is usually allied with the Owl and the Dragon. Since its long-term animosity to the Giraffe was patched up, the Caterpillar has no enemies – at present. It is allied to the Porcupine, the Shell and the Tower. These ancient intricacies are well understood by every Sienese and they often influence the outcome of races. Outsiders are left wondering. But the alliances allow proxy support. The narrow race-track in the Campo has room for only ten runners and so seven *contrade* have to sit out any one Palio. They automatically qualify for the next one, while the remaining three places are allocated by lot.

On the nights before a race jockeys are sometimes ambushed in the streets, despite having bodyguards from their *contrada*. Somewhere out of sight they are persuaded not to attempt to win the race, and horses are sometimes doped (occasionally by jockeys who have been persuaded) to achieve the same non-result. None of this is done in fun. The Owl has not won a *palio* in more than thirty years and the other *contrade* jeer '*Nonna! Nonna!*' Literally meaning 'grandmother', it is an insult to the proud men and women in red, black and white. The Owls will do anything to win.

It is 7 p.m. in the Campo. The Corteo Storico has passed and the bell of the Palazzo Pubblico has tolled the hour. Hushed, expectant, the packed crowd waits. Millions of euros have been risked in bets. Rumours of fixes fly around the piazza like swooping swallows. How much did which jockey take? Has the Shell's horse been nobbled? And then, as though from nowhere, the runners and riders appear. Like a wave rolling across the Campo, a roar fills the evening air and the horses shy and skitter sideways.

The start for the Palio is near the Fonte Gaia on the long high side. A cannon is primed. Nine of the horses are held in a small area between two ropes while one is free and circles behind them. This is the *rincorso* and the race will only begin when the jockey charges the other nine from behind at a moment of his choosing. This is when the sharp-eyed can detect a fix. The *rincorso* may wait until an allied *contrada*'s horse is facing the right way or is in a good position before making his move. When at last he does, the cannon booms, the ropes drop – and it is a false start. The crowd groans. Some arcane rule, some minor infraction brings the horses back. And often, as soon as they assemble, the *rincorso* suddenly charges again and they really are away.

Flying around the first corner, the hoofbeats thunder, and then downhill to the Palazzo Pubblico corner and up the shaded side. Only three circuits, the Palio lasts 90 seconds. The sole prohibition during the race is snatching the reins of a rival. Otherwise the jockeys barge each other, whip opponents' horses and kick for dear life, bouncing bareback at breakneck speed. When the winner crosses the line, there is near-delirium.

Then the parties begin. And the post-mortems and recriminations. The winning horse is paraded around the streets of the city (its jockey is usually nowhere to be seen, probably counting his money and staying away from those who bribed him to throw the race), its head raised, the white of its eyes showing its terror at all the chaos around it. And the race is re-run endlessly on television.

The passion of the Palio is absolutely authentic, entirely undimmed over at least seven centuries. And more, it shows vividly how a medieval city celebrated itself, its customs and traditions already old. The costumes, the colours and the processions are all eloquent about the past, showing what it looked like, but it is the persistence of medieval habits of mind in Siena which is so fascinating. The cut-throat rivalry inside the city recalls the ceaseless feuding of the thirteenth and fourteenth centuries, the loyalty to the *contrada*, an extended family, is an ingrained impulse and the sheer, unbridled pride of belonging is attractive in the alienated, urban world of the early twenty-first century.

The Palio is run on the site of the Roman forum of the town of Sena Julia, and while little else remains from antiquity, it is still the focus of urban life. In northern Italy there were almost 100 substantial Roman towns, some of them large and prosperous like Milan and Bologna, and by AD 1000 nearly seventy were still functioning as communities, although much reduced in size.

By the twelfth century the Tuscan towns were beginning to boom. Some of the most hard-wearing and fine wool was reared in the hills around Siena and in the western foothills of the Apennines, the countryside close to Lucca, Florence and Arezzo. Cloth production came to be organised on a semi-industrial basis, turning out large volumes for trade. This in turn produced cash surpluses and led to a growth in banking, particularly in Siena and Florence. With the purchase of a silver mine from the old Etruscan town of Volterra in the 1160s, local mints were able to produce a sound and relatively plentiful coinage for Siena. The city still boasts the world's oldest bank, the Monte dei Paschi di Siena, founded in the fifteenth century and a successor to an even older institution.

Well-organised textile production and high cash balances were not the only stimuli to the gathering phenomenon of urban growth in medieval Tuscany. International politics played a central role in making the great cities more independent and economically dynamic.

The Investiture Contest which flared into such dramatic life with the humiliation of the Emperor Henry IV in the snows at Canossa continued throughout the Middle Ages. The German emperors and the popes exchanged advantages over hundreds of years and two parties of supporters gathered around each. Named after the German royal house of Hohenstaufen von Weiblingen, the Ghibellines backed the imperial cause in Italy, and the Guelfs became the papal party. In seeking more and more independence, the Tuscan cities opposed interference from any quarter but since they lay to the north of the directly controlled Papal States and were formally part of the Holy Roman Empire, they were usually Guelfs, of course. Those few cities who had Ghibelline sympathies sometimes only adopted them for the sake of preserving their freedom from each other. Siena had originally been Guelf but in the thirteenth century crossed over to avoid being in the same camp as its hated rival, Florence.

In rejecting the rule of the German emperors, the Tuscan cities began to talk of concepts like freedom, and in devising a conceptual, constitutional framework to enshrine it, lawyers and the law grew in importance. After Pisa pioneered the 'Customs of the Sea' in 1077, others followed suit. The death of the powerful Countess Matilda, the protectress of Pope Gregory VII, in her castle at Canossa, was Florence's cue to seek greater independence. By 1115 the city was breaking away from the control of the nobility, especially the Alberti family, the counts of Guidi. Siena elected its first consuls in 1125, and by 1169 its bishops had ceased to be significant figures in government. At the same time Arezzo wrested power from its bishop.

A predecessor had made a very significant and entirely non-political cultural contribution through an act of enlightened patronage. Church music was an integral, even inspiring part of worship and what became known as Gregorian chant was sung by large choirs in the cathedrals and churches of the Tuscan cities. The Bishop of Arezzo, Tedald, was especially proud of his singers, and in 1025 he began to encourage the innovative work of a Benedictine monk, Guido d'Arezzo.

The problem for large choirs was a restricted repertoire. Each new piece of music had to be taught by ear, and often performances were uneven because of the simple fact of some singers being better able to remember the sequences of notes than others. By inventing written notation and an easily memorable scale, Guido d'Arezzo revolutionised the learning and singing of religious music.

Using the first syllables of the opening stanza of the hymn, *Ut queant laxis*, the monk compiled the hexachord, the scale first known as *ut, re, mi, fa, sol, la*. *Doh* was later substituted for *ut* and *ti* and another *doh* at the end of the sequence added. Guido also developed a four-line staff, the precursor of the modern five-line version. Using it he was able to write down all the notes of the antiphoner, a book containing all the chants needed for the daily monastic offices: Matins, Lauds, Prime, Terce, Sext, Nones, Vespers and Compline.

Pope John XIX was impressed and invited Guido d'Arezzo to Rome, almost certainly to show the papal court how the new techniques worked and what their uses could be. The Eternal City was not, however, congenial and Guido began to suffer poor health. By 1028 he had returned to Arezzo and probably died there sometime after 1030 at the bishop's palace.

Inside the walls of the medieval cities less peaceful and creative pursuits were being followed. In many places there was fierce faction fighting between Guelf and Ghibelline. The landed nobility, whose hilltop castles punctuated the landscape, were mostly Ghibellines, supporters of the German emperors who had originally conferred their titles and estates and were likely to underpin their continuing dominance. But at the same time they, too, valued independence. During the long periods when the emperors were distracted by politics north of the Alps, when they were forced to ignore Italy, Tuscan counts and lords became used to their own version of freedom.

When the cities began to grow and produce wealth (largely from the produce of the land), the landed gentry had no hesitation in setting up town houses from which they could protect their interests and influence local politics. This led immediately to friction. Between 1177 and 1179 Florence was torn into near-anarchy as noble families fought each other. Crossbowmen were shooting in the streets. There were pitched battles in the piazze, buildings were set alight and assassination was a constant threat.

Often families would find allies. There was a great deal of intermarriage within a restricted circle and the unity of an extended family would sometimes focus on the patronage of a particular church or chapel. In Florence the Pazzi Chapel and the Medici Chapel are later examples. Quarters of the city were seen as distinct territories and the likes of the Peruzzi family lived in houses around a single piazza. But the most striking legacy of these volatile times was the tall towers built inside the city walls. In the early thirteenth century the skyline of Florence was pierced by at least 150 and there were many in Pisa, Lucca, Siena and Arezzo. Famously, in the small town of San Gimignano, fifteen towers still stand.

When several families came together, they formed what were known as *consorterie*. And it was these organisations which pooled resources to build the great towers. Useful both as a secure place of refuge and as a means of attack, they could sometimes soar to 50 metres. The taller the tower the better to place archers and even catapults on its roof. These could fire down on other towers or into the street. Sometimes the members of *consorterie* who built them would sign contracts and in Lucca one of these notes that in times of crisis, they should decide whether to serve the commune or to serve every one of his friends. It was a characteristic tension, one which still disconnects national, local and personal politics in 21st-century Italy.

In 1095 Pope Urban II preached the First Crusade in Clermont, in central France. It was an event whose historical significance also rippled into the twenty-first century, and more immediately, it transformed the fortunes of the great Italian maritime cities. Concerned by the endemic violence in medieval society, particularly in France, where the military culture of knighthood had caused continuing trouble, Urban wanted to channel all that aggression into the service of God, and the papacy. Jerusalem had fallen to Muslim forces and the holy places needed Europe's warriors to ride to its rescue. Immensely powerful religious symbolism came into play. Christians saw Jerusalem as an earthly gateway to Heaven, the site of the Passion, where God had walked in the garden. Now the sacred city had been defiled by the hands of unbelievers.

No-one, not even Pope Urban, could have predicted the reaction to his call for a crusade. At Clermont the huge crowd below the papal dais, knights, bishops and ordinary people, was inspired, roaring *Dios lo volt* ('God wills it!') A torrent of profound fervour was suddenly released. A cardinal fell to his knees and made confession. Thousands came forward for Urban's blessing and to join the Way of God, to take the cross and become a fighting pilgrim in the holy war. The pope promised forgiveness for the sins of all who went to *outremer*, across the sea to fight the unbelievers and restore Jerusalem. Many marched and walked across Europe, through what is now Turkey and down to Palestine. Others travelled by sea and the growing navies of Genoa, Venice and Pisa were happy, for a fee and concessions, to transport crusaders to the east. Transformed overnight into an admiral, the Archbishop of Pisa personally led his city's ships to the shores of the Holy Land. In return for this vital logistical link, the Italian cities saw their trading horizons open up as never before.

Ship-owning merchants began to make fortunes. The easternmost coasts of the Mediterranean, known as the Levant, were where the spice roads reached the sea. And it was a fabulously lucrative trade. In a Europe before refrigeration, food was only fresh for a short time and meat usually very salty from the only reliable preservation agent.

And so spices were more than just an option in cookery, at least for those who could afford them. They also had an important role in medicine as admixtures. Most attractive of all to the Italians, spices were the best sort of cargo. High-value, not perishable, light and not bulky, they could be delivered in quantity on the quaysides of Venice, Genoa and Pisa and fetch vast prices. All that merchants and their sea-captains had to ensure was a safe passage through pirate-infested waters from a Levantine port to their customers in Italy, and then they could be sure of making their profits. Investors queued up.

As trade settled into a pattern, and naval cover improved after the success of the First Crusade, merchants became powerful as well as rich. And not only in the coastal cities. Inland, in Florence, Siena, Arezzo and elsewhere, a mercantile class made money from the textile trade. Perhaps aping the Roman formula, in Florence this group began to call themselves Il Popolo, 'the People'. In reality they meant to contrast themselves with the Senate, the aristocracy, and describe themselves as the free people of the city, something like 'the Citizens'. In any case they sought actively to challenge the power of the nobility and carve out a share of political power.

In the shadows of their great towers, the aristocratic factions were growing ever more fractious. Often they used the language and habits of chivalry. Honour could be impugned by insults and these could ignite blood feuds between the offender and the offended. Any wider political dimension sometimes came later. It was said by contemporaries that the bitter rivalry of the Guelfs and Ghibellines in Florence actually began over a matter of family honour. On the Ponte Vecchio a young nobleman, Buondelmonte de' Buondelmonti, was murdered by assassins sent by the Uberti family because he had been persuaded to break off an engagement to one of their daughters (and thereby wrecking any future marriage prospects for her) and marrying into the Donati family. Honour was satisfied but a long and bloody political feud followed.

Too much was at stake for this to be allowed to continue, and as the thirteenth century wore on, the noble families were gradually removed from any role in the government of Florence. Between 1248 and 1259 Il Primo Popolo established a stable regime. It was underpinned by the great craft guilds. Divided into seven major guilds and fourteen minor ones, these organisations represented different industries, textiles being the most important.

The most prestigious was the Arte dei Giudici e Notai, the lawyers' guild. As ever, they made money when an economy boomed; contracts had to be drawn up and notarised, and disputes settled. Most of their corporate clients came from the three textile guilds, the wool, silk and cloth merchants, the Arte della Lana, the Arte di Por Santa Maria, and the Arte di Calimala. The bankers' guild, the Arte del Cambio, grew in importance throughout the Middle Ages. The Arte dei Medici, Speziali e Merciai eventually admitted more than doctors, apothecaries and shopkeepers. As artists and sculptors were better and better paid, emerging as more than paint- and dust-spattered tradesmen, they were allowed to join. The seventh major guild also charged high prices. The furriers and leather workers were members of the Arte dei Vaccai e Pellicciai. Butchers, tailors, masons and many more humble crafts formed the fourteen lesser guilds.

The church of Orsanmichele in Florence is a fascinating monument to all that early trade unionism. Its walls are decorated with sculptures of the saints and the Madonna, many made by great Florentine masters, men like Ghiberti, Donatello and Verrocchio and paid for by the members of the guilds. There was of course a row about who did what. Niches had been allocated but in sixty years of wrangling and inaction, only one had been filled. A ten-year deadline was imposed, and in a relative frenzy of commissioning, some stunning work was produced. Made for the *corazzai*, the armourers, Donatello's *St George* is justly believed to be one of the most beautiful sculptures he made.

The guilds were wealthy enough not only to pay for great art but also to maintain small companies of soldiers and to buy more military backing if they needed it. Florence had enlarged the circuit of its medieval walls several times, growing into one of the very largest cities in Europe, with more than 100,000 souls. And it was the richest. By sheer weight of numbers and resources, the Popolo simply dominated the aristocracy.

Towards the end of the thirteenth century, the leading seven guilds, gli Arti Maggiore, promulgated a new constitution. *Gli Ordinamenti della Giustizia* of 1293 confirmed existing practices and at last formally excluded the noble families. Dante Alighieri, the great poet, was unimpressed and compared Florence's politics to a sick man forever shifting his position in bed. But in reality the settlement of 1293 was very successful in that it lasted more or less intact until

1534. For two and a half centuries the city remained a republic ruled by an oligarchy.

The foundations of a new building were laid in 1299 to house the new government. Now known as Il Palazzo Vecchio, the 'Old Palace', it still stands, dominating the eastern side of the Piazza della Signoria. Every two months it saw a new government. In a remarkable system, the council which controlled the city was chosen by lot in a public ceremony. Mostly selected from the members of the seven major guilds, names were placed in eight leather bags (kept under lock and key in the sacristy of the Franciscan church of Santa Croce) and then drawn out. For eight weeks the nine men chosen at random met in the Palazzo Vecchio in near-continuous session, only emerging at the end of their tenure of office. As they sat and debated, they were fed, waited upon, closely guarded and even occasionally entertained. A *buffone*, a professional clown, was permanently employed in the palazzo.

This governing committee, the Priori or Signori, was chaired and led by the *gonfaloniere*, the city's standard bearer. One of their most important duties was the nomination of a series of sub-committees to oversee different aspects of civic life such as security, commerce and so on. All were supported by a permanent civil service headed by a chancellor, an office once held by Niccolò Machiavelli. In times of crisis a *podestà* could be appointed from another city (supposedly with no loyalties to any faction) and he assumed dictatorial powers. When the Vacca sounded, the great bell of the Palazzo Vecchio whose deep note was thought to be like the lowing of a cow, then the times were really desperate and all Florentine citizens over the age of fourteen were summoned to a *parlamento* in the piazza.

In reality the random system of choosing by lot was routinely manipulated by the major guilds and the powerful mercantile families. By carefully controlling the names inserted in the leather bags at Santa Croce, they could ensure a consistently like-minded and sympathetic city government. Even though this republican constitution was corrupt and excluded not only Il Popolo Minuto, literally the 'small people', Florence's proletariat, but also I Grandi, the nobility, its survival and success are a testament to subtlety. Because of the skill of the Peruzzi, the Strozzi, the Medici and the Albizzi, the city was basically stable, wealthy and ready to witness an astonishing cultural flowering in the centuries to come.

Only once in the fourteenth century did the system break down significantly. In 1378 Florence was suddenly engulfed in a storm of street violence which quickly became a revolution. The lowliest group of wool-workers, those who washed and carded the raw fleeces so that they could be wound more easily into yarn, rose up against their employers and their starvation wages. Known as I Ciompi, from the noise made by their wooden clogs on the paved floors of the wool-washing houses, they attacked the comfortable houses of the wool merchants and drove the Signori and their officials out of the city. For four years the Ciompi ruled Florence and their principal demand was the freedom to form their own guilds so that they could protect their interests and share in the prosperity of the wool trade. Even though their Sienese brethren also rose up, their efforts failed and in 1382 the leather bags were once more taken out of the sacristy of Santa Croce.

Overwhelmed by the money and resourcefulness of the Florentine middle classes, the Ciompi were unlikely ever to succeed. Alongside the textile industry which so ruthlessly exploited the wool carders, another business had first been stimulated by Tuscan manufacturing and then outstripped it. Banking became centrally important in all the Italian merchant cities, but especially in Genoa, Venice, Pisa, Siena and ultimately Florence.

The Crusades triggered a new need for cash movement. Large sums were required to pay for the wars in the east and transporting gold and silver coins over long distances was both awkward and dangerous. And all around the Mediterranean shore, sometimes from city to city, there were differences in denomination and relative values were difficult to work out. Money changers occupied a pivotal position and, with astute calculation and manipulation, could accrue vast profits.

A different approach to cash transfers was needed, and the first recorded paper transaction took place in 1156. Two brothers borrowed 115 pounds in Genoa and agreed to a contract obliging them to repay the loan – in Byzantium. One month after entering the city, the brothers were bound to reimburse the Genoese bank's agents with 460 bezants. This gold coinage, minted in the Byzantine empire, was considered the most pure and stable available in the east. Clearly the brothers had bought a cargo for 115 pounds, shipped it eastwards and hoped to sell it in Byzantium, or nearby, for more than the 460 bezants.

What this early example shows is, in essence, the use of a paper currency. Backed by coinage made from precious metals, the contract issued in Genoa not only had an equivalent value 1,000 miles to the east, it also had value in itself.

The Crusades also saw the establishment of chivalric orders of knights. Perhaps the most famous were the soldier-monks known as the Knights Templar. Richly endowed by a flood of donations from the pious and the anxious, they spread all over Europe in the twelfth century. In each major European city a temple was set up. Often strongly fortified, it also had a chapel protected by a force of soldier-monks. When patrons donated cash (as well as lands and services), the Templars sometimes needed to move it around and they, almost inadvertently, became bankers, all the more trusted because of their religious role as guardians of the Temple in Jerusalem.

Merchants, pilgrims and crusaders began to accept what were called demand notes from the Templars in return for deposits of local currency. These could be cashed in any Temple in any city for the equivalent value. For travellers demand notes were obviously much less risky to carry than coins, and if they did happen to be robbed, it was unlikely that bandits would attempt to present one. Most important was the fact that a religious order could charge a marginal fee for the use of this service.

Usury, or the charging of interest on loans, was specifically forbidden by the Church. That was the reason for the importance of Europe's Jews in the money economy. But a charge could legitimately be made for a service, and through this loophole most of the Tuscan banking families cheerfully climbed, after the Templars were suppressed in 1307.

Despite the popularity of paper money, coin remained vital. The problem was that there was too little, Europe being poor in silver and gold deposits. This in turn had forced governments of all sorts (who controlled mints) sometimes to debase their coinage and issue bronze and copper money which had a low intrinsic value. With typical élan, the growing Italian cities solved the problem by enterprise, by locating a new source of gold – from Africa.

The stories were legendary. 'King Solomon's Mines' and 'Prester John' are more modern variants on the myths of fabulous wealth in the heart of Africa. But the Genoese, the Venetians and the Florentines knew that there was substance to the tales. The divine kings who ruled at Great Zimbabwe were fabulously wealthy. Between 1250 and 1450 their acropolis city near Lake Mutirikwi gathered in much of the gold mined in the provinces of Matabeleland and Mashonaland. Traders from the Muslim port of Sofala, now in modern Mozambique, came to barter for the ingots and take the first step on their journey to Zanzibar, Mogadishu and the Mediterranean.

The Arab historian, Muhammad Al-Idrisi, wrote that the West African kings of Ghana tethered their horses to bricks of gold. The mines on the banks of the Sirba sent bullion across the Sahara to the ports at Tunis and Algiers, and further west Arab traders took Senegalese and Guinea gold to Ceuta and across the straits to southern Spain. A faint memory of this ancient route still lingers in the old English word 'guinea' for a gold coin worth 21 shillings.

By the end of the thirteenth century a great deal of pure African gold had found its way into the heart of the European economy. And in the astute hands of Tuscan and Venetian merchants, the effect was not inflationary – but revolutionary. The Italian cities saw a great opportunity. Florence minted a pure gold coinage, the florin, which became a standard unit of reliable value in western Europe, and in the east the Venetian ducat was recognised as a stable currency.

Another vital element in the development of banking came out of Africa in the thirteenth century. A Pisan merchant, Guglielmo Bonaccio, had established himself in a trading post (perhaps as a customs official) near Algiers in what was then the territory of the Almohad sultanate. His wife died young and so Guglielmo had his son brought over from Pisa to live with him. Only nine years old, the boy showed a precocious interest in arithmetic, something which no doubt delighted his father. But it was not the clumsy Roman numerals which fascinated Leonardo. Based on the fingers and hands ('I' is one finger held up, 'V' is the nick between the index finger and the thumb while 'X' is two index fingers crossed to make 10), the ancient way of counting looked dignified on memorials and triumphal arches, but it must have seemed awkward and very primitive when all sorts of mercantile calculations were required.

Arabic numerals, the ancestors of modern numbers, were in common currency in North Africa, and it seems that young Leonardo recognised how much better suited they were for the conduct of business. Travelling throughout the southern Mediterranean as a trader, he talked to Arab mathematicians wherever he met them and gradually made a thorough study of their methods. In 1202 Leonardo Fibonacci (his name was a contraction of *figlio Bonaccio*, 'son of Bonaccio') published a revolutionary treatise. The *Liber Abaci*, the 'Book of the Abacus' (the most common instrument then used for calculation), became a standard reference as it introduced the use of Arabic numerals to Italy and Europe.

The methods outlined in the *Book of the Abacus* made all aspects of arithmetic much easier, in particular multiplication and the working out of fractions. When Arabic numbers were used to calculate rates and amounts of interest, correct weights and measures and rates of currency exchange, all parties could understand a deal or contract much more readily. The introduction of the idea of 'zero' also allowed the use of large numbers in what is known as the place-value system, the place where the zero appears.

Record-keeping also improved enormously, since it was so much simpler to do. At the end of the thirteenth century a Genoese merchant was strongly advised: 'You must always remember to write down all that you do. Write it down immediately before it slips your mind.' And in the fourteenth century a Florentine merchant insisted that 'One must never be lazy about writing.' Proper business systems were slowly being put in place.

One of the most important of these had become current by the end of the thirteenth century. Using Fibonacci's numbers, a Florentine merchant called Amatino Manucci was keeping business records by means of what came to be known as double-entry book-keeping. Each time a transaction was agreed the sale or purchase was ultimately recorded in separate columns, and usually at the end of a month or so, or on a quarter day, these were totalled and transferred to a ledger. By looking at, say, a year's worth of debits and credits and from them calculating a balance sheet and profit and loss account, a merchant could quickly understand the state of his business, how much he had made, how much he owed and was owed and what the value of his assets was.

Most thirteenth-century merchants used three books: a memorandum book, a journal and a ledger. In the first they made a rudimentary record of a transaction, usually on the day it was agreed. *Memorandum* is a Latin term which simply means 'for remembering'. The journal was usually where a better and tidier record of each day's transactions was kept and it was here that double entries were listed. The left-hand side was headed *in dare* for debts and the right-hand *in havere* for credits. In the ledger more organisation was added and on each page or set of pages accounts for each individual or business were recorded separately, with running balances and any cross-reference which seemed relevant. As each transaction was completed or account closed, a merchant could work out how much money he had made from the deal and then make another transfer to a running total which acted as a summary of how well, or how badly, his business was doing.

Banks kept more complex records, but in essence used the same principles to make sense of their activities. They still do. Or should. Alongside the widespread use of demand notes or bills of exchange, as they were more commonly known, the development of double-entry book-keeping and the related concept of credit had the effect of expanding the money supply well beyond the actual value and amount of gold and silver coinage in circulation. As it does now, the system depended on trust between people and their businesses and confidence in them and the future productivity of the economy. Those who loaned cash, for a fee, had to believe that their debtors would ultimately repay the capital sum. But sometimes they did not.

At the end of the thirteenth and for most of the fourteenth centuries, the kings of England and France were at war, often with each other. Unable to sustain long campaigns with a feudal host raised on the basis of obligation, usually only for a summer, they began to use mercenaries and needed cash to pay them, and the other related costs of conflict. It was difficult to say no to a king, especially if a bank had agents in England or France, and so when royal agents approached the Tuscan banks, they were more or less forced to make loans. The consequences were disastrous. In 1294 the Riccardi of Lucca were bankrupted when the English and French kings repudiated their loans. Then the Bonsignori bank in Siena was forced into liquidation in 1298 because it too had lent cash to royalty. And forty years later Edward III of England ruined the Bardi and Peruzzi banks in Florence when he refused to pay back what he had borrowed. The Tuscans were in no position to insist.

Despite the availablity of African gold, there was still too little liquidity in the medieval European economy. A great deal of coin was travelling eastwards to pay for incoming spices and such silver mines as there were (the most productive were in Bohemia, at Kutna Hora, and along the Elbe at Annaberg and Freiberg) could not keep pace with demand. The Tuscan banks were forced to increase the paper money supply to perilous levels. Between 1303 and 1400 the public debt supported by the civic government of Florence spiralled from 50,000 gold florins to 3,000,000.

War was expensive, and the Tuscan cities of the thirteenth and fourteenth centuries fought with each other a great deal. Pisa, Arezzo, Siena and Florence, with a short cameo role for Lucca, were the main actors in the struggle for control of the region.

As the Arno began to silt up, Pisa found it increasingly difficult to function as a port, and her trade was slowly strangled. A Ghibelline city, a supporter of the imperial faction in Italy, Pisa was opposed to Guelf Florence, on the side of the papacy. But as time went on, the city took a less active part in urban conflicts. To avoid an uncomfortable alliance with her northern neighbour, Siena switched to the Ghibelline camp, and matters came to a head in 1260. A Florentine herald rode to the gates of the city and demanded that Siena's walls be cast down and the Ghibelline exiles sheltering behind them be surrendered. At his back there was a huge army, 40,000 men from Florence and the Guelf League were camped in the hills to the north.

The Sienese leaders threw open the doors of their cathedral, laid the keys of their city on the high altar and dedicated themselves to the grace and mercy of the Virgin Mary. And then they rode out of the gates with a small army to Montaperti where they cut the Florentines to pieces. Despite overwhelming odds, the Sienese inflicted a devastating defeat on their hated rivals. So complete was the victory that Florence lay entirely undefended and the city could have been utterly destroyed, its buildings razed to the ground and, in classical fashion, the ground sown with salt. According to the great Florentine poet, Dante Alighieri, it was the Ghibelline exiles who persuaded vengeful Siena to relent. The chance would never come again.

In 1314 the Pisans roused themselves to attack and seize the old Roman city of Lucca. What must have seemed like a routine episode of local warfare prompted a remarkable response. Having been exiled as a boy from Lucca, Castruccio Castracani had made a career as a mercenary soldier in the service of the kings of France and England. When he heard of the Pisan seizure of his home city, he and some of his comrades rode to the rescue.

A seasoned and wily campaigner, Castracani carved out an unlikely Luccan state, and became Duke of Pistoia, Volterra, Luni and his home-town. Later he took Pisa and was appointed Imperial Vicar of the city. But Florence was the dominant regional power and by 1325 Castracani was strong enough to attack. Having defeated a Florentine army, he laid siege to the city – but before he could take it, malaria took him.

Niccolò Machiavelli wrote a life of this charismatic adventurer, and his actions resonated down the centuries. Lucca managed to negotiate its continuing independence until the nineteenth century, passing into the Grand Duchy of Tuscany only just before the unification of Italy began.

Castracani almost certainly fought as a heavily armoured mounted knight whose principal weapon was a lance. Most western European armies of the period depended on a small squadron of knights and they hoped their thunderous charges would settle any battle. As a mercenary in English and French service, Castracani would have seen ranks of knights rumble into the gallop many times, and perhaps he was one of them. There were only two effective deterrents to this medieval equivalent of tank warfare: archery and closely packed and well-armed and armoured infantry bristling with long spears or pikes. In Italy crossbows were often preferred to longbows and some could send their quarrels straight through all but the thickest plate armour. After an initial charge by heavy cavalry, a battle often became a hand-to-hand melee, and those fighting with swords tried to go for weak points in an opponent's armour or chain-mail: the neck, arms or legs. In the forges of Pistoia a particularly vicious long dagger known as a *pistolese* was made, and when these gave way to firearms, the term 'pistol' somehow stuck.

Most of the Tuscan cities conscripted men between the ages of fifteen and fifty into their armies, and although these soldiers were often trained and had decent weapons and armour, they were in essence amateurs. Castracani's brilliant but short-lived success was probably based on his own and a small cadre's professionalism which they passed on to their comrades. In 1289 Florence fought Arezzo at the Battle of Campaldino. It turned out to be a bloody and expensive exchange. The Florentines prevailed, but so many were killed that the cost in citizen manpower was tremendous and industrial output suffered badly. Campaldino turned out to be one of the last times an army of conscripts would take the field to fight for the cause of a Tuscan city. The days of the *condottieri* were coming.

These were companies of mercenary soldiers whose leaders hired out their services to kings, aristocrats and the governments of the Italian cities. One of the most famous of these hard-bitten commanders is depicted on the north wall of the nave of the Duomo in Florence. Sir John Hawkwood was an Englishman who led the White Company across the Alps from Burgundy to fight for the Marquis of Montferrato in his war against the Visconti rulers of Milan. Like many mercenaries of the times, he and his men had been blooded in the Hundred Years War between England and France, and Hawkwood may have fought at Crécy and Poitiers.

Italians knew him as Giovanni Acuto. It may have been a version of his English surname, but *acuto* also translates as 'keen', in the sense of sharp-witted, and that was certainly a description of the *condottiere*'s reputation. Available for hire by any city which could pay, the pope or the emperor, Hawkwood often succeeded in being paid twice. Once he received a contract (usually a formal, written contract which had to be read out to the illiterate soldier), he would sometimes accept cash from the aggressor and then approach the other side for a payment not to attack them. In 1375 the pope's agents employed the White Company to make war on Florence, but the Signori offered a contract to delay hostilities for three months, which Hawkwood promptly accepted.

Condottieri were dangerous to employers and their enemies but surprisingly lenient with each other. Whenever Hawkwood, or John of Bohemia or Guidoriccio da Fogliano or any of the other commanders found themselves fighting against other mercenaries, which must have been often, the outcome of a battle was sometimes agreed before too much unnecessary killing took place. A sort of victory on points. As professional soldiers, these men had no interest in annihilating other members of the same profession. War was their business and in fourteenth- and fifteenth-century Tuscany, the *condottieri* knew that the continued viability of other companies was essential.

By the 1390s Florence had become the dominant city and had the cash to offer Sir John a long-term contract as commander-in-chief of their armies. The Visconti of Milan presented a serious threat but the old general pre-empted it by marching his battle-hard veterans across the Apennines and defeating the Milanese in their own territory. Given a hero's welcome on his triumphant return, the Englishman was made a citizen of Florence, and given a state pension and a villa in the countryside. Old for a *condottiere*, Hawkwood was 74 when he died in 1394. The Florentines had promised a bronze equestrian statue in his honour. But it was later thought to be a bit too dear, and since the old warrior was no longer on hand to object, the skinflint Signori opted for a much cheaper fresco by Paolo Uccello. The reason it was painted in a strange grey-green colour, *terra verde*, was because it was supposed to resemble a sculpture made in bronze. But it looks exactly like what it is: the cheaper option.

The battle at Campaldino, which brought the *condottieri* to Tuscany, was significant for another reason. Fighting in the front rank of the Florentine cavalry was one of the city's most famous sons. Dante Alighieri was born in 1265 into a prominent family. His name later appears in voting records and he took a full but ultimately unsuccessful part in the political life of Florence. It was his sublime poetry which made him famous, even in his own lifetime. Dante is also the first Tuscan with a substantial historical personality. His writings contain a good deal of biographical material and he was centrally involved in and deeply affected by the convoluted politics of the age. And his private passions were also clear and poignantly memorable.

When only a boy, Dante fell helplessly in love with Beatrice Portinari at first sight, the origin of the phrase. It was some time before he could speak to her, and in any case both had been betrothed early to other people. In the streets of Florence, Dante would catch a glimpse of Beatrice often but was only able to exchange greetings. Apparently she knew nothing of his feelings and they never became more than acquaintances. When Beatrice died young, in 1290, Dante was devastated and began to retreat into the interior world of his poetry.

At the end of the thirteenth century Florence was once again riven by faction-fighting. The Guelf party had split into two opposing wings, the Blacks and the Whites. In 1301 Dante was sent on a diplomatic mission to the papacy in Rome on behalf of the White leadership and during his absence the Blacks took over. All of the family property was confiscated and Dante was sentenced to death by burning at the stake. He never returned to Florence, to the streets where he had first seen his beloved Beatrice and died in 1321 in Ravenna.

His greatest work, *La Divina Commedia* ('The Divine Comedy'), was the first major literary work to be written in Italian and not Latin. It helped to establish the Tuscan dialect as standard Italian and came to be seen as the very greatest work written in the developing language. Here is a passage describing the pain of exile:

> You shall leave everything you love most:
> this is the arrow that the bow of exile
> shoots first. You are to know the bitter taste
> of others' bread, how salty it is, and know
> how hard a path it is for one who goes
> ascending and descending others' stairs . . .

Dante's writing may seem formal and sometimes obscure, but his life and work are one of the first to leave a sense of passion, of personal feelings and to offer a role for the individual in the wash of history across the landscape. Increasingly in the thirteenth century the Tuscan cities produced more graphic personalities, people rather than merely names, who took part in the workings of political forces, and in the narrow streets and piazzas history began to come alive.

Despite the turmoil of the times, there was prosperity and population growth. But as the Tuscan economy boomed, the position of the Church grew more and more ambivalent. The profits made by enterprising merchants had long been thought suspect, close to usury and often formally frowned upon. A medieval sculpture in Rome shows a merchant being dragged down to hell by the purse around his neck. The Crusades changed attitudes radically, and with the soldier-monks of the Knights Templar deeply involved in the money economy, the Church softened its stance. Here is Thomas of Cobham, an English cleric writing at the beginning of the thirteenth century: 'There would be great hardship in many localities if merchants did not bring what is plentiful in one place to another place where that commodity is lacking. So they have a perfect right to be paid for their work. Large-scale international trade is now a necessity willed by God; it is part of the scheme of Providence.'

Running parallel were important changes in religious doctrine. The Church began to encourage the concept of purgatory, a sort of antechamber to heaven where un-confessed earthly sins had to be atoned and paid for before the gates of Paradise could swing open. Purgatory was not hell, from which there was no release, but it was not comfortable either. The time spent there could be significantly shortened by prayers offered up by surviving relatives and others, and also by good works on earth. The latter was a particularly attractive notion, especially to those merchants who had made a great deal of money and thereby risked the residual stain of usury. They could afford to endow good works and absolutely guarantee a shorter sentence before a warm welcome on High. When loyalty to and love of their native cities were added to these spiritual encouragements, the results in Tuscany were spectacular.

Siena's banking community had been consistently successful and in the thirteenth century it began to provide the funds for the adornment of the city in every sense. At Santa Maria della Scala, the merchants established what was probably Europe's first urban hospital. Close to the Via Francigena, there had long been a hospital providing shelter, or hospitality, for pilgrims on their way to and from Rome. The old road passed just below the walls of Siena. When private donations began to flow, Santa Maria della Scala developed a role caring for the sick and for poor people. In hard times it acted as a soup kitchen, and in good times the hospital expanded, building its own church and commissioning devotional work from Siena's greatest painters.

Between 1295 and 1310 the Palazzo Pubblico was completed, its huge bell-tower dominating the south-eastern side of the Campo and affording long views not only over the city but most of the territory of the Republic in southern Tuscany. It quickly became known as the Torre di Mangia, literally, the 'Tower of Eating'. Apparently the buildings' costs were so high that the reference was to *mangia guadagni* – 'eating the profits'.

Much more likely to shorten any stay in purgatory were the work and expense lavished on Siena's stunning cathedral. Built on the highest point of the city, the Terza di Città, it was begun around 1200 and most of it was completed by 1270. The façade and other facings are made in black and white marble arranged in beautiful geometric patterns, and the great sculptor, Giovanni Pisano, was commissioned to fill the niches with saints and prophets. Inside, a pulpit was carved from Carrara marble by another Pisan, Nicola Pisano, and from the

1280s onwards a wonderful series of inlaid marble pavements was laid down depicting sages and mythological and biblical figures.

The interior centrepiece for the new cathedral was commissioned from Siena's greatest painter, Duccio di Buoninsegna. Known as the *Maestà*, it was a large panel intended to be hung behind the high altar and it shows the Virgin Mary enthroned and flanked by rows of adoring saints. With no expense spared, the materials are gorgeous: expensive ultramarine blues against a background of gold leaf. Siena's love and reverence for God's Mother is still remembered in the Palio when each year's winning *contrada* takes the pall painted with her image. Such was the intensity of civic pride and investment in the *Maestà* that when Duccio had completed his masterpiece in the summer of 1311, it was carried through the streets from his studio to the cathedral amidst huge and cheering crowds.

Master masons, architects, sculptors and painters were also very busy in Florence. The end of the thirteenth century saw the foundation stones laid for many of the city's most famous monuments. The cathedral, the Duomo, was designed and begun under the direction of Arnolfo di Cambio, an architect who may have worked at Siena. 'It will be so magnificent in size and beauty', announced the Florentines, 'as to surpass anything built by the Greeks and the Romans.' And it was not empty bluster. Arnolfo set out what was to be the largest church in all Christendom. The octagonal crossing was an unprecedented 44.5 metres in diameter, but sadly di Cambio died before he had worked out how to cover it with what needed to be the biggest dome ever built.

Building work commenced on the Franciscan church of Santa Croce in 1295 and the old Baptistry of St John was renovated and redecorated in the years after 1296. It is an ancient building, its core perhaps begun in the Dark Ages, between the sixth and ninth centuries, and ever since it has been the focus and fusion of civic and religious life in the city. On New Year's Day Florentine families used to bring all of the babies born the preceding year year to be baptised at St John's in a communal ceremony. They could be neither Florentines nor Christians until they had been blessed at the old church. Even now the baptistry is seen as a symbol of the city's long history and part of its soul.

In 1970 archaeologists made an extraordinary discovery. While looking for the remains of Santa Reparata, the much older church demolished by Arnolfo di Cambio to make way for the new cathedral, they came across a burial under some paving stones. No marker with a handy inscription could be found, but forensic scientists were able to date the remains to the first half of the fourteenth century. An assembly of the skeleton indicated a very small male, perhaps only a little over 4 feet tall. The skull was large and disproportionate, perhaps indicating a form of congenital dwarfism and it seemed that the man had a prominent hooked nose and one eye was clearly recessed. Pathologists were intrigued by other unusual features of the skull. The teeth were worn down in such a way as to suggest that something hard was often held between them. And this was many centuries before pipe-smoking produced a similar pattern of wear. The top vertebrae of the neck also showed a curious configuration: it seemed that this small man was in the habit of tilting his head backwards a great deal. All of the pieces of this fascinating investigation finally fell into place when a chemical analysis of the bones showed a very high absorption of lead and arsenic, two elements commonly found in paint.

Professor Francesco Mallegni and his team were certain that they could identify the skeleton. It was Giotto di Bondone, one of the greatest painters Florence, or indeed the world, had ever seen. He had died in 1337, and the sixteenth-century art historian, Giorgio Vasari, recorded that he had been buried in the Duomo, Santa Maria dei Fiori, near the main entrance. Another source claimed, in an apparent contradiction, that Giotto had been buried in Santa Reparata. Both were correct because, as the new Duomo rose, the old church which would eventually disappear under it was still in use.

Across the city at Santa Croce, in one of his fresco cycles, there is a painting of a dwarf, and a powerful tradition insists that it was a self-portrait of the artist. Giotto's irreverent contemporary, the great writer Boccaccio, reckoned that there was no uglier man in the city of Florence. And because he had to work quickly in fresco (before the plaster on which he painted dried), using different brushes for different colours, the little man held them between his teeth and often tilted his head back to check on progress.

Giotto was undoubtedly an immensely talented and innovative painter, his work breaking free from the old, stiff, hieratic style of the Middle Ages, and it still has the power to move all who look on it. But as important, he was recognised during his lifetime as a great artist. Before the fourteenth century, European painters, architects and sculptors were all but anonymous, and were in any case seen as craftsmen rather than creative artists. In the Tuscan cities their status began to rise and the development of the cultural background which enabled and encouraged their emergence is central to any understanding of the most famous time in the region's history, the Renaissance.

Despite what Dante characterised as the poisonous politics of Florence in particular – in 'L'Inferno' he wrote of 'Three sparks from Hell – Avarice, Envy, Pride/ In all men's bosoms sowed the fiery seed' – the mercantile middle classes grew and prospered. In addition to numeracy and acumen, their businesses involved two related skills: literacy and an understanding of the law. The latter contributed to the rise of some of the earliest European universities at Bologna, Padua and Pisa, and less formally, at Florence. Founded by papal decrees and dominated for centuries by the Church, these institutions nevertheless became central to the retrieval of classical texts, particularly those which had recorded Roman law. When models were required, even precedents, medieval Italian jurists tended to reach for ancient texts. And this in turn fostered a better understanding of classical Latin, as compared with the less sophisticated medieval versions.

As the mercantile classes became more literate in pursuit of profits, they too developed an interest in Roman (and eventually Greek) literature. Aside from religious works, there were few enough manuscripts for a lay reader to enjoy, and very little in any of the vernacular languages such as Italian. Dante's great success was undoubtedly deserved and the quality of his writing still sparkles, but when his *Divina Commedia* appeared, it had few rivals. History was a much-favoured genre amongst the literate laity and what survived from Livy and the other Romans was especially prized. And as contemporary historiography developed – it appears that Tuscans never tired of stories about their cities and their heroes from the past – it adopted classical texts as models.

Exiled from Florence in 1302 for the sin of being part of the White Guelf party, in the same purge which expelled Dante, the Petrarca family settled in Arezzo. In 1304 Francesco was born, and after an abortive education in the law, he gradually discovered his talents as a writer and poet. A canon of more than 300 sonnets forms the basis of his modern reputation but it was as a historian that he first came to prominence. Taking the epic story of Scipio Africanus, the conqueror of Carthage and Hannibal, he wrote (but failed to complete) one of the earliest studies of Rome and its republican empire. The book was the basis on which Petrarch was crowned as the first poet laureate since antiquity. On the Capitoline Hill, amongst the ruins of Rome, sponsored by King Robert of Naples, the laurel wreath was placed on his head in 1341. Even though there is more than a hint of self-aggrandisement and self-consciousness about the revival of the ceremony in Rome, Petrarch was by that time the most famous living writer in Europe and, like Giotto, was seen as a creative artist who deserved substantial as well as ceremonial reward for his creativity. Fame as much as wealth was what he craved.

Like Dante, he pined from unrequited love. Her name was Laura, and it appears that she was married to a French aristocrat, Hugues de Sade. Petrarch was in any case nominally a cleric (he lived off benefices given by the Church) and was probably not in a position to take a wife, if the object of his affection had been available. His sonnets dwelt often on his love for the beautiful and unattainable Laura, and when she died in 1348, his despair turned to inconsolable grief.

Petrarch's innermost feelings are not a matter of interpretation or conjecture. In a private memoir, his *Secretum*, and his *Letter to Posterity*, he makes them clear: 'In my younger days I struggled constantly with an overwhelming but pure love affair – my only one, and I would have struggled with it longer had not premature death, bitter but salutary for me, extinguished the cooling flames. I certainly wish I could say that I have always been entirely free from desires of the flesh, but I would be lying if I did.'

In the *Secretum* he chides himself for seeking fame and for his pride and prickly preciousness as a writer. And Petrarch saw himself as very special, different from the common run of men, but recognised at the same time that he craved popular approval. Depression sometimes struck him down, and lust assailed him, but the great man appears to have had a talent for friendship and some real personal warmth can be sensed. It is very striking how fresh these private thoughts appear – across seven centuries.

History knew a great deal about Petrarch, perhaps more than any other famous figure who came before him. In fourteenth-century Tuscany painters, sculptors and architects also acquired vivid personalities, and for similar reasons – which need to be unpacked.

As Petrarch travelled around Europe (something which he seemed to enjoy for its own sake), he searched for ancient manuscripts buried in monastic libraries. Blowing the dust off crumbling parchments, he had the learning to recognise lost treasures. In 1345, at Verona, he found a series of letters from the great Roman politician and orator, Cicero, and his reaction encapsulated his reasons for what was a lifelong quest:

> Each famous author of antiquity whom I recover places a new offence and another cause of dishonour to the charge of earlier generations, who, not satisfied with their own disgraceful barrenness, permitted the fruit of other minds, and the writings that their ancestors had produced by toil and application, to perish through insufferable neglect. Although they had nothing of their own to hand down to those who were to come after, they robbed posterity of its ancestral heritage.

The term Middle Ages at first described the time between the first coming of Christ and his second, but Petrarch labelled the centuries after the fall of Rome and his own day as the Dark Ages. It was this palpable sense of recovery, the reclaiming of the glories of the past and the rebirth of its standards and values, which animated the best minds of the fourteenth century in Tuscany. And these ideas were applied to painting, architecture and sculpture. Giotto, Dante, Petrarch – all were pioneers, better and fresher than the medieval mediocrity of the immediate past, and ready to carry on where the ancients had left off, and perhaps even exceed them.

Petrarch died in 1374 but his work continued to influence many. In a heavy-handed imitation of classical Latin (his friend, Colluccio Salutati, made many corrections to his manuscript), Filippo Villani wrote a history of his native city, *On the Origins of the City of Florence and its Famous Citizens*. This passage is an apposite example of the way these men saw their new world. It first harks back to the golden age of ancient painters and sculptors, and then leaps over a thousand years of European art before the tradition of excellence is picked up by Cimabue, the master who taught Giotto. Written in 1381–82, it helped set the intellectual framework for art history for centuries:

> The ancients, who wrote admirable records of events, included in their books the best painters and sculptors of images and statues

along with other famous men. The ancient poets too, marvelling at the talent and diligence of Prometheus, represented him in their tales as making men from the mud of the earth. These most wise men thought, so I infer, that imitators of nature who endeavoured to fashion likenesses of men from stone and bronze could not be unendowed with noble talent and exceptional memory, and with much delightful skill of hand. For this reason, along with the other distinguished men in their annals they put Zeuxis ... Phidias, Praxiteles, Myron, Apelles of Cos ... and others distinguished in this sort of skill. So let it be proper for me, with the mocker's leave, to introduce here the excellent Florentine painters, men who have rekindled an art that was pale and almost extinguished.

First among whom John, whose surname was Cimabue, summoned back with skill and talent the decayed art of painting, wantonly straying far from the likeness of nature as this was, since for many centuries previously Greek and Latin painting had been subject to the ministrations of but clumsy skills, as the figures and images we see decorating the churches of the saints, both on panels and on walls, plainly show.

After John, the road to new things lying open, Giotto – who is not only by virtue of his great fame to be compared with the ancient painters, but is even to be preferred to them for skill and talent – restored painting to its former worth and great reputation. For images formed by his brush agree so well with the lineaments of nature as to seem to the beholder to live and breathe: and his pictures appear to form actions and movements so exactly as to seem from a little way off actually speaking, weeping, rejoicing, and doing other things, not without pleasure for him who beholds and praises the talent and skill of the artist. Many people judge – and not foolishly indeed – that painters are of a talent no lower than those whom the Liberal Arts have rendered *magistri*, 'masters', since these latter may learn by means of study and instruction written rules of their arts while the painters derive such rules as they find in their art only from a profound natural talent and a tenacious memory. Yet Giotto was a man of great understanding even apart from the art of painting, and one who had experience in many things. Beside having a full knowledge of history, he showed himself so far a rival of poetry that keen judges consider he painted what most poets represent in words. He was also, as was proper to a prudent man, anxious for fame rather than gain. Thus, with the desire of making his name widely known, he painted something in prominent places in almost every famous city in Italy, and at Rome particularly in the atrium of the Basilica of St Peter, where he represented most skilfully in mosaic the Apostles in peril on the boat, so as to make a public demonstration of his skill and power to the whole world that flocks to the city. He also painted with the help of mirrors himself and his coeval the poet Dante Alighieri on a wall of the chapel of the Palazzo del Podestà.

When portraiture first reappeared in the early fourteenth century, it seems at first to have chimed with the new sense of the individual, his fame, the rounded-out personalities of Dante, Petrarch and Giotto himself. While this may be so – and seems certain to be the case in the example of the double portrait of Dante and Giotto – the emergence of likenesses of real people probably has a more prosaic origin.

When Giotto was commissioned by the great Florentine banking families of Bardi and Peruzzi to decorate their side chapels at Santa Croce with scenes from the life of St Francis, it appears that he included portraits of his patrons. This was less a celebration of the individual than a way of clearly commemorating who it was who paid for the work. The same thing happened in other large-scale public commissions. Where crowd scenes were involved, in the likes of Crucifixions or the Adoration of the Magi, it did no harm to include portraits of the important people from whichever wealthy family was attempting to cut short their time in purgatory. Genuine portraits do appear later, but these early examples serve as an aid to authenticity. Because they were representations of real people, they did, in Villani's phrase, make the pictures seem to live and breathe.

In 1316 an embattled papacy fled the city of Rome to take up temporary residence at Avignon, in the Rhône valley. It stayed for sixty years. At the same time the power of the German emperors north of the Alps declined and, no longer sandwiched between powerful rivals, the Tuscan cities enjoyed greater freedom than ever before. They used it to intensify their internal squabbles and to fight with each other: Guelf and Ghibelline splintered into factions and companies of *condottieri* rode the dusty highways between bitter enemies. But business seemed barely interrupted and the grand building projects proceeded apace.

In Florence the bell-tower for the Duomo, designed by Giotto, was completed and the Ponte Vecchio across the Arno rebuilt. Ever competitive with its loathed neighbour, Siena planned to put all of that grandeur firmly in the shade. To the north of its cathedral, modern visitors see a wall of black and white marble connected to the nave and running off to the right – but serving no obvious purpose, too grand to be a retaining or boundary wall. Opposite are other fragments now built into the walls of houses around the Piazza Jacopo della Quercia. These were the dimensions of an immense ambition. In 1339 Siena planned a huge new cathedral, much larger than the half-finished, half-baked Duomo in Florence, one which would leave no doubts about which was the most significant, magnificent, pious and powerful city in Tuscany – in fact in all Christendom. The prosperity of the early fourteenth century had made the great banking houses fabulously wealthy and the textile trade was booming. The city crackled with excitement.

Nine years after the plans were made public, the run of the walls pegged out and building work begun, the project was suddenly and entirely abandoned. A catastrophe struck Siena, Tuscany and the rest of Europe. A catastrophe from which Siena would never recover.

Far to the east, on the peninsula of the Crimea in the Black Sea, the Genoese trading colony of Caffa was under siege. It was the late summer of 1346. Without the engines and battering rams needed to breach the walls, the Tartar khan, Janibeg, ordered the use of a much more deadly weapon. Plague had broken out in East Asia, a much more virulent pestilence than anyone had ever seen, and it had swept westwards along the Silk Road to the shores of the Black Sea. Many Tartar warriors had died astonishingly quickly and in terrible pain, and Janibeg had their rotting corpses catapulted over the walls and into Caffa.

The Genoese panicked and immediately began boarding their galleys and putting to sea. They knew about the deadly disease – but failed to escape its grip. Some of their sailors had become infected, and in any case the black rats scuttling in the holds of their ships were infected with fleas which bit humans and passed on the fatal bacillus. By the time the Genoese fleet reached Messina in Sicily, all of the crew members of some of the ships had died and their vessels were found run aground on the beaches, washed up beyond the tidemarks, stinking with putrefying corpses. Others limped into port with only a few exhausted survivors manning the sails and the rudder, having heaved over the side many of their shipmates.

Looters swarmed over the ghost ships on the Sicilian beaches and many of them quickly contracted the disease. When the remaining ships of the fleet were refused landing at Messina, they sailed on up through the Tyrrhenian Sea to their home port of Genoa, where again they were refused permission to disembark. Many would have had families waiting on the quays. They were forced to sail on westwards, growing ever more desperate, putting in at Marseilles and Valencia. They carried the Black Death across the Mediterranean, the most devastating epidemic ever known in Europe, and it spread like wildfire.

By January 1348 people had begun to die in their thousands in Genoa, despite having turned away the infected fleet from Caffa. The plague struck Venice at the same time and then quickly spread to Pisa, Florence and inland Tuscany. At Siena, Agnolo di Tura wrote down what he saw:

> Father abandoned child, wife husband, one brother another; for this illness seemed to strike through the breath and sight. And so they died. And none could be found to bury the dead for money or friendship. Members of a household brought their dead to a ditch as best they could, without priest, without divine offices . . . great pits were dug and piled deep with the multitude of dead. And they died by the hundreds both day and night . . . And as soon as those ditches were filled more were dug . . . And I, Agnolo di Tura, called the Fat, buried my five children with my own hands. And there were also those who were so sparsely covered with earth that the dogs dragged them forth and devoured many bodies throughout the city. There was no-one who wept for any death, for all awaited death. And so many died that all believed it was the end of the world. This situation continued from May until September.

All over Europe many millions died. Despite the fact that the vast majority lived in the countryside, in farms and small villages, and did not travel far, there appeared to be nowhere the appalling suffering could not reach. In the narrow streets and the packed, ramshackle tenements of the Tuscan cities, the death toll was even greater. In Florence the plague found another eloquent chronicler. Giovanni

Boccaccio is revered for his beautiful, lyrical poetry on the vicissitudes of romantic love and the great tales of mythology. *Diana the Hunter* is amongst his most famous works, and *Il Filostrato* and *Teseida delle Nozze d'Emilia* were the source for Geoffery Chaucer's *Troilus and Cressida* and *The Knight's Tale*. But in 1348 he watched the poison of the Black Death destroy his native city.

> The plight of the lower and most of the middle classes was even more pitiful to behold. Most of them remained in their houses, either through poverty or in hopes of safety, and fell sick by the thousands. Since they received no care and attention, almost all of them died. Many ended their lives in the streets both at night and during the day; and many others who died in their houses were only known to be dead because the neighbours smelled their decaying bodies. Dead bodies filled every corner. Most of them were treated in the same manner by the survivors, who were more concerned to get rid of their rotting bodies than moved by charity towards the dead. With the aid of porters, if they could get them, they carried the bodies out of the houses and laid them at the door; where every morning quantities of the dead might be seen. They then were laid on biers or, as these were often lacking, on tables.

The apocalyptic scenes on the streets affected those left alive in different ways:

> Some thought that moderate living and the avoidance of all superfluity would preserve them from the epidemic. They formed small communities, living entirely separate from everyone else. They shut themselves up in houses where there were no sick, eating the finest food and drinking the best wine very temperately, avoiding all excess, allowing no news or discussion of death and sickness, and passing the time in music and suchlike pleasures.
>
> Others thought just the opposite. They thought the sure cure for the plague was to drink and be merry, to go about singing and amusing themselves, satisfying every appetite they could, laughing and jesting at what had happened. They put their words into practice, spent day and night going from tavern to tavern, drinking immoderately, or went into other people's houses, doing

only those things which pleased them. This they could easily do because everyone felt doomed and had abandoned his property, so that most houses became common property and any stranger who went in made use of them as if he had owned them. And with all this bestial behaviour, they avoided the sick as much as possible.

In Florence the Black Death raged on for four years and historians reckon that it reduced the population by more than half, from 110,000 souls to only 50,000 by 1351. Many fled, including Boccaccio. His greatest and most famous work, the *Decameron*, was written in the dark shadow of the pandemic, and as a direct consequence of it. It tells the story of ten people, three women and seven men, who abandoned Florence for a remote castle in the countryside. To amuse themselves, they told each other a series of tales, a hundred in all, and they dealt with many subjects, some of them racy and humorous. Like Dante and Petrarch, Boccaccio wrote in an unfussy and spare Italian, a style which remains very accessible and entertaining.

Neither he nor any of his contemporaries understood how the Black Death was transmitted, or indeed knew much about the nature of the disease except for its dramatic symptoms. Many believed that it was carried on miasma, or foul air, and that the incredible speed of its spread was due to the fact that birds were infected. Others did not trouble with any forensic considerations and simply ascribed the pandemic to the Wrath of God, or perhaps the work of the Devil. In some of the cities cats were caught and burned alive because desperate, half-deranged people thought them to be the agents of Satan. For quite another reason, aside from its extreme cruelty, it was a crazy thing to do.

There were three sorts of plague stalking the streets and highways of Europe and the most common, bubonic plague, was spread by rats. The culling of the urban cat population simply allowed them to breed and increase unchecked. More precisely, it was the fleas who lived in the fur of black rats, known as ship rats, which carried the disease. They had come in the holds of the plague fleet from Caffa, and in the Tuscan cities these fast-reproducing vectors found their ideal environment.

Rats have always lived and thrived in the shadow of human beings. It is said that no modern city dweller is further than a few yards from a rat, and in Florence, Pisa, Siena and Arezzo, people were a lot closer. As the economy boomed and the fourteenth-century cities mushroomed, so did the rodent population. Black rats were able to tolerate the bite of infected fleas because their blood was able to withstand high concentrations of the bacillus. But even they died of plague and, in need of fresh blood, the fleas transferred to new hosts, either human beings or other animals.

When symptoms first appeared, there was no doubt about the onset of bubonic plague. Sufferers found that the lymph glands in their neck, groin and under the armpits quickly swelled into what were known as buboes. Boccaccio either observed what happened or spoke to someone who had:

> It began in both men and women with certain swellings in the groin and under the armpit. They grew to the size of a small apple or egg, more or less, and were vulgarly called tumours. In a short space of time these tumours spread from the two parts named all over the body. Soon after this the symptoms changed and black or purple spots appeared on the arms or thighs or any other part of the body, sometimes a few large ones, sometimes many little ones. These spots were a certain sign of death, just as the original tumour had been and still remained.

The spots were the outwards marks of internal haemorrhages as blood vessels burst. It must have been agony. At Viterbo some grim humour described the marks as freckles.

Less common were deaths from the two other variants of the Black Death. Septicaemic plague was a form of blood poisoning and it too was carried by the fleas of black rats. Pneumonic plague was transmitted through the air and people could be easily infected by the breath of those suffering from it. Affecting the lungs, it was especially fast and always lethal.

The overwhelming popular reaction was to abandon immediately anyone who exhibited symptoms. Almost all of the victims died in great pain and alone. No last rites were administered by a priest and no comfort given by friends and family members gathered at the bedside. It was too dangerous. Historians now believe that perhaps a quarter of all those infected with bubonic plague might have had a chance of survival; but left to die alone, unable to move, many would have perished from thirst or starved to death.

These were hellish times. Between 1347 and 1351 three-quarters of the population of Italy may have died, and it must have seemed as though Dante's 'L'Inferno' had come to pass on earth. Death came much more often to the towns than to the countryside; isolated places did avoid the plague. In the Pyrenees, high valleys escaped and there may have been remote communities in the Apennines where it failed to reach. But the effects of the pandemic were profound and long-lasting.

Historians believe that the Black Death hastened the end of the feudal way of life, a military society based on an interlocking pattern of obligations and services. Cash became a much more important means of exchange and gradually workers, even on the land, came to be paid in coin rather than in kind. The transition was not smooth and in the decades following the pandemic (it returned regularly but less severely with nine outbreaks in the fifteenth century), there were popular uprisings all over Europe, like the Ciompi in Florence and Siena. The trend towards a cash economy only played to the habits and skills developed in the Tuscan cities.

Equally profound changes in attitude took place. In the *Decameron*, Boccaccio appeared to advocate living in the present, for the moment, rather than enduring life in the hope of better times and a life in the hereafter. Because the Black Death was widely seen as an epic manifestation of the Wrath of God, sobriety and restraint became cardinal virtues. In Florence and in Venice, sumptuary laws forbade ostentatious dress. The wealthy were compelled by statute to embrace the new black, to wear only dark, undecorated clothes, and in other matters of taste they showed a serious-minded bent.

As often happens, the new severity became fashionable and even princes and kings disdained to show off their rank and wealth in what they wore. Others, even Tuscans, were behind the trend. The mid-fifteenth-century Florentine bookseller, Vespasiano da Bisticci, recounted an illustrative incident:

> There was a Sienese ambassador at Naples who was, as the Sienese tend to be, very grand. Now King Alfonso usually dressed in black, with just a buckle in his cap and a gold chain around his neck; he did not use brocades or silk clothes much. This ambassador dressed in gold brocade, very rich, and when he came to see the King he always wore this gold brocade. Among his own people the King

often made fun of these brocade clothes. One day he said, laughing to one of his gentlemen, 'I think we should change the colour of that brocade.' So he arranged to give audience one day in a mean little room, summoned all the ambassadors, and also arranged with some of his own people that in the throng everyone should jostle against the Sienese ambassador and rub against his brocade. And on the day it was so handled and rubbed, not just by the other ambassadors, but by the King himself, that when they came out of the room no-one could help laughing when they saw the brocade, because it was crimson now, with the pile all crushed and the gold fallen off it, just yellow silk left: it looked like the ugliest rag in the world. When he saw him go out of the room with his brocade all ruined and messed, the King could not stop laughing . . .

Exuberance and show were not acceptable, often mocked and condemned in Tuscany itself, and in the aftermath of God's wrath, an interest in the severe delights of classical Latin texts was encouraged. The austerity of republican Rome would be reflected in republican Florence as the city grew increasingly powerful in Tuscany.

Siena could not stand in the way of its old rival. The city had been ruled by an oligarchy, the Nine, and stable government had encouraged enterprise and growth. But after being ravaged by the Black Death and abandoning the expansion of its cathedral, Siena never recovered. In 1355 the Nine were overthrown by an aristocratic coup, and after the wool-workers' rebellion of 1371 (they were known as the Compagnia del Bruco), the city became prey to the companies of *condottieri* and their threats and blackmail.

But amidst the ruins of Sienese ambition, sanctity flourished. Two remarkable, charismatic people lived exemplary lives in the second half of the fourteenth century. Catherine Benin was born in 1347 in Siena, just as the Black Death was about to rage through Italy. She was the last of twenty-five children brought into the world by the long-suffering Lapa Piagenti, the obliging wife of a cloth dyer, Giacomo di Benincasa.

In her early teens, it appeared that Catherine experienced an irresistible religious calling, and despite the objections of the order itself, she took the habit of the Dominican Tertiaries. Developed from the original Dominican order of preachers, these were men and women who devoted themselves to good works. After what she described as a mystical marriage to Christ when she was nineteen, Catherine began to take part in the life of the world. In the terrible wake of the Black Death, Siena needed brave and selfless people and her work among the poor and the dying was tireless. Catherine's simple virtue and her ability to communicate the love of Christ began to attract a following of men and women who became intensely loyal to her. At the same time she also attracted the attention of the leaders of the Dominican order in Florence. After being interrogated in 1374, Catherine was not only allowed to continue her work but was encouraged to travel widely.

More than 300 letters survive, and they are evidence of Catherine's learning (an unusual achievement for a woman at that time) and of her diplomatic skills. She wrote to the pope (calling him 'Babbo' or 'Daddy'), exhorting him to reform the Church and its growing laxities, and to secular rulers, encouraging them to turn to peace rather than continue the ceaseless hostilities between Italian cities. Her influence, her fame and her legacy extended far beyond the Alps. In Edinburgh, street names remember the great saint of Siena. Sciennes is a compressed version of St Catherine of Siena and it was the site of a nunnery dedicated to her on the south side of the city. After her death in 1380, almost certainly from a brain haemorrhage, Catherine was quickly canonised and is, fittingly, the patron saint of nurses.

Born in the year of her death, Bernardino Albizeschi was clearly inspired by Catherine's example. When plague returned to poison Siena once more in 1400, he worked at the hospital of Santa Maria della Scala and eventually contracted the deadly disease. But he survived, by what he probably believed to be a miracle, and soon after joined the strict Franciscan order known as the Observants. Like Catherine, Bernardino began to travel and preach all over Italy. His particular theme was devotion to the Holy Name of Jesus, something still recalled in many churches all over the Christian world. Pulpits, altar tables, and lecterns often have a cloth draped over them with the embroidered monogram of 'IHS' and this is the most obvious legacy of Bernardino. *Ihesus* was how the name of Jesus was written in the Middle Ages and IHS became a common abbreviation.

In 1425 the great preacher was in Siena. Every day for seven weeks, Bernardino gave sermons around the *contrade* of the city and he attracted a tremendous following. As often, the papal court was suspicious of such popularity and a summons to a trial for heresy was issued. Bernardino was acquitted and he began another tour of the Tuscan cities. This time his theme was homosexuality and a record of his railing has survived: 'Italy, how much more than any other province have you become contaminated! Go to the Germans, and hear what lovely things they say about the Italians! They say there are no people in this world that are greater sodomites than the Italians.'

In Santa Croce, in Florence, Bernardino attacked the city's tolerance of gay men: 'Whenever you hear sodomy mentioned, each and every one of you spit on the ground and clean your mouth out as well. If they don't want to change their ways by any other means, maybe they will change when they are made fools of. Spit hard! Maybe the water of your spit will extinguish their fire.'

Bernardino told the Florentines that in Genoa and Venice gays had been burned alive, and later he raged that the Sienese should do the same, even if they had to burn every male in the city.

Despite the fire and brimstone, Bernardino, and Catherine in particular, preached the cause of peace. Rivalry between Italian cities had brought little but ruin, and the saints implored the powerful to damp down their ambition. But their words were, of course, ineffective, and their native city of Siena suffered more than most. By 1399 the ruler of Milan, Giangaleazzo Visconti, led an army south and claimed possession. Having shrunk from a high of 80,000, in 1700 only 15,000 people lived amongst the magnificence of medieval Siena.

6

In the Name of God and of Profit

In the centre of the town of Prato, 10 kilometres west of Florence, stands a well-preserved late fourteenth-century palazzo. On the lintel above the main entrance there is an inscription:

Almshouse of Francesco, son of Marco,
Merchant of Christ's Poor,
Of which the Commune of Prato
is trustee.
Bequeathed in the year 1410.

Along with his house, Francesco left his entire fortune for the relief of the poor people of his home town. It was 70,000 gold florins, a huge sum and enough to ensure that the almshouse could be maintained and the old merchant's wishes carried out. More than four centuries later, a remarkable discovery was made; Francesco di Marco had left another bequest, this time of incalculable value.

In 1870 some officials of the commune were inspecting the premises and the condition of the occupants. A photograph of 1900 shows at least forty standing outside the main door, most of them women and small children. Under a back staircase, unnoticed for hundreds of years, several dust-covered sacks were pulled out. Inside was one of the most remarkable, extensive and detailed historical archives ever to come to light until modern times.

Nibbled a little by mice and insects but largely intact were more than 140,000 letters, 500 account ledgers, 400 insurance policies, 300 deeds of partnership and many bills of lading and exchange. They were collected and filed over a lifetime of trade by Francesco di Marco, known as Datini, and they supply an unparalleled record of business and society in the second half of the fourteenth century.

And on the title-page of the ledgers is inscribed a guiding motto: 'In the Name of God and of Profit.'

Francesco's parents both died in the first and most savage visitation of the Black Death in 1348. Only he and his brother, Stefano, survived and while their inheritance, a house, a small parcel of land and 47 gold florins, was looked after by a guardian, the boys, only thirteen and eleven, went to live with Monna Piera di Pratese Boschetti. She looked after them well and some of Monna Piera's letters were found in the dusty sacks. 'Your mother in love' was how she signed herself.

As his extraordinary archive shows again and again, Francesco was very well educated. At Prato and the other Tuscan towns and cities, boys were schooled in two clear stages. From the age of six or seven they went first to the *botteghuzza*, the primary school, where they were taught to read and write. In addition, the little boys learned to set out a business letter and frame a rudimentary contract, usually following models set out in primers. Many of these have survived.

Education was entirely vocational, and to equip budding merchants and businessmen, the *abbaco*, or secondary school, concentrated heavily on mathematical skills. Proficiency in both arithmetic and geometry was vital to a successful career and the principles were drummed into the boys by rote-learning and the rod.

At the age of fourten or fifteen, as soon as his secondary education was completed, Francesco took himself to Florence, from a country town to a big city. It was early in the year 1350 and the baleful aftermath of the Black Death must still have been obvious: empty and boarded-up houses, the vast mass graves and the continuing (but diminishing) toll of victims. Although people were still dying of plague, it is striking how quickly the economy began to recover. Despite the dearth of farm-workers, harvests were somehow gathered in and animals driven to market. The wool clip still sent fleeces and woolfells to the weavers, dyers and finishers in Prato and Florence, and merchants still tried to make a profit.

Ever resourceful – and ruthless – Tuscans turned to the slave trade to make up the labour shortfall. When the young Francesco Datini walked into Florence, he would have seen sallow-skinned, slant-eyed Tartars, Circassians, Greeks, Russians and Georgians. Bought from the slavers in the east, especially around the shores of the Black Sea, who abducted and traded for thousands of children (and some men and women), the Venetian and Genoese merchant ships often brought a human cargo as well as spices and silks. It was a very lucrative business. In 1401 Francesco Datini himself insured a particularly valuable Tartar slave, called Margherita, who was to be taken by ship to a buyer in Barcelona. For a large sum, 50 gold florins, she was insured against any risk from the hand of God, the sea, human beings, barter or her master. But specifically excluded in the policy was the risk of loss through flight or suicide. If Margherita threw herself into the sea of her own accord, then no compensation was payable. It must have happened too often.

Still large, despite the devastation of the plague, the Tuscan cities were nevertheless intimately linked to the countryside around them, their *contado*. It was where most of their food came from, every day. City-dwellers grew what they could. Inside the long circuit of Florence's walls there were vegetable gardens, some close to the centre, and, to supply both dappled shade and sweet grapes, vines grew everywhere. Pots of spices and herbs on windowsills and in doorways were watered every morning and up the walls of courtyards, and anywhere enclosed, espaliered apple, pear and plum trees were trained. Larger orchards, vineyards and small wheat fields were planted in the suburbs, in the open spaces behind the street frontages.

Outside the walls farmers gathered produce for sale and slung it over the wooden pack-saddles of their mules. At the city gates tolls were levied and no doubt a good deal was routinely concealed or under-declared. Sacks of cereals, baskets of vegetables, water-skins full of live fish and nets of small birds were brought to market. Meat mostly walked to the butchers' slabs.

When sheep, cattle, goats, pigs and geese came a distance to a city market, the animals often had to be shod. Most had been reared on grass and consequently their feet were soft and unused to the hard surfaces of roads and tracks. And lameness cost money. Half-shoes were nailed onto the cloven hooves of cattle, and pigs wore socks knitted out of tough grasses. Perhaps the most ingenious footwear was designed for geese. They were first driven through hot pitch or tar, then across a patch of grit or sand, and to fix the mixture and cool it off, they finally splashed into a pond.

In the narrow streets and lanes of Florence, Pisa, Siena and Arezzo, life was lived outside, in full view of neighbours and passers-by. Those who worked at intricate trades requiring good light to see by, like cobblers or tailors, brought their work and a stool into the street. Their shops, the *botteghe*, rarely had any windows. Sellers of food and drink often set up outdoor stalls in the morning and packed them away in the evening. Cloth needing to be bleached white in the sun or stretched on tenterhooks was taken out of doors. And when butchers slaughtered an animal they cut its throat in the street so as not to make a mess inside their shops. It was not the blood they wanted to see flush down the commune's inadequate drains, that was valuable for making puddings. In the moments before death most trussed-up and terrified animals defecated.

A few good smells also filled the air (although dung was dropped continually by horses, mules and other draught animals) and when bakers took their loaves out of the communal ovens and street sellers roasted meat with herbs, it was easier to take a deep breath. Tanners and blacksmiths usually found themselves expelled to the outskirts or even beyond the walls. Forges and sparks could set a whole city alight and the foul-smelling mixture of urine and dog turds used to cure leather was too strong even for a fourteenth-century nose.

Like all the Tuscan towns and cities, Florence had its own rhythms. On appointed days religious festivals and processions filled the streets with piety, gaiety and music, and news and official proclamations were regularly bellowed out in the piazzas and at crossroads, often preceded by fanfares or drum-rolls. When criminals were condemned to death, the noose, the block or the bonfire were not the only terrifying prospects they had to face. Justice was a drawn-out ritual, needing to be seen to be done in all its awful cruelty to have any deterrent effect. The condemned were sometimes tied to a low frame or hurdle and dragged through the streets to the scaffold. The grim procession often stopped to allow jeering citizens to urinate on the victim or tip a pot of night-soil over his head. Prostitutes and petty thieves were stripped naked, their hands tied, and then whipped through the streets. These and other appalling scenes were frequent events and enormously popular.

The drama of the streets mixed with the everyday business of life to produce a community which knew itself intimately. Talk was incessant, gossip endemic, privacy almost impossible and news travelled across the city like electricity, sparking and short-circuiting. As Francesco Datini made his way from the Porta al Prato through the narrow streets to the centre of Florence, his eyes would have been wide.

Most likely through family connections, the young man had found an apprenticeship in a *bottega,* a cloth-merchant's shop. A contemporary description of Signor Francesco da Bene's establishment in the Via di Calimala has survived and the place where Datini began his long career probably looked similar.

In addition to cloth folded on shelves, kept off the floor to ensure it stayed dry, the *bottega* sold silks, velvets and table linen as well as scissors and needles. Shop furniture was rudimentary. A row of benches lined the walls, there were tables for showing off cloth (samples would often have been taken outside for inspection in better light) and a desk and a few stools. At the back sat the clerk with his ledgers and abacus. Yardsticks, checked and approved by officials from the guild, were used for measuring out what clients had decided upon.

What was stored in the shop was valuable – and vulnerable. Often one of the apprentices slept overnight on a palliasse so that intruders might be discouraged, if not deterred. If young Francesco had been given that job, he would have been listening hard to the night-time noises of medieval Florence, hoping it was rats he could hear and not burglars.

News was the life-blood of the city and its mercantile community. Outside the doors of the *bottega*, men heard and talked of events, not discussing them in the abstract but in direct connection with their business. Wars and rumours of wars inhibited movement and markets, plague shut city gates and a coronation or royal birth was good for trade. In 1373 Tuscany suffered a calamitous harvest and famine gripped the land and its cities. The neighbouring Papal States had a surplus of corn, but the cardinal-legate, Guillaume de Nollet, refused to allow its export. Florence declared war on the pope, who in turn brought all his spiritual firepower to bear upon the scene. Not only was the city laid under the dead hand of interdict, which compelled churches to cease sanctifying baptism, marriage and funerals, and all the everyday needs of life in a devout community, but Florence's merchants also attracted the Holy Father's particular spite. He called on Christian kings to expel them all, and further insisted that it was no longer a sin to attack and rob the Florentines of their merchandise.

In the narrow streets of the city news like this was evaluated, added to by passers-by and its implications caused merchants to make plans, or change them or shelve them. In 1350 and 1351, Francesco must have heard a good deal of talk about the French town of Avignon. Standing on the banks of the great River Rhône, it had become the seat of the papacy in 1305. Claiming that continuing instability in Rome and central Italy had made it impossible for Christ's Vicar to return to the see of St Peter, succeeding popes stayed in France until 1377. The reality was that they were all Frenchmen and that the Church had largely fallen under French control.

Nevertheless, their presence made Avignon an economic and political magnet. Most of Europe's ecclesiastical taxation and revenue was collected and redirected by the papal bureaucracy, the great offices of the Church (including the papacy) were bestowed in Le Palais des Papes, and decisions, alliances and plots swirled around its ante-chambers and porticos. And a college of wealthy cardinals and other princes of the Church attended the papal court. For a merchant with the right merchandise, there was tremendous opportunity in Avignon. Many of the men who stood in the street outside Francesco Datini's *bottega* would no doubt have nodded their heads. Avignon was the place to be.

Wrapped in a crimson cloak, only fifteen years old, Francesco set out on the road to France, and to fortune. It was 1351, the worst of the Black Death was past, and he had persuaded his guardian in Prato to sell some land on his behalf. In his purse, secured under his cloak, he carried his capital of 150 gold florins.

Travel in the fourteenth century could be very dangerous. Even though many of the old straight roads laid down by Roman legionaries were still in use (at least their courses had survived, if not their metalling), the wide clearings on either side had long overgrown and there were many bands of brigands lurking in the countryside. Pilgrims had travelled through Tuscany on the Via Francigena for generations but they had some nominal protection, wearing badges and emblems of the saints. Even so, they tramped the roads in companies, the larger the better. Merchants did the same, especially if they were carrying goods or cash. Datini almost certainly made his way to Avignon *all'ombra del Signore*, 'in the shadow of a powerful man'. If a large company left Florence in the spring or summer of 1351, they may have made for Pisa and boarded a ship bound for the mouth of the Rhône. Shallow-draught medieval boats could make their way up the river to the quays at Avignon, and while there were pirates and storms to contend with, it was faster and safer than a journey on land.

For a fifteen-year-old with only a little experience in business, it must have been a daunting undertaking. And yet Francesco would not have found himself entirely amongst strangers in Avignon. When the papacy moved, Italian merchants did not hesitate to move with them. The prospect of a market which could afford all sorts of goods drew many across the Alps or the sea. At Avignon in 1351 there were at least 600 Italian families in residence and even several from Francesco's home-town of Prato. And a Pratese cardinal sat in the papal Curia.

These expatriate communities kept to themselves, in city groupings, and not only through cultural or insular instincts. There were sound business reasons. Each city dealt in a different currency (although the florin was widely accepted since it was minted in pure gold and consistently weighed 54 grains) and the whole community was also held severally responsible for the individual conduct of its members. If a Florentine or Pratese merchant defaulted on a deal then every trading company from the same city was bound to make it good. This not only gave rise to a co-operative and relatively open consensus, it also enforced honesty, fair-dealing and self-regulation.

By 1361 Francesco had established himself securely in Avignon, but not as a cloth merchant. He dealt in armour and arms. The archive lists huge quantities of helmets, breastplates, mail coats and other items passing through his hands. Much of this was imported from the forges of Milan and other northern Italian towns, and Francesco sold it on to whoever had the ready cash. As with modern arms dealers, politics played no part in his business, and when opportunities arose he moved quickly. Having heard news that a company of *condottieri* had been defeated in Liguria in 1382, Francesco immediately instructed his agent in Pisa to buy up as much kit as he could, second-hand. 'When peace is made,' wrote Francesco, 'they often sell all their armour.' *Condottieri* were regular customers, both as buyers and sellers.

One of Francesco's most regular correspondents, and perhaps his only constant friend, was Ser Lapo Mazzei. He was a notary, and letters flowed between the two Pratesi for many years. Occasionally Mazzei gently chided his old friend, describing him as a man who has known all the pleasures of the body, and a man who kept women and lived only on partridges, adoring art and money, and forgetting his Creator and himself.

Monna Piera also wrote to Francesco about his behaviour, and encouraged him to leave behind the fleshpots of Avignon and come home to a more wholesome life in Prato. Only his reply survives:

> I obtained your letter by means of certain pilgrims from Prato, and was glad. As to your words, I know them to be true; and it weighs on no-one in the world as much as on me, since I know I am doing wrong. But sometimes one cannot do better. Man proposes and God disposes. Sometimes it is necessary, when one is dancing, to finish the measure, and there is a women's proverb: 'Struggle a little longer, and give birth to a male child.' Thus I, too, intend to struggle a little longer, and to satisfy myself and those who love me ... May Our Lord grant me grace in His mercy, to do what is best, both for body and soul.

By the time the papacy left Avignon, in 1377, Datini had made a great deal of money, and by the sound of things, spent a little of it unwisely. But he was about to make a great deal more. When the papacy interdicted Florence, her merchant community was evicted en masse from Avignon. Many entrusted their goods and businesses to Datini and as his operations expanded overnight, he quickly became very wealthy indeed.

Six years later he finally made his way back to Prato and the wagging finger of Monna Piera. He did not stay long. Despite having taken a wife, the redoubtable Monna Margherita, Francesco was restless, anxious to make and take business opportunities. It was what he lived for. In 1382 he went to Florence to set up a warehouse and, with several partners, began to import wool and trade in cloth, leather, spices, wine, anything which would fetch a good price and turn a profit. Datini joined one of the major guilds, the silk merchants, L'Arte di Por Santa Maria. Then a shop was opened, and eventually branches of the trading company were established in Pisa, Genoa, Spain and the Balearic Islands. Money was certainly made and business transacted, but the young partners sent out from Tuscany did not always comport themselves as Francesco wished. He had evidently entirely forgotten his own conduct in Avignon.

Cristofano di Bartolo ran the company branch in Majorca, and seems to have had a grand time. In his house, the official company premises, he kept his concubines and – this appears to be what irritated Datini most – continued to keep them after their inevitable pregnancies:

> Let every compagno of mine get it out of his head that in any place I have to do with, he can boast of keeping a woman in the house or a child at the breast – for in good faith I know not, had I one of my own, if I would keep it with me. Even in Prato and Florence there are few men who keep a child at the breast in the house, even among the very rich . . . You once said to me, you would like to be the head of a branch, to show your ability; but I now believe . . . you spoke like that, in order to do what you pleased and to live at ease and make merry and have as much pleasure and beget bastards . . . Perhaps, had you ruled yourself according to my counsels, you would by now have several children . . . and you would be cared for by the hand of a wife, and not of a slave.

It was slack behaviour and bad for business, and in a letter of 1398, Francesco became very exercised and promised Cristofano 'that you shall have such a caning from me as leaves a mark'. But this was not for licentiousness. The young man had incurred business losses, the most heinous crime of all. Another of Francesco's partners became well used to his complaints and lists of instructions and replied bitterly: 'Did you not bite me in each letter, you would feel you had not done right.'

The vast Datini archive paints a vivid picture of the man. He seems to have been characteristic of his era and his peers. Because he had grown rich from humble beginnings, a self-made man, Francesco was eternally anxious, believing all his hard-won wealth could disappear in a moment. And so he was tough, shrewd and versatile, trading in any commodity which would turn a florin, switching from one transaction to another with, for the times, surprising speed. Trusting no-one, except perhaps his old friend Mazzei, he drove hard bargains but took high risks.

Alongside all that commercial ruthlessness ran the conventional pieties, the keeping of saints' days and fasts and contributing generously to the church. Worried about the consequences of his

Above. Morning in Pitigliano, the sun lighting the site of the Etruscan citadel.

Below. Pitigliano seems to grow directly out of its tufa cliffs.

Right. The Medici aqueduct and the Orsini fortress at Pitigliano.

Below. A narrow medieval lane in Pitigliano.

Right. Niches from one of the complexes of Etruscan tombs in southern Tuscany.

Below. The massive walls of Tarquinia, built on Etruscan foundations.

Above. One of the medieval towers of Tarquinia.

Left. Bolsena, the new city of the Volsinii on Lake Bolsena.

Left. The narrow lanes of medieval Bolsena.

Below. Fiesole, the Etruscan city in the hills north of Florence.

Above. The Roman/Etruscan gateway into Saturnia, the terminus of the Via Clodia.

Right. The flagpole at the top is the sole perpendicular line on the leaning tower of Pisa.

Above. The beautiful early medieval cathedral of Pisa and its leaning bell tower.

Left. Ornate architecture in the city of Pisa shows its ancient prosperity.

Right. Madonna and Child at
Pisa Cathedral.

Below. The courtyard at Pisa Town Hall.

Above. The Arno flows lazily through Pisa.

Below. Pisan defence works by the Arno.

bove. Massive defences kept Lucca independent for many centuries.

elow. Now glazed and decorated, this gateway is one of four guarding access to Lucca.

Above. The portcullis still survives.

Right. The magnificent town hall, the Palazzo Pubblico, of Siena in the Campo.

Left. The Palio, the great annual horse race, is run around the perimeter of the Campo.

Below. A bronze sculpture in Siena of Romulus and Remus being suckled by the She-wolf.

Above. The gorgeously decorated façade of Siena Cathedral.

Left. A elaborate portal to an inner courtyard off one of Siena's narrow streets.

Above. The famous medieval towers of San Gimignano.

Below. The Florentine skyline. Above the line of the Arno, the Palazzo Vecchio and the cathedral.

Above. The Franciscan church of Santa Croce in Florence.

Left. Brunelleschi's dome for Florence Cathedral.

Right. Rich decoration on the façade of Florence Cathedral.

Below. Florence Cathedral and its bell tower, designed by Giotto.

Above. A view looking down the Arno as it flows west through Florence.

Left. Some vestiges of Florence's massive defences remain.

Right. Michelangelo's David, the copy in the Piazza della Signoria.

Below. The Ponte Vecchio with the windows of the Corridoio Vasariano on the first floor.

Above. The town hall at Montepulciano.

Right. The medieval streets of Montepulciano.

Right. The villa of La Foce, the wartime home of Iris Origo and her family.

Below. The lush produce of Tuscan farmland and market gardens.

Left. The butcher's shop in Pitigliano run by the Polidori family.

Below, opposite and overleaf. Views of the intensively cultivated and stunningly beautiful Tuscan countryside.

usurious and technically sinful business practices and the length of any sentence in Purgatory, Francesco paid for good works often. Childless at the end of a hard-working life, he took out his last insurance policy when he left everything to charity. Perhaps the gift of his house and fortune to the poor of Prato was a memory of a fate he himself avoided. After the death of his parents in 1348 from plague, Francesco could easily have become impoverished, dependent on the kindness of others. Many of his letters are revealing, but this one, written in 1398 to his wife, shows how business consumed him, even when he was asleep:

> I dreamed last night of a house which had fallen to pieces, and all my household were inside it ... And the meaning of this dream gives me much to ponder on, for there are no tidings of a galley that left Venice more than two months ago, bound for Catalonia; and I had insured her for three hundred florins, as I did the other ship for Domenico di Cambio, which perished the next day ... I am so vexed by many matters, it is a wonder I am not out of my mind, for the more I seek the less I find. And God knows what will befall me.

When Francesco had his small palazzo built in Prato, he repeatedly enquired after costs and materials, frequently firing off irritated letters. Like most of his mercantile contemporaries, he commissioned interior decoration in the form of frescoes. Two can still be seen. In the main hallway there is a St Christopher. Just as travellers wear his likeness as a pendant, householders also believed that the saint's presence was protective. In 1394 Francesco wrote that although the fresco had been started by Niccolò Gerini, two young painters were to be paid ten florins to finish it. The other painting is a portrait of the master of the house. Its inscription makes the point:

> I am Francesco di Marco
> Who left my Pratesi as heirs of all my fortune,
> Because I loved my city above all things.

While much exercised by costs, Datini had nothing to say about the quality of the paintings he commissioned. Few merchants of the time did, but that does not mean that they saw them as formulaic wallpaper, something which scarcely engaged their attention. Especially in Tuscany, painters were very well aware of mercantile tastes and interests and tried to incorporate them into their work.

A good example is the now largely lost skill of 'gauging', something which Francesco Datini would have been expert at. Since the nineteenth century almost all quantities, whether packets, sacks or bottles, bought in shops or from specialised merchants, have come in standard sizes. Nowadays we buy a litre of milk, half a kilo of sugar or 75 centilitres of wine. No more and no less. In the fourteenth century and for a long time afterwards, each barrel, sack or bale was unique. No commodity was sold as a standard unit. Two woolpacks, or bales of fleeces, might each contain the same number but because no two sheep were exactly the same size, one might yield a lot more wool than the other. Weight might be influenced by dampness or particularly oily fleeces, or dry fleeces. Any two bolts of cloth might be of differing widths and lengths, or barrels of wine might be made with thicker or thinner staves even when they looked as though they were the same girth and height.

Francesco Datini and his fellow merchants dealt with this sort of complexity every day of their working lives and were immensely skilled at gauging quantities. If mistakes were made, profit might turn into loss. At the *abbaco*, their secondary schools, boys were taught the geometric formulae needed to work out relative volumes. And they were usually able to do these calculations in their heads. On a quayside or in a marketplace, a merchant would often find himself bidding for commodities against others, and fiddling about with ready-reckoners might have led to fatal hesitations.

Painters understood the principles of gauging very well. The great Tuscan, Piero della Francesca, wrote a teaching handbook with illustrations. Often frescoes contained exercises in gauging in their compositions. This was done for amusement and as an acknowledgement of the skills of the wealthy merchants who had commissioned the work. One of the most striking examples is Paolo Uccello's vast painting of *The Battle of San Romano*, which now hangs in the National Gallery in London. In the centre of the picture, surrounded by armoured knights and a forest of lances, rides Niccolò da Tolentino. Unlike the helmeted men around him, the *condottiere* is wearing a splendid hat made out of what looks like furnishing fabric and shaped like an upside-down cottage loaf. Why? Made from two voluminous polygons painted in precise perspective on a two-dimensional surface, Niccolò's hat is unlikely to have protected him from the maces and swords brandished by his enemies. It is in fact an exercise in gauging. And it would have amused the merchants who looked at it.

What was known as the 'Golden Rule' also influenced painting very much, especially proportion and composition. Also called the 'Rule of Three' or the 'Merchant's Key', it is explained in Piero della Francesca's handbook:

> The Rule of Three says that one has to multiply the thing one wants to know about by the thing that is dissimilar to it, and one divides the product by the remaining thing. And the number that comes from this is of the nature of that which is dissimilar to the first term; and the divisor is always similar to the thing which one wants to know about.
>
> For example: seven bracci of cloth are worth nine lire; how much will five bracci be worth?
>
> Do it as follows: multiply the quantity you want to know about by that quantity which seven bracci of cloth are worth – namely, nine. Five times nine makes forty-five. Divide by seven and the result is six and three sevenths.

Simple. At least after a great deal of repetition and re-reading. Made possible by Leonardo Fibonacci, the Golden Rule instilled, literally, a sense of proportion into the mercantile classes, the people who paid for paintings and new buildings. And the painters and architects responded by working within its harmonies and sequences. Any failure to do that would have jarred, seemed somehow awkward.

The artistic glories of the Italian Renaissance were largely paid for by a very small group of wealthy people who had made their money in trade and banking. The now obscure skills of gauging and calculating by the Rule of Three were very well known to them all, had formed a central part of their education and were used every day of their working lives. Understanding what has been called a 'period eye', a way of seeing fifteenth-century art in the way that the fifteenth century saw it, helps in turn to understand how all those wonderful buildings, sculptures and paintings came to look the way they do.

At the same time as Francesco Datini was having his palazzo built in Prato, another ambitious and hard-working Tuscan was laying the foundations of a banking dynasty in Florence. In 1397 Giovanni di Bicci de' Medici invested 5,500 florins in a new bank, having persuaded relatives to come up with a further 4,500 to make up the opening capital of 10,000. Originally from the Mugello, the countryside north of Florence, in the foothills of the Apennines, the Medici had risen to prominence, if not great wealth. In 1296 Ardingo de' Medici had been elected *gonfaloniere*, the leading citizen, and two other family members followed him in 1299 and 1314. The canny Giovanni would eventually establish the Medici as sufficiently wealthy and well-connected to become the dominant power in Tuscany, their hegemony lasting for 300 years.

By the end of the fourteenth century the family was more like a clan, with twenty or so branches, most of whom lived in the neighbourhood around the church of San Lorenzo, just to the north of the Piazza Duomo and the dusty building site that would eventually become Florence's new cathedral. The Medici often gave their sons the name of Lorenzo.

Giovanni di Bicci was cautious in his lending and investment, and efficient in running the banking business. His first year of operation realised a 10 per cent profit and he wisely invested it in some land in the Mugello. The Medici premises in Florence were not grand, nothing like the great monuments to banking of the nineteenth and twentieth centuries. More like a shop, no bigger than the cloth-merchant's *bottega* run by Francesco Datini, the first Medici bank probably had a broad counter, the name of which gave away its function as a flat surface on which counting was done. In Italian a counter is a *banco*, the origin of the English word. Behind the counter sat clerks and book-keepers with their abacuses and ledgers, and it was rare for more than five or six to work in a bank. Even after Giovanni had opened branches in Venice, Rome, Naples and Gaeta (south-east of Naples), there were never more than seventeen employees. The Medici operation did not approach the scale of the Bardi or Peruzzi banks of the early fourteenth century.

But then they and others had crashed, and Giovanni was determined to proceed carefully, at least most of the time. In 1402 he took what seemed to be a wild and uncharacteristic risk. Baldassare Cossa was a penniless aristocrat from Naples whom Giovanni had met in Rome. He was a remarkable man – and Giovanni must have seen something in him. Having made a great deal of money as a successful pirate, Cossa then took what seems a dizzying change of direction when he matriculated as a law student at the university of Bologna before buying his way into the Church hierarchy. Which he found very congenial, just the sort of milieu where a retired pirate with a law degree might prosper. The papacy and the Church were in chaos, cut-throat chaos. After the return to Rome from Avignon in 1377 and the death of Gregory IX a year later, what became known as the Great Schism began. The Italian Church elected Urban VI, who based his court in Rome, and the French cardinals withdrew and elected an antipope, Clement VII, who returned to Le Palais des Papes in Avignon. The kings and princes of Christendom lined up on each side. And then in 1409, at the Council of Pisa, convened to resolve the Schism, a third pope was elected – Alexander V. Amidst all the faction-fighting, intrigue, coup and counter-coup, Baldassare Cossa was thriving.

When Giovanni di Bicci was asked by Cossa to loan him 12,000 gold florins, Florence was astonished when the wily old banker agreed. In the deeply corrupt Church, it was the price of a cardinal's hat. It appeared to matter little that Cossa was famously dissolute, and when he duly became cardinal-legate at Bologna, his residence was soon home to whores and disreputables of all sorts. A contemporary rated his interest in matters spiritual as zero or minus zero. When Giovanni di Bicci's florins disappeared, the cardinal requested more loans to pay for more debauchery. And the Medici bank obliged. It seemed a crazy waste of cash, thrown away by an otherwise frugal man.

But Giovanni di Bicci knew exactly what he was doing. Cardinal Cossa was positioning himself to succeed the Roman pope, Urban VI, and in 1410 the old man died. More Medici florins bought the election and the former pirate ascended the throne of St Peter as Pope John XXIII, and Giovanni di Bicci became the Church's banker. The rewards would be huge.

The proceeds of the sale of relics, of Church offices, of the right to collect ecclesiastical taxes and of indulgences (paper guarantees of the forgiveness of sins) flowed to Rome from much of Europe. The Medici bank organised the collection of all this cash and took a handsome commission for its services. Between 1397 and 1420 the Rome branch alone made a profit of 79,195 florins. Cardinals, archbishops, abbots and other prelates who attended John XXIII's court also banked with Giovanni, and although many were overdrawn most of the time, their status ensured security for the loans. At one point the Medici held a priceless, jewel-encrusted papal tiara as security against sums advanced to Cossa himself.

The chaos came to an end in 1414 when the German emperor, Sigismund, called a council of the Church at Constance in Switzerland. To protect Medici interests, Giovanni sent his son, Cosimo, with John XXIII's entourage. It proved an impossible commission. Along with the other two popes, John was deposed. Even more seriously, he was then arrested as he attempted to flee and then thrown into prison. A ransom of 35,000 florins was demanded, and despite the certainty that there was no prospect of repayment, Giovanni obliged once more. There was one condition, however, something which hinted at a motive. When Baldassare came to Florence he was to take part in a public reconciliation with the new and undisputed pope, Martin V. It was a clever ploy, showing how well Giovanni di Bicci played the long game.

Martin had made the Spini, a rival Florentine family, his bankers, but when they went out of business in 1424, the pope remembered the loyalty of the Medici to his disgraced but reconciled predecessor. And so Giovanni regained the most lucrative banking contract in Europe. An astute espousal of apparently hopeless causes had manoeuvred the Medici into an immensely powerful position.

It was time for the old man to retire and he handed over the running of the bank to his sons, Lorenzo and Cosimo. He was sixty years old and contented himself with an advisory role. When news came to Florence that the former manager of the Medici bank in Venice, Neri Tornaquinci, was living in poverty in Cracow, in Poland, Giovanni ordered that 36 gold florins be sent to him immediately. It was more than a wealthy old man's act of kindness to a former employee; it spoke of an attitude to life and its vicissitudes.

Twenty years or so before, Giovanni had written to all of the managers of the bank's branches instructing them never to lend to Germans. They were backward and untrustworthy. But Neri Tornaquinci ignored the letter and advanced a large sum to a group of German traders, who promptly defaulted and fled back across the Alps. Too terrified to inform head office, Neri borrowed cash at exorbitant rates of interest to fill the hole in the accounts. When the discrepancy finally showed up, Neri was summoned to Florence, ordered to sell all his assets, including his house, to reimburse the bank, and was then dismissed.

With nothing to lose, the wretched Tornaquinci set off in belated pursuit of the defaulting Germans. Astonishingly, he caught up with them in Cracow and retrieved part of what was owed. Perhaps he had hired some local muscle. But rather than return to Florence and hand over the cash, Neri decided to stay in Poland and start a new life. Clearly he failed. When Giovanni di Bicci heard of his dire straits, he saw no point in anything other than an act of kindness. But an act of kindness which has come down to us, and which was probably well known to contemporaries. Another example of Medici loyalty and a snippet which played well with posterity – and at the time.

By 1428 the old man had begun to fail. Having taken to his bed, he gave some parting and eloquent advice to his sons. The words may be apocryphal but the sentiment sums up Giovanni's cautious and un-showy attitude to business and survival:

> Never hang around the Palazzo della Signoria as if it is the place where you do business. Only go there when you are summoned, and only accept the offices which are bestowed upon you. Never make a show before the people, but if this is unavoidable, let it be the least necessary. Keep out of the public gaze, and never go against the will of the people – unless they are advocating some disastrous project.

Cosimo took part of his father's advice. In his stewardship of the Medici bank he showed the same sort of canny caution, but at the same time realised that in order to maintain the family's pre-eminence, it was vital to be active politically. There were other differences. Educated at the monastery school of Santa Maria degli Angeli, Cosimo became aware of and then keenly interested in classical literature. On his ill-fated mission to the Council of Constance, the banker slipped away to visit some of the ancient Swiss monasteries. In their dusty libraries scrolls and codices had lain unopened and uncatalogued for many centuries. Texts by eminent Roman and Greek philosophers, poets and politicians awaited rediscovery, and Cosimo took an energetic part in the search for the knowledge of the ancients. For perhaps the first time since the zenith of the Roman Empire, a powerful and wealthy individual had become as cultured as the intellectuals and artists he patronised. Increasingly, Florentines had seen themselves as successors to the Romans, and as observed by Giovanni Villani, the city was rising and achieving great things, whereas Rome was declining. And Cosimo de' Medici was about to lead Florence and much of Tuscany into the glories of the Italian Renaissance, a unique flowering of creativity.

7

Cosimo and the Florentine Renaissance

Twenty miles north of Florence, up in the green hills of the Mugello, around Trebbia and Cafaggiolo, the Medici had owned land for many generations. It was seen as their ancestral home and Cosimo de' Medici often left the heat of the summer city for the peace of his villa at Il Trebbio. In May and June 1433, it offered more than a spiritual sanctuary. At the dead of night, while the Medici and their servants were fast asle_ _ _ _ _ _ _ ie doors of their palazzo in the Piazza Duomo had been dau_ _ _ _ _ _ th blood. Cosimo and his family left the city immediately for _ _ _ _ bio.

Trouble was coming. The ox blood smeared by their enemies' thugs might become _ _ dici blood. Florence had been involved in a disastrous, unnecessary and expensive war with Lucca, a crazy enterprise which Cosimo had at first spoken against but later was forced to support. Unlike the other great cities of the Val d'Arno, Lucca was still independent and, wishing to remain so, had allied itself with Giangalleazo Visconti, Duke of Milan. A hawkish faction in Florence saw the alliance as a good reason to launch an attack on its neighbour. When an army marched down the Arno, Milan dispatched the *condottiere* Francesco Sforza to hurry to the aid of Lucca. The disconcerted Florentines offered a huge bribe of 50,000 florins and when the mercenaries duly left a mad plan was hatched.

Three artists were commissioned to design and oversee the building of an enormous earthen dam. The River Serchio runs down a narrow valley from the Apennines which widens out just above the city of Lucca and the architects, Filippo Brunelleschi and Michelozzo Michelozzi, and surprisingly, the sculptor, Donatello, were instructed to stop its flow. One night would be enough for a massive volume of water to back up, and in the morning it would be suddenly released so that a tremendous torrent would wash away the walls of Lucca. And then the Florentines would march over the rubble. Simple. Instead, under cover of darkness the Lucchese stole out of the city and broke down the dam at another point. And a tremendous torrent washed away the Florentine camp.

The instigator of this embarrassing farce had been Rinaldo degli Albizzi, an ambitious Florentine aristocrat from an old family. While clearly lacking military acumen, he nevertheless had excellent political instincts, and far from being seen as the author of the city's misfortunes, Rinaldo managed to shift the blame onto the Medici. Even before the blood was smeared on his doors, Cosimo had sniffed conspiracy and danger. In the early summer of 1433 Medici money was moving. On 30th May 2,400 gold florins were taken for safe-keeping to the monks at San Miniato al Monte, south of the walls, and 4,700 went to the Dominicans at San Marco. No-one would dare violate the sacred precincts. The head office of the Medici bank transferred 15,000 florins to the Venice branch and valuable stocks and documents went down to Rome. By June Cosimo had removed most of his fortune beyond the reach of ██fiscation, and he had removed himself and his family to Il Tr███o. Unlike the villa at Cafaggiolo, this house was well defended. Illustrations show a tower and crenellated battlements.

Meanwhile Rinaldo degli Albizzi had been busy. By means of blatant rigging of the names to be drawn out of the leather bags by lot, he had ensured that seven of the nine-man Signoria were Albizzi supporters, and had also paid the overdue taxes of Bernardo Guadagni so that he could legally become *gonfaloniere*. The Palazzo della Signoria was under Rinaldo's control. All the pieces were in place.

A horseman galloped out of the city and up into the Mugello with a dispatch from the Signoria. Cosimo de' Medici was commanded to appear 'so that some important decisions could be made'. Not noted for his courage but recognising that any future his family might have lay in Florence, Cosimo had little choice but to comply.

Immediately on arrival, on 4 September, he went to see Gonfalonier Guadagni and the Signoria. There were rumours of a coup d'état, of a plot to destroy the de' Medici: 'When I told them what I had heard, they denied it, and told me to be of good cheer, as they hoped to leave the city in the same condition as they had found it when their time was up.'

There would be another meeting of the Signoria on 7 September, and Cosimo would have an opportunity to speak then. Believing none of these blandishments and showing characteristic caution, he went to the Medici bank and replaced himself with his wife's cousin, Lipaccio de' Bardi, as manager of head office and all the branches.

Meanwhile, in the shadowy depths of the Bargello, Florence's medieval prison, only a few hundred yards from the Piazza della Signoria, the rackmaster was busy. A rectangular wooden frame, raised off the flagstones, the rack had a drum-like roller at one end with ratcheted gearing attached. To be tightened smoothly, the roller needed to be oiled before use.

Niccolò Tinucci was a poet, part of the intellectual circle around Cosimo de' Medici which met to discuss classical texts, Roman and Greek literature and history, the new discoveries which came to light each year. Also qualified in law, he had occasionally acted as a notary for the Signoria. When Rinaldo degli Albizzi's men banged on the door of his house near Giotto's campanile in the Piazza Duomo, Tinucci would have protested at his arrest, perhaps even struggled. When they dragged him into the rackmaster's torture chamber in the Bargello, he must have been wide-eyed with terror.

So that humiliation and vulnerability were intensified, the rackmaster's men probably stripped the trembling Tinucci naked before lifting him onto the rack. His ankles were clamped into iron manacles attached to a stout beam at the foot of the frame and his hands chained to the roller at its head. As the rackmaster turned to the first notch, interrogators would have put the first question. 'It was true, was it not, that Cosimo de' Medici had often talked of taking over the government of the city entirely?'

The rack was a preferred method of extracting confessions because it inflicted constant and excruciating pain while allowing interrogation to go on, at least in the intervals when the victims did not scream. And even though many soiled themselves, there was no blood. As the rackmaster turned the ratchet, muscles were first stretched so far that they would be irretrievably torn and would lose the ability to contract. This made them useless after the torture ceased, leaving arms and legs floppy and rendering the victims immobile. As the rollers pulled ever tighter, joints dislocated and there were usually loud popping noises as cartilage, ligaments and even bones snapped. In their agony, many mercifully lost consciousness as their bodies were destroyed.

Niccolò Tinucci confessed: 'Many times I heard Cosimo and Averardo [one of his cousins] say that the way to keep oneself powerful is to keep the commune in a state of war and to serve the needs of the war economy.' His name does not appear in Florence's municipal records after 1433, and it may be that Albizzi's torturers killed Tinucci, or he committed suicide.

On the appointed day, 7 September, Cosimo de' Medici walked from his palazzo near the Duomo through the narrow streets to the Palazzo della Signoria to appear before Gonfalonier Guadagni and his colleagues. The meeting never took place. When Cosimo made his way through the archway and into the courtyard, an official asked him to wait. Presently the Captain of the Guard came, and instead of being escorted to the Council Chamber, Cosimo was led up the steep stairs of the great bell-tower, bundled into a cell near the top and the door locked behind him. Known as the Alberghettino, the 'Little Inn', its slitted window looked out over the city. Perhaps one of the first things to occur to Cosimo was that in times past prisoners had been thrown from the bell-tower. He had been 'arrested on good grounds, as would soon be made clear'. At least that implied some sort of process, and not a summary execution.

As Niccolò Tinucci screamed in the Bargello and Cosimo de' Medici pondered his prospects, Rinaldo degli Albizzi was persuading the Signoria to call a *parlamento*. In times of crisis, this ad hoc assembly of citizens in the Piazza della Signoria was summoned. Usually it was asked to approve the election of a *balia*, a council of 200 who would deal with whatever emergency had arisen.

In his tiny cell Cosimo fretted. Suspecting poison, he refused to eat, and peering out of the narrow window, tried to guess what was taking place below. On his arrest, Medici supporters had sent messages out of the city, to the pope in Rome and the doge in Venice, and wherever else Cosimo was held in high esteem. People owed him favours, and money. The *condottiere* Niccolò da Tolentino was alerted and his men began to march up the valley of the Arno towards Florence.

Rinaldo degli Albizzi knew that time was short and he insisted that the Signoria meet to pass sentence on their prisoner. Some semblance of legality was important. The charge reads oddly. Cosimo de' Medici was accused of 'attempting to raise himself above the rank of an ordinary citizen', and the punishment was death. Spooked by what they had already done, and no doubt aware of support beginning to rally to Cosimo, the Signoria could not bring themselves to have him executed. The sentence would be banishment for five years.

Degli Albizzi was disgusted but determined to go ahead with the summons of the *parlamento*. On 9 September Cosimo heard the deafening boom of the Vacca, the huge bell in the tower above his head, calling the citizens to assemble in the piazza below. At each of its entrances Albizzi's armed men were preventing Medici supporters from attending. Although only a paltry twenty-three eventually gathered, a *balia* was agreed and degli Albizzi would make sure that it was packed with his people.

In his *History of Florence*, Niccolò Machiavelli takes up the story, foregrounding the role of the sympathetic jailer, Federigo Malavolti:

> In this place, hearing the assembly of the Councils, the noise of arms which proceeded from the piazza, and the frequent ringing of the bell to assemble the Balia, he was greatly apprehensive for his safety, but still more lest his private enemies cause him to be put to death in some unusual manner. He scarcely took any food, so that in four days he ate only a small quantity of bread. Federigo, observing his anxiety, said to him, 'Cosimo, you are afraid of being poisoned, and are evidently hastening your end with hunger. You wrong me if you think I would be party to such an atrocious act. I do not imagine your life to be in danger, since you have so many friends both within the palace and without; but if you should eventually lose it, be assured they will use some other medium than myself for that purpose, for I will never imbue my hands in the blood of any, still less in yours, who never injured me; therefore cheer up, take some food, and preserve your life for your friends and your country. And that you may do so with greater assurance, I will partake of your meals with you.' These words were a great relief to Cosimo, who, with tears in his eyes, embraced and kissed Federigo, earnestly thanking him for so kind and affectionate conduct, and promising, if ever the opportunity were given him, he would not be ungrateful.

Federigo's judgement of the mood in the Signoria and the streets is eloquent. The immediate crisis seemed to be passing, or was at least stalled. The hand-picked *balia* was divided. Degli Albizzi's ultras called loudly for the death penalty while a moderate group preferred banishment, ten years rather than five.

Up in the bell-tower cell, conditions continued to slacken. Federigo Malavolti brought in a man called Il Farnagaccio (literally, the 'Crazy Guy') to amuse Cosimo. He was probably the resident clown, the *buffone* hired to amuse the Signoria during its two-month term of office. And he turned out not to be so crazy. Cosimo gave Il Farnagaccio a note and instructed him to take it to the director of the Santa Maria Nuova Hospital, who would immediately hand over 1,100 Venetian ducats. The clown was to keep 100 for himself and quietly pass 1,000 to the *gonfaloniere*, Bernardo Guadagni. The Medici were beginning to mobilise their money and buy their way out of trouble, and more bribes were accepted by other members of the Signoria.

Outsiders involved themselves. Three Venetian ambassadors arrived in Florence to plead for Cosimo's release and Pope Eugenius IV sent his local representative, Ambrogio Traversari, to intercede. Most worrying for the Albizzi faction were reports that Niccolò da Tolentino had camped at Lastra, only six miles west of the city, and was awaiting instructions.

It was at this point, it seems, that Rinaldo produced the confession of Niccolò Tinucci and demanded the death penalty. Cosimo was clearly guilty of high treason, of wishing to take over the city. It was glaringly obvious – his soldiers were within a short march from the gates. Degli Albizzi's invective convinced very few. It appears to have been widely known that Tinucci's testimony had been extracted on the rack, and it was discounted. The Signoria confirmed that Cosimo and other leading members of his family were to be sentenced to banishment. On 3 October, after almost a month in the tiny cell at the top of the bell-tower, the prisoner was led into the council chamber to hear the verdict read out. Cosimo sounded relieved, but anxious about any supposed accident which might befall him:

> As you have decided I am to go to Padua, I declare that I am content to go, and stay wherever you command, not only in the Trevisian state, but should you send me to live amongst the Arabs, or any other people alien to our customs, I would go most willingly. As disaster comes to me by your orders, I accept it as a boon, and as a benefit to me and my belongings . . . Every trouble will be easy to bear as long as I know that my adversity will bring peace and happiness to the city . . . One thing I beg of you, Signori, that seeing

you intend to preserve my life, you take care that it should not be taken by wicked citizens, and thus you be put to shame ... Have a care that those who stand outside in the piazza with arms in their hands anxiously desiring my blood should not have their way with me. My pain would be small, but you would earn perpetual infamy.

If Cosimo sounds ingratiating, even pathetic, it is as well to remember that despite all his support he stood alone in front of the rulers of Florence with some sort of mob baying outside the windows. Words were cheap, defiance a dangerous luxury. At nightfall armed guards led Cosimo out of the city by the Porta San Gallo and they rode 40 miles north-east to the borders of the republic, high in the Apennines.

As their patron made his disconsolate way to Padua, Medici supporters began to suffer at the hands of the all-powerful Albizzi. By far the most important and most obvious civic building project was the completion of the new cathedral, and in August 1434 its architect, Filippo Brunelleschi, was arrested and thrown into prison. The pretext was so flimsy that the motives must have been political. The architect's membership of the masons' guild was apparently in arrears, by the piffling sum of 12 *soldi,* what a labourer would earn for a day's work.

It was a strange episode. The completion of the Duomo was not a Medici commission but something supported by the whole city, a matter of communal pride. As long ago as 1296 the foundation stone had been laid and a design by Arnolfo di Cambio accepted. Two old churches and several blocks of houses were demolished to make way for what would be the grandest cathedral anywhere. But work had gone on by fits and starts, and after the Black Death of 1348 and its return visitations, it was suspended entirely for a time. By 1366 the nave was eventually roofed over and it was the east end of the church which remained unfinished. There was a substantial problem. The original plans drawn up by Arnolfo di Cambio appear to have been lost and a new architect, Neri di Fioravanti, was asked to supply a new design.

Instead, he seemed at first to have created a problem. In proposing to cover the crossing with a huge dome, the broadest and highest built since the time of the Romans, he offered a crowning, inspiring glory to finish off the cathedral. The problem was no-one knew how to build it, how to solve the immense engineering difficulties. How could such a dome be prevented from falling in on itself?

Neri built a large model, 15 feet high and 30 feet long. The dome was not to be hemispherical but slightly pointed and made in a series of tapering sections to be topped by a large lantern. To complicate construction further, there were to be two domes, an inner and an outer shell.

Everyone was deeply impressed. When the overseers of the cathedral works, the Wool Merchants' Guild, met each New Year's Day, they laid hands on the model and swore an annual oath to make sure the cathedral was completed according to Neri's design. They were forced to do this because of the inconvenient fact that the architect had died before he could begin to convert his concept into bricks and mortar.

For almost fifty years the dome perplexed the wool guild's overseers and architects had begun to believe that the design was impossible to execute. In 1418 another project was announced, and once again models were made. The selection process narrowed the number of candidates to two: Filippo Brunelleschi and Lorenzo Ghiberti. They were bitter rivals. In yet another competition, in 1401, Ghiberti had triumphed over Brunelleschi to win the commission to make new bronze doors for Florence's ancient baptistry, San Giovanni. What became known as the 'Doors of Paradise' were the result, not only a very beautiful set of panels depicting biblical scenes, but also technologically brilliant.

Casting in bronze involved what was known as the 'lost wax' process, and was extremely difficult to execute properly. The reliefs for the baptistry doors were first modelled in clay and then more finely etched in a layer of wax. Then a foul-smelling, protective film of iron filings, cow dung and burnt horn was carefully painted over the wax and allowed to dry. Layers of clay were applied and once they had dried, the whole package was tied tightly with iron straps. After the mould had been baked in a kiln, the clay dried even harder and as the wax melted and dripped out of the bottom, a thin gap was left over the area of the sculpted surface. Into this mould molten bronze was poured, making sure it reached every corner. When all was cool and the clay broken apart, a perfectly cast bronze relief emerged. Usually. Sometimes the process misfired, and Michelangelo was famously superstitious about the lost wax process.

More technology lay at the heart of the competition to design and build the cathedral dome. Because Neri di Fioravanti had stipulated a pointed structure, formed by a series of what were essentially inward curving and pointed arches, the most fundamental issue revolved around centring. As they were built up, all arches were laid on a removable wooden frame known as 'centring', and what exercised the architects involved was the vast scale of the centring needed to support the dome. It had a diameter of 143 feet 6 inches and the forming of the stonework to make it began at an extraordinary 170 feet off the ground.

There was another engineering problem. All domes are prey to what is called 'hoop stress'. As gravity pulls down on the unsupported centre of a dome, the weight of all that curving stonework pushes the sides outwards. They bulge, like a cushion when someone sits on it. For the Romans, reducing the overall weight of the centre worked well, and at the Pantheon in Rome, the oldest and largest surviving domed building from antiquity, the architects used pumice stone and even empty amphorae to achieve a lighter shell. Coffering also helped: the shrinking of the volume of the shell of the dome by making it from a series of interlocking and ever-decreasing sunken panels of masonry.

Brunelleschi's design solved all of these problems very simply. There would be no centring at all, and by adapting Neri di Fioravanti's concepts of a double skin and a series of stone-built hoops, the dome would rise, slowly but surely. Despite the fact that the irascible Brunelleschi refused to divulge the precise details of his scheme, he was awarded the contract. However, the wool merchants hedged their apparently reckless bet by appointing Lorenzo Ghiberti as joint overseer of the building work. Brunelleschi was furious, but he accepted the commission.

In 1420, on the morning of 7 August, the masons and labourers hired to build the dome climbed up to the top of the drum on which it would sit. Before they began work, the men enjoyed a feast to mark the start of the great enterprise. Looking over the city rooftops, 140 feet up, they ate bread and melons, washing down the unusual combination with some Trebbia wine.

They certainly needed something to give them courage. As the sides of the dome rose, the masons worked off flimsy platforms made from willow withes stuck into previous courses of stonework. They

were called *ponti*, or 'bridges', and soon Brunelleschi was being told
how dangerous and difficult they were. As much to prevent the men
from looking down as to provide a safety net, a *parapetto*, a scaffold
of wider boards was suspended from the masonry so that it lay below
the *ponti*.

The dome was built very slowly, *di giro in giro*, 'circle by circle',
as courses of bricks were laid and then allowed to set before more
were added. Brunelleschi had promised the wool merchants that he
would review the issue of centring when the sides of the dome began
to curve inwards at the critical angle of 30 degrees. He did, and they
carried on without it.

All that confidence had a basis in more than bad-tempered
bravado. In the years before he won the commission for the Duomo,
Brunelleschi had spent a great deal of time in Rome examining
classical ruins. His interests were more than antiquarian. By precise
measurement and an analysis of materials, the architect aimed to
understand ancient techniques and apply them to his own times.
With the unfinished cathedral in mind, he made a particular study
of the Pantheon. Brunelleschi became so skilled at surveying and
transferring his research onto paper that he became a master at the
lost art of perspective drawing.

When he won the contract for the dome in 1418, Brunelleschi
was already famous for a remarkable illusion. Using the drawing
skills developed while surveying ancient buildings, he made a small
painting of the Baptistry of San Giovanni which amazed all who saw
it. Perspective drawing is founded on the principle of the vanishing
point, the place, usually in the middle of the painting, where all the
parallel lines appear to lead the eye into the distance, the point where
they seem to converge.

To make his painting, Brunelleschi took up a position inside
the central door of the unfinished cathedral, where he was exactly
115 feet from the baptistry and could use the doorway as a frame.
Using the techniques of perspective painting, he created as accurate
a representation of the little church as he could. For the sky, he
attached a strip of polished silver so that real clouds and sunshine
were reflected. Then he bored a small hole precisely at the vanishing
point. The experiment was ready.

Subjects were told to stand exactly on the spot from where
Brunelleschi had painted the baptistry, given the small painting to

hold in one hand and asked to reverse it and look through the hole. In the other hand, they held up a mirror. The effect was disconcerting, as though it was possible to see a real building – and when they were asked to take away the mirror, almost exactly the same scene was magically revealed. People must have been astounded, and painters profoundly influenced.

One of the first to adopt the principles of perspective was also one of the greatest. Tommaso di Ser Giovanni di Mone Cassai was mercifully known as Masaccio, or 'Big Tom', and in early fifteenth-century Florence he painted masterpieces. His most obvious debt to Brunelleschi was *The Holy Trinity*, a fresco in the church of Santa Maria Novella. God the Father appears to support his dying son on the cross, while the Virgin Mary and St John kneel on either side. Much of the dominating power of the image comes from its setting of a coffered vault which suggests an illusory side chapel on the flat wall of the real church. Looming out of this background, the Trinity seems to hover over the viewer, more like sculpture than painting. But perhaps the most complete of Masaccio's achievements is the *Tribute Money* fresco cycle in the Brancacci Chapel.

As a 'testimony to the standing of the family and a symbol of its solid prosperity', Piero di Piuvichese Brancacci gave money for the building and decoration of a new chapel in the church of Santa Maria del Carmine on the south side of the River Arno. Work began in 1387 and forty years later Felice Brancacci commissioned Masaccio and Masolino, 'Big Tom' and 'Little Tom', to paint frescoes on the subject of the life of St Peter. The *Tribute Money*, the episode when Christ was confronted by a tax collector, must have seemed appropriate to a merchant. Masaccio was twenty-two, Masolino forty, and they divided the work between them.

Fresco is a technique which demands thorough preparation and rapid execution. First a large cartoon, or paper drawing, is made and a satisfactory composition of the main figures arranged on it. Pigments are ground and mixed with water or with egg whites to make what was called egg tempera. The egg bound the colour and made it stick when the wall was plastered and allowed to dry. When water-based paint was used, the wet plaster acted as the fixative. That was how Masaccio and Masolino worked at the Brancacci Chapel. There, the gesso, or plaster, was slathered onto the wall and made even with a float (not too smooth; slightly roughened plaster acted as a key), and the cartoon quickly pegged up to give the painter a rough guide to composition. Then work began quickly. On a fresco the size of the *Tribute Money,* Masaccio would have had approximately seven hours at a time before the plaster dried. Economy of brush strokes was important and a sureness of touch vital. Behind the group around Christ, the figure of St Peter taking a coin from the mouth of a fish is achieved with dazzling simplicity and the whole panel still shows the vigour of working at speed.

Those who looked at the frescoes in the fifteenth century saw all that skill and bravura, but they saw other things that we have now lost or no longer understand. Most early fifteenth-century representations of Jesus look broadly similar because it was believed that a genuine description had survived from antiquity. But what follows was in fact a much later work of the imagination purporting to be a report to the Roman Senate from a fictional governor of Judaea, Lentulus:

A man of average or moderate height, and very distinguished. He has an impressive appearance, so that those who look on him love and fear him. His hair is the colour of a ripe hazelnut. It falls straight almost to the level of his ears; from there down it curls thickly and is rather more luxuriant, and this hangs down to his shoulders. In front his hair is parted into two, with the parting in the centre in the Nazarene manner. His forehead is wide, smooth and serene, and his face is without wrinkles or any marks. It is graced by a slightly reddish tinge, a faint colour. His nose and mouth are faultless. His beard is thick and like a young man's first beard, of the same colour as his hair; it is not particularly long and is parted in the middle. His aspect is simple and mature. His eyes are brilliant, clear, mobile, splendid. He is terrible when he reprehends, quiet and kindly when he admonishes. He is quick in his movements but always keeps his dignity. No-one ever saw him laugh, but he has been seen to weep. He is broad in the chest and upstanding; his hands and arms are fine. In speech he is serious, sparing and modest. He is the most beautiful amongst the children of men.

It is an image, a prescription for divinity that has never fallen out of use. To the left of the scene featuring Christ and the tax collector in the Brancacci Chapel, Masaccio painted perhaps the most compelling image in the whole fresco cycle. It is the moment of the expulsion of Adam and Eve from the Garden of Eden. Once again it is based on an iconography whose origins are obscure. The two nudes, in themselves innovative, are not only a series of cylinders which gauging merchants might have enjoyed looking at, they also depend for their effect on gestures with medieval origins.

One of the most successful of the reformed orders of monks, the Benedictines, insisted on periods of silence for prayer or contemplation. So that communication did not cease entirely, the brothers developed a mime language of simple gestures. Masaccio has used two of the more dramatic for Adam and Eve. With his hands over his eyes, Adam expresses the emotion of shame while with her hand on her breast, Eve is grief-stricken. Her other hand covers her pudendum, 'her shame', as the Bible has it, when she suddenly realises she is naked. Therefore a combination of a Benedictine sign and scripture tells those who looked at the fresco exactly what Eve was feeling at that time. Several of the monastic signs have found their way into modern culture. A hand on the chest can mean at least two things. When accompanied by a smile the gesture expresses thanks and pleasure, and when the eyes are cast upwards, the emotion is interpreted as relief. The monks would have been casting their eyes heavenwards.

Many Florentines expressed great relief in 1434. Without Medici money to lubricate the engines of state, Florence had virtually gone bust during the year of Rinaldo degli Albizzi's rule. With no cash left for bribery, the aristocratic faction was unable to prevent Medici supporters being selected for the Signoria. Despite mustering a large armed band and terrorising the centre of the city, degli Albizzi could see that control was leaking fast. Pope Eugenius IV was in temporary residence in Florence and he appears to have counselled persuasively against bloodshed. The Vacca tolled once more, a *balia* was appointed and it voted overwhelmingly to invite Cosimo de' Medici to return from exile.

Degli Albizzi's attempted coup left the Medici stronger than ever. The invitation to come back in effect recognised that Cosimo was ruler of the republic. But he refused to create or accept high office of any kind. Instead, Cosimo sought to remain in the shadows, and while retaining an iron grip on political power, he did not attempt to change the constitution. The Signoria and the *gonfaloniere* would still be selected in the usual way, but they would constantly be measuring their decisions against Cosimo's approval or disapproval. Appearances were kept up so that 'whenever he wished to achieve something he saw to it, in order to escape envy as much as possible, that the initiative appeared to come from others and not from him'.

On 25 March, on the Feast of the Annunciation, in 1436, Pope Eugenius IV, seven cardinals, thirty-seven bishops, the Signoria and Cosimo de' Medici, a private citizen, processed through the streets of Florence to the cathedral of Santa Maria del Fiore. In order to elevate the gorgeously robed clerics above the crowds, in every sense, Brunelleschi had had a 6-foot-high wooden walkway built from the papal residence at Santa Maria Novella to the Piazza Duomo. Usually coins were scattered into the crowds in the narrow streets to clear a passage for a procession but perhaps Cosimo and his architect felt the occasion demanded a little more dignity.

The dome had not yet been capped by its tall, white lantern or its outer surface faced with tiles, but the interior looked complete. Since Cosimo's return and Brunelleschi's release from prison, the masons on their precarious ponti had been busy. Five months later the dome itself was complete, and when the Bishop of Fiesole consecrated it in August 1436, the great cathedral was at last a reality, 140 years after the foundations had been laid. Florence rejoiced, and Cosimo smiled.

Paolo Toscanelli was also pleased to see the lantern finished, but for different reasons. A mathematician and astronomer, he had taught Brunelleschi the principles of Euclidean geometry, and now that the cathedral was complete, he contemplated a scientific use for the 300-foot-high dome. Much later, in 1475, Toscanelli had a bronze plate fitted into the base of the lantern. Through a hole in its centre the sun's rays shone down onto the floor of the great church where the mathematician had laid out a calibrated gauge. This allowed him to measure the passage of the sun across the sky very precisely and to work out the exact times and dates of the equinoxes. This turned out to be very important for the developing science of navigation.

Using tables of these precise measurements and better instruments, sailors could check their position on the sea without constant reference to the coastline or any islands they could see. Toscanelli also made more accurate maps and began to evolve a theory that India could be reached by sailing westwards. Like virtually all of his contemporaries and many medieval scholars, he had long accepted that the world was round. Toscanelli was contacted by a Genoese sea captain who was very interested in his ideas. Christopher Columbus and the old mathematician corresponded and at one point a map was sent to Genoa. If Cosimo de' Medici could have imagined that the discovery of America and those immense commercial opportunities had been linked to the building of the most impressive cathedral in Christendom, he would have smiled even more broadly.

Toscanelli was a pioneer in another sense. The degree of accuracy his bronze plate allowed added to a developing sense that notions of time had to be standardised. When Julius Caesar reformed the calendar in 45 BC, his mathematicians overestimated the length of the year by eleven minutes. The cumulative effect was an extra day every 128 years. By 1454 the spring equinox had moved back from Caesar's date of 28 March to 12 March and the crucial date for the Church's main festival, at Easter, from which all other religious holidays were reckoned, had drifted far from its original placing at the first Sunday after the spring full moon, i.e., on or after 21 March.

All of this confusion was compounded by the fact that the different northern Italian cities operated different calendars. It was possible to set out from Venice on 1 March 1454, the first day of the Venetian year, and on arrival in Florence find that it was 1453. If, after a few days in the city, a traveller made the short journey down the Arno to Pisa, he could find himself in 1455. And if he continued west into Provence, he would have arrived, magically, back in 1453. How merchants managed to do business efficiently is a mystery. It was not until the late sixteenth century that the Church insisted on reform with the new Gregorian calendar, and it was not adopted by some Protestant countries (suspecting a popish plot) until the mid eighteenth century.

By 1444 (according to Florentine time) the Palazzo Medici was also complete. Cosimo had had a design from Brunelleschi but he considered it too showy, too ornate for the residence of a private citizen. Instead the plans submitted by Michelozzo were preferred and behind the austere façade near the Piazza Duomo the old man ran the city.

Outward appearances were not quite everything. In the courtyard enclosed by Michelozzo's plain architecture stood one of the most sexually suggestive works of art ever made. David, the slayer of Goliath, was seen as a biblical figure who symbolised Florence, like a patron saint. He was graceful, beautiful, intelligent, brave and able to kill Philistine giants. The first free-standing bronze nude to be cast since antiquity, it is a deliberately erotic, even fanciful representation of an Old Testament king in his youth, and it must have scandalised many. Wearing a large but elegant helmet and nothing else but knee-length boots, this very feminine boy stands over the severed head of Goliath. But not in triumph exactly. All of his weight is on one leg (in an attitude known as 'classical contrapposto') and while one hand holds a sword, the other is placed nonchalantly on his hip. Under long and luxuriant hair, David's expression is a sort of sexy half-smile and his behind looks as though it might have belonged to a female model. The dark lustre of the bronze somehow adds to the overpowering sensuality.

The *David* was made by Donato di Niccolò de Betto Bardi, known as Donatello, the first really great Renaissance sculptor, a friend of Brunelleschi's and an artist valued and supported by Cosimo de' Medici. He came from very humble beginnings, and his father was a wool carder, involved in the rebellion of the Ciompi. The librarian, Vespasiano da Bisticci, went into detail about Donatello's relationship with Cosimo:

> When he [Cosimo] had dealings with painters or sculptors he knew a good deal about it and possessed in his home something from the hand of the outstanding masters. He was a great expert on sculpture and much favoured the sculptors and all the worthy artists. He was a great friend to Donatello and to all the painters and sculptors, and since in his time the art of sculpture suffered some lack of employment, Cosimo, to prevent this happening to Donatello, commissioned him to make certain pulpits of bronze for San Lorenzo and made him make certain doors which are in the Sacristy, and gave orders to his bank to allow him a certain sum of money every week, enough for him and his four apprentices, and in this way he kept him. Since Donatello did not dress as Cosimo would have liked him to, Cosimo gave him a red cloak with a hood, and a gown under the cloak, and dressed him all afresh. One morning of a feast day he sent it all to him to make him wear it. He did, once or twice, and then put it aside and did not want to wear it any more, for it seemed too dandified to him. Cosimo used the same liberality to any body who possessed some 'virtù',

because he loved such people. To turn to architecture: he was most experienced in it, as can be seen from many buildings he had built, because nothing was built or made without his opinion and judgement being asked; and several who had to build something went to him for his opinion.

Cosimo appeared to be more concerned with Donatello's clothes than with the fact that he seems to have been an openly gay man and that his *David* could be seen as a very beautiful hymn to homosexuality. The point was that it was beautiful, and nothing else mattered much, not even the laws of the Church and the commune.

Although it was illegal and in theory carried dire punishments, homosexuality was tolerated in Florence. In fact the city was literally a byword; in German slang '*ein Florenzer*' meant a gay man. San Bernardino of Siena preached that the terrible fate of Sodom and Gomorrah awaited Florence, although as a Sienese he had his own agenda. Nevertheless the Signoria took such infamy seriously and introduced a municipal vice squad to suppress gay activity and, slightly surprisingly, to promote female prostitution by licensing brothels around the old marketplace.

This was seen as a solution to a structural social problem. Tuscan men tended to marry later, in their late twenties, thirties and beyond. In the long period before they could enjoy the delights of marital sex and when they were at their most potent, there was precious little of the pre-marital sort available. Women married young, in their late teens, and if they were not virgins when they did, there could be tremendous difficulties. The upshot was that there was a shortage of available women, a shortage of extra-marital sex and, it was thought, a consequent growth in homosexuality. More whores, properly licensed and regulated, would fill that awkward gap and set the young men of Florence on a more wholesome path.

It was not only Donatello's genuine homosexuality that set him apart. He was also one of the first artists to be recorded as behaving temperamentally, like a mad genius, like the modern cliché of a creative person. Famous for flying into ungovernable rages (he once pursued an apprentice who left him, threatening murder), he was also scruffy, cared nothing for money and was single-minded in pursuit of his art. Cosimo could see all that, and as a practical man made sensible provision for this volatile but inspired artist.

These attitudes and exchanges signalled a profound change. At the outset of the fifteenth century patrons like Cosomo were very meticulous in their contracts with artists about the cost and quantity of materials and rather less concerned with what might be seen now as issues around skill and even talent. In 1408 the painter, Gherardo Starnina, was commissioned to execute a fresco cycle on the subject of the life of the Virgin Mary for the church of San Stefano at Empoli, 25 miles west of Florence. The blue pigment known as ultramarine, made from crushed lapis lazuli, was the most expensive and often used for the robes of the Virgin. Starnina was contracted specifically to paint those with ultramarine to the value of two florins an ounce, and for the rest of the painting, one florin an ounce would do.

When Cosimo paid Donatello what was in effect a salary, that was a sign of changing views. The sculptor took more of the decisions about a piece himself and the cost of his skill and talent was becoming as important as the cost of the bronze or the marble he worked in. In 1445 Piero della Francesca agreed to paint another Virgin Mary for the Prior of Santa Maria della Misericordia in San Sepolcro. At the foot of the detailed contract a striking stipulation appeared: 'no painter might put his hand to the brush other than Piero himself'. By 1499 the insistence on a particular artist was absolutely clear and unambiguous. For frescoes at Orvieto Cathedral, Luca Signorelli, and none of his assistants, or any other painter, would do the work:

> The said master Luca is bound and promises to paint all the figures to be done on the said vault, and especially the faces and all the parts of the figures from the middle of each figure upwards, and that no painting should be done on it without Luca himself being present . . . And it is agreed that all the mixing of colours should be done by the said master Luca himself.

Sometimes a patron rejected a piece of work. The painter, Fra Filippo Lippi, had taken holy orders, but in name only, and he regularly failed to complete commissions. At one point he was given a room in the Palazzo Medici and locked in until he finished the work. (He escaped out of the window using a rope of bedsheets.) When Piero de' Medici, Cosimo's son, refused to pay Lippi for a panel, he received a wonderfully abject letter:

I am one of the poorest monks there is in Florence, that is me, and God has left me with six nieces [more likely daughters] on my hands, all sick and useless . . . If you could only send me from your household a little grain and wine which you might sell to me, it would be a great joy and you might debit my account for it. I get tears in my eyes when I think that if I die I can leave it to these poor kids . . .

As Cosimo grew old, he began to reflect more and more on mortality, and on his prospects of paradise. His wealth and usurious means of acquisition weighed heavily on his conscience. 'Only have patience with me, my Lord, and I shall return it all to you', he was heard to say, and there is a palpable sense of buying a place in heaven or at least a shorter stay in purgatory. Cosimo's grandson, Lorenzo de' Medici, added it all up:

I find we have spent a large sum of money from 1434 up to 1471, as appears from an account book covering that period. It shows an incredible sum, for it amounts to 663,755 florins spent on buildings, charities and taxes, not counting other expenses, nor would I complain about this, for though many a man would like to have even part of the sum in his purse I think it gave great lustre to the state and this money seems to be well spent and I am very satisfied.

Vespasiano da Bisticci reckoned that almost 200,000 florins had gone on buildings, sculpture and art. Part of this vast sum was also spent on the Medici library and Cosimo's fascination with manuscripts from antiquity. Agents scoured Europe and regularly sent items of interest to Florence. In 1460, towards the end of Cosimo's life, a Greek monk from Macedonia arrived at the Palazzo Medici with a manuscript thought to be of incalculable value, the most profound, most significant ever to come to light.

It was not a lost work of Plato, or Aristotle, or Cicero, or Livy but the *Corpus Hermeticum*, the writings of Hermes Trismegistus, a figure who fascinated the Renaissance, and who has slipped once more into obscurity.

Just as Christian scholars believed that the older a gospel or a letter was, the closer it would be to the purity of the period of Christ himself, classicists valued manuscripts for their great age. These impulses combined in the search for the *priscus theologus*, the 'first theologian', the person who pre-figured Plato, Aristotle and the teachings of the New Testament. All of these streams of philosophy were thought to be connected. Classical scholars in the fifteenth century could justify or excuse their great interest in Plato, for example, a pagan thinker, by seeing him as a prototype for certain Christian beliefs. Hermes Trismegistus, an Egyptian sage, was believed to have been the earliest of all, the *priscus theologus*, but his writings had been long lost in the mists of the past, until a far-travelled Greek monk turned up in Florence in 1460.

When Marsilio Ficino, a member of Cosimo's circle, saw the manuscripts, he could see what they might be. Unusually, he could read Greek and it quickly became clear that here at last was the *priscus theologus*, the first stirrings of what would become Platonism and then develop into Christianity. Ficino explains:

> He is called the first author of theology: he was succeeded by Orpheus, who came second amongst ancient theologians: Alglaophemus, who had been initiated into the sacred teachings of Orpheus, was succeeded in theology by Pythagoras, whose disciple was Philolaus, the teacher of our Divine Plato. Hence there is one ancient theology ... taking its origin in Hermes and culminating in the Divine Plato.

By 1463 Cosimo de' Medici realised he was dying, and in order to read the works of the *priscus theologus*, he ordered Ficino to put aside his work and begin translating the Hermetic texts as quickly as possible. There is a real sense of the old man hoping for some sort of epiphany, the gaining of a pure knowledge that might somehow ease his passage into the hereafter.

It is to be hoped that Cosimo met his death more peacefully after he had read Ficino's translation, not least because the whole exercise had been entirely futile. Hermes Trismegistus almost certainly never existed and the texts which found their way to Florence were not earlier than Plato or Christ, but significantly later. Compiled between AD 100 and AD 300, probably in Alexandria, they contained elements of Platonic and Christian thinking because their authors were well aware of both pre-existing traditions. Nevertheless, Ficino's translation was one of the earliest printed books in Italy, published in 1471, and it circulated widely before the radical error of dating was discovered.

On Cosimo's death in 1464, his son, Piero, became head of the family, the Medici bank and the unchallenged ruler of Florence. No vote or even any acclamation was involved; an elder son had followed his father in princely fashion on the principle of primogeniture. Trouble would soon come, but not at the traditionally volatile moment when power passed from one autocrat to a successor. Piero's greatest problem was not so much politics as illness. Throughout his adult life he suffered from gout. It was an inherited ailment; Cosimo had had it and Giovanni di Bicci may also have been a victim. Gout can be extremely painful and there is no doubt that Piero endured periods when he was virtually paralysed, but by sheer strength of character he clung to power.

Caused by the retention of uric acid and the consequent build-up of crystalline deposits around the joints (particularly the smaller joints, the toes and fingers), gout can restrict movement severely. Sufferers are simply unable to bear any pressure on their limbs when the inflammation is at its most acute. The Medici acquired soubriquets. Cosimo was Il Vecchio, 'The Old Man', and Piero, unfortunately, was Il Gottoso, 'The Gouty'. Often he had to be carried around in a litter and a report from an ambassador visiting the Palazzo Medici before Cosimo's death confirmed that an audience was held with three of the Medici lying side by side on a large bed. Piero, his brother, Giovanni, and Cosimo were all suffering bad attacks at the same time.

When confined to his palazzo, Piero found consolation in his family's possessions and collections. Like a bored aristocrat, he would take pleasure in ownership, and a fascinating glimpse of these episodes of enforced idleness has survived. The architect, Filarete, spoke to the Medici ambassador to Milan and wrote down what he said:

He tells me that Piero takes great pleasure in whiling away his time by having himself carried to his studio ... there he would look at his books as if they were a pile of gold ... let us not talk about his readings. One day he may simply want for his pleasure to let his eyes pass along these volumes to while away the time and give recreation to the eye. The next day, then, according to what I am told, he takes out some of the effigies and images of all the Emperors and Worthies of the past, some made of gold, some of silver, some of bronze, of precious stones or of marble and other materials, which are wonderful to behold. Their worth is such that they give the greatest enjoyment and pleasure to the eye ... The next day he would look at his jewels and precious stones of which he has a marvellous quantity of great value, some engraved in various ways, some not. He takes great pleasure and delight in looking at those and in discussing their various powers and excellences. The next day, maybe, he inspects his vases of gold and silver and other precious metals and praises their noble worth and the skill of the masters who wrought them. All in all when it is a matter of acquiring worthy or strange objects he does not look at the price ... I am told that he has such a wealth and variety of things that if he wanted to look at each of them in turn it would take him a whole month and he could then begin afresh and they would again give him pleasure.

Turning these objects over in his hands, holding them up to the light or simply running his fingers over them, Piero sounds like a distracted, disengaged figure, and there is a sense of emptiness amongst all those fabulous riches. They were not only tokens of power but actually useful in its exercise. The Medici often sent lavish gifts to kings and aristocrats. A much clearer sense of Piero's personal taste in art comes through in his correspondence. The painter Matteo de' Pasti shows a canny sense of the sort of thing his client might like, well understanding his love of pomp and splendour:

I want to tell you that since I arrived in Venice I have learnt something which would be particularly suitable for the work you commissioned me to do, a technique of using powdered gold like any other colour; and I have already begun to paint the triumphs in this way so that they will look different from anything you have seen before. The highlights in the foliage are all in gold, and I have embroidered the costume of the little lady in a thousand ways. Now please send me the instruction for the other triumph so that I can go ahead ... I have got the instructions for the Triumph of Fame but I do not know if you want the sitting woman in a simple dress

or in a cloak as I would like her to be. The rest I know: there are to
be four elephants pulling her chariot; but please tell me if you want
only young men and ladies in her train or also famous old men.

These were paintings of a series of poems by Petrarch called *The
Triumphs*, and it is clear that Piero and his painter had discussed the
work in detail. Matteo de' Pasti was not an artist of the stature of
Donatello and Piero treated him differently.

Donatello was becoming a famous old man. When de' Pasti wrote
to Piero in 1441, the great sculptor was fifty-five and renowned
throughout Italy. Florentine artists had been commissioned by other
cities and there is a sense of new ideas and new techniques in art
flowing from the city. Siena had not abandoned dreams of returning
glory and for the baptistry of their unfinished cathedral the merchants
approached the great Donatello to make a bronze relief for the font.
Appropriately, it was to be a scene from the life of St John the Baptist,
but perhaps less appropriately, it depicted the gruesome moment
when the head of St John was brought to King Herod on a platter.
Even more alarming was the manner in which Donatello dealt with
the drama of the scene. Gone are the hieratic arrangements of solemn
figures, and instead the relief looks like a freeze frame, a moment
captured by the artist's skill and imagination.

What Donatello did was not to ask the patrons where they thought
figures might be disposed, as Matteo did with Piero. The great sculptor
attempted to visualise what might have actually happened when the
executioner brought the head of the Baptist to Herod. Figures recoil
in shock, almost exclaiming, and the mother of Salome, the instigator
of the terrible deed, tries to explain. Herod throws up his hands in
horror, children are terrified and run away, another covers his eyes.
The use of perspective, the creation of the illusion that the scene is
taking place in a Roman-style royal palace simply adds to the drama.
In Siena, where older styles of painting and sculpture hung on for
much longer, contemporaries must have been astonished. And there
is a suspicion that Donatello made the panel he wanted to make, and
that the Sienese accepted it as the latest thing despite the fact that
babies were to be baptised next to the aftermath of a decapitation.

Apart from the republics of Siena and Lucca, Medicean Florence
dominated Tuscany in the fifteenth century. Much of Cosimo and
Piero's power depended on their wealth and an astute deployment

of gifts, bribes and payment for mercenary soldiers. But at Cosimo's death in 1464 the Medici bank was found to be over-extended, having lent to Edward IV of England and other unreliable clients. Piero called in some debts, steadied the ship and immediately got lucky.

Alum was a vital chemical agent in the cloth industry. A mineral salt, it was used in great volumes to fix dyes so that colours did not run when cloth became wet. There was only one source, the mines on the Genoese island of Chios off the coast of what is now Turkey. By the fourteenth century it was no longer under Italian control, and the advancing Ottomans had taken over the alum trade and were making a fortune from the monopoly, more than 300,000 florins a year. Ironically, these revenues coming from Italy and western Europe were financing the Turkish wars of conquest in the Balkans.

In the early 1460s alum was discovered in the Monti della Tolfa near Civitavecchia in the Papal States. As bankers to the popes, the Medici were able to distribute and sell about half of the output through their bank's branches while the Vatican's own agents sold the rest. It should have been an immediate bonanza, especially when the pope turned the Tolfa supply into a new monopoly by threatening to excommunicate anyone who bought Turkish alum. But Piero and his colleagues found that the papacy was an unsophisticated business partner. Often they flooded the market and drove prices down. But by 1466 the Medici had gained control of the entire selling operation and everyone began to make a great deal of money; 70,000 florins a year came back to Piero.

The Florentine economy was booming and merchants were becoming very wealthy. Giovanni Rucellai commissioned the architect, Leon Battista Alberti, to design and build a new palazzo. With arches, pilasters and architraves in the Roman style and a perfectly proportioned façade, it is a masterpiece of Renaissance architecture. Giovanni was delighted, almost child-like:

> I have also spent a great deal of money on my house and on the façade of the church of Santa Maria Novella and on the tomb I had made in the church of San Pancrazio, and also on the gold brocade vestments for the said church, which cost me more than a thousand ducats, and on the loggia opposite my house and on the house and garden of my place at Quaracci and at Poggio a Caiano.

All the above-mentioned things have given and give me the greatest satisfaction and pleasure, because in part they serve the honour of God as well as the honour of the city and the commemoration of myself.

It is generally said, and I agree with it, that earning and spending are among the greatest pleasures that men enjoy in this life and it is difficult to say which gives greater pleasure. I myself, who have done nothing for the last fifty years but earn and spend, as I describe above, have had the greatest pleasure and satisfaction from both, and I really think that it is even more pleasurable to spend than to earn.

So there. That wonderfully open and unaffected entry comes from Rucellai's *zibaldone*, a commonplace book kept by the merchant. A mixture of a diary, quotations and comments, it is a rich and very different source for Renaissance Florence. In 1470 Giovanni celebrated the glories of his native city, and even allowing for a substantial vein of smugness, it is not an inaccurate portrait:

For the reasons and causes which are written below, it is my opinion that our age has more to commend it than any other age since Florence was built. Beginning with the masters of warfare, it is said that nowadays this is restored to the Italians, whereas before it was with the Northerners. These Italians outstrip the Northerners in natural talent, astuteness, wickedness and sagacity in conquering territory and in land battles. In our age there have been more outstanding men of learning, in Greek, Latin and Hebrew; with its polished and ornate Latin, our literature is the best since the age of Cicero. These men have brought back to light the ancient grace of a lost and forgotten style. More outstanding than in any other age are the citizens in our administration, and the Signoria is larger, because in the fifteenth century Florence has conquered Pisa, Cortona, Borgo san Sepolcro, Poppi and some lands in Castentino. The city and the contado are more beautiful with churches, hospitals, buildings and palaces decorated both inside and out with stonework 'alla Romanesca', that is, in the manner in which the ancient Romans made it. In this age we have been well endowed with architects and with sculptors of both intaglio and marquetry in the way it is done throughout all Italy. Not since pagan times have there been equally good masters in woodwork, intarsia and the like, and with such skill in perspective that it could not be done better with a brush. We also have outstanding painters and draughtsmen with such great skill, accuracy and order that Giotto and Cimabue would not have been worthy pupils. And there are many other very notable craftsmen who could be named. In our age men and women wear only rich clothes which are beautifully made and finished. The women are more ornately dressed with brooches, embroidered clothes, jewels, pearls and hats after the French style – one of these could cost 200 florins. In this age there is a great interest in sailing across the sea in large merchant galleys which are very useful to our city, bringing honour and good reputation throughout the world.

8

Murder in the Cathedral

On the morning of Sunday, 26 April 1478 a young man rode down the Via Larga. Raffaele Riario was seventeen, a student at the University of Pisa, and as his horse clattered over the paving stones, under the arched gateway into the Palazzo Medici, he did not want to keep his host waiting. Having dismounted in the courtyard, he went quickly upstairs to change into his cardinal's robes. Raffaele's great-uncle was Sixtus IV, Francesco della Rovere, one of the most corrupt of the worldly popes of the fifteenth century. No fewer than seven of his 'nephews' and nephews had been elevated to the College of Cardinals. When the young man reappeared in his scarlet silk vestments and hat, Lorenzo de' Medici was waiting for him at the foot of the stairs. The bells of Santa Maria del Fiore were ringing out over the morning city, summoning the people of Florence to mass.

Francesco Salviati, Archbishop of Pisa, joined Lorenzo and his young friend. As they made their way to the Piazza Duomo, the crowds may have noted a contrast. Walking beside the gorgeously robed clerics, Salviati in his episcopal purple and Riario in scarlet, the most powerful and wealthy man in Tuscany wore a simple dark gown, and his friends were similarly attired. The archbishop's company on the way to church was more than serendipitous. Despite the fact that the de' Medici had agreed with the papacy that all ecclesiastical appointments in their part of Tuscany needed the approval of the government of the republic of Florence, Sixtus had given Salviati the see of Pisa without consultation. Lorenzo had retaliated by refusing to allow him entry into the republic and so the new archbishop did not see his cathedral for three years, being forced to seethe in idleness – and penury – in Rome. But an accommodation was eventually reached, the archbishop was finally consecrated, and it was good for the two men to be seen together in public.

When the party reached the main doors of the Duomo, a strange thing happened. Salviati suddenly announced that he would not after all hear mass that day. Lorenzo was surprised. The archbishop explained that his mother was gravely ill and he needed to go and attend to her. Cardinal Riario, Lorenzo and four of his friends continued on into the cool of the great church, and they walked up to the high altar. In common with all churches at that time there were no pews or chairs but an enormous open space which was slowly beginning to fill with people. As it still is, church-going in fifteenth-century Italy was not sombre, but a social occasion. People greeted each other, chattered loudly and gossiped quietly. Lorenzo led young Riario through the wooden rood screen designed by Ghiberti and left him at the altar rail while he strolled around, talking to groups of people. Perhaps the cardinal knelt to pray.

Francesco de' Pazzi and Bernardo Bandini Baroncelli were becoming agitated. Neither of them could see Lorenzo's brother, Giuliano, anywhere in the cathedral. They hurried out and made their way to the nearby Palazzo Medici. Giuliano had not yet recovered from a nagging pain in his leg, probably sciatica, and he had decided not to attend mass. But Francesco and Bernardo would help. He could lean on them and easily be there before the service began. It was not far. Having been persuaded and perhaps charmed, Giuliano limped down the Via Larga. With a supportive arm around his shoulder, de' Pazzi realised that the invalid was not wearing a mail shirt or any sort of protection under his gown, and he had neglected to buckle on a sword or dagger.

The three men entered Santa Maria by the main doors and moved across the nave to the northern wall, near the door to the Via de' Servi. Sir John Hawkwood glowered down from Uccello's fresco on the wall above where they stood and talked. The cathedral was becoming more crowded. At the high altar under Brunelleschi's dome Lorenzo had rejoined Cardinal Riario and his friends, Filippo Strozzi, Antonio Ridolfi, Lorenzo Cavalcanti and Francesco Nori. Standing directly behind were two priests, their hands folded inside their robes. The mass began.

Congregations in vast cathedrals in the fifteenth century were rarely hushed in reverence. As the priests processed in and the rituals began, people continued to talk, look around and greet their neighbours. But before the Host was raised from the high altar, the sacristy bell rang for silence. And then all hell broke loose.

As Giuliano de' Medici bowed his head, his companions pulled out their daggers and began a frenzied attack. Baroncelli struck so hard that his blow split open Giuliano's skull in a shower of blood, and de' Pazzi stabbed so viciously at the falling body that he accidentally pierced his own thigh. The congregation shrank back in shock.

The two priests behind Lorenzo hesitated fatally, one of them clamping his hand on his victim's shoulder. This allowed a crucial moment for Lorenzo to turn around and, by good fortune, take only a cut in his neck and not the severance of his carotid artery. Ripping off his cloak and whirling it around his forearm to act as a shield, Lorenzo drew his sword. Maffei and Stefano, the priests, were pushed back, giving him time to leap over the altar rail and run towards the sacristy.

From the north wall of the cathedral Baroncelli saw what was happening and he raced down the nave, his sword drawn, to cut Lorenzo off before he could reach the sacristy doors. Francesco Nori attempted to block his path and Baroncelli ran him through with one thrust, and then slashed at Lorenzo Cavalcanti, cutting him badly in the forearm. But Lorenzo de' Medici and his remaining friends made it and heaved the heavy bronze doors shut, barricading themselves in.

The cathedral was in uproar. People panicked and fled for the doors, some shouting that the dome was falling. Others gawped at the pool of blood around Giuliano's lifeless and mutilated body. And amidst the chaos the seventeen-year-old Raffaele Riario stood stock still at the high altar, unable to comprehend what had happened.

In the safety of the sacristy Antonio Ridolfo took hold of Lorenzo and began to suck at his wound in his neck, spitting out the bloody mess, shouting that the priest's dagger might have been poisoned. Another friend, Sigismondo della Stufa, climbed up to the beautiful choir made by Luca della Robbia. He could see that the assassin-priests and the wounded Francesco de' Pazzi and Bernardo Baroncelli had escaped into the crowds. Guglielmo de' Pazzi was shouting to anyone who would listen that he had had nothing to do with the attack. And young Riario still stood, lost, at the high altar.

Meanwhile Archbishop Salviati had gone nowhere near his mother. Instead, he had kept a rendezvous with a band of Perugian mercenaries and they marched quickly through the streets to the Palazzo Vecchio. Once the rulers of Florence had been murdered in the cathedral, the Signoria appointed by them had also to be speedily removed. At the arched gatehouse, Salviati demanded to see the *gonfaloniere*, Cesare Petrucci. He was at dinner but allowed the archbishop to be taken to a reception room. Wisely, the captain of the guard directed the Perugians into a separate chamber, which was immediately locked and could not be opened from the inside, the handles having been removed. In the corridor a few other attendants waited with Salviati's lieutenant, Jacopo di Poggio Bracciolini.

When Petrucci finally met the archbishop, he realised immediately that something was amiss. As he stood before the *gonfaloniere* to deliver what purported to be a message from Pope Sixtus IV, the man was shaking, stammering and mumbling, clearly terrified. When Petrucci summoned his guards, Salviati rushed out screaming that the moment had come. Bracciolini attacked the *gonfaloniere* but found himself taken by the hair and thrown to the ground. Picking up a roasting spit from a fireplace, Petrucci whirled it around his head, shouting for his fellow members of the Signoria. As they heard the Perugians using their weapons to hack their way out of the locked chamber, the *gonfaloniere* and his colleagues fought their way to the bell-tower stairs and chained the door behind them. They began to toll the Vacca, the great mooing bell, to summon Florentines to the Piazza della Signoria.

The city was erupting. Armed Pazzi supporters rode through the streets shouting '*Libertà! Popolo e Libertà! Abasso i Medici!*' But it was quickly becoming clear that the coup was faltering. Petrucci and his *signoria* were raining stones down from the bell-tower on Pazzi soldiers, and a band of armed Medici supporters joined with the guards at the Palazzo Vecchio and slaughtered Salviati's hapless Perugians. With their heads impaled on swords and lances, dripping with blood, the guards rushed in triumph into the Piazza della Signoria. The crowd cheered, shouting '*Palle! Palle! Palle!*', the name of the Medici coat of arms.

When news came to Petrucci that Giuliano had been assassinated but Lorenzo was still alive, he took decisive and brutal action. A rope was secured around a window transom on the second floor of the Palazzo Vecchio and the other end knotted around Jacopo di Poggio Bracciolini's neck. With his hands tied behind his back, the struggling prisoner was lifted up to the window sill and thrown out. The crowd howled with joy as he squirmed and spun, choking to death. Francesco de' Pazzi had been found, and he was next. Stripped naked so that the mob could watch him defecate and with his thigh still streaming blood, he was bundled out, banging off the rough stone walls. In his archbishop's purple robes, trembling and begging for immunity or mercy, Salviati had his hands tied with a leather belt, the first thing Petrucci's men could find, and he too was tumbled out of the window. As his eyes bulged in their sockets and his face turned blue, Salviati tried to bite de' Pazzi's naked body in a crazed attempt to take the fatal pressure off his neck. The crowd below screamed with glee.

The Medici mob ran riot. Lorenzo appeared on a balcony at his palazzo, his neck bandaged, to show himself and to appeal for calm. His supporters cheered and then resumed the rampage. When the two assassin-priests were discovered hiding in the Badia, the abbey near the Piazza della Signoria, they were dragged out, had their robes stripped off and were castrated before being strung up. The *condottiere* hired to give military backing to the coup, Gian Battista da Montesecco, was tortured at length for information but given a soldier's death when he was decapitated at the Bargello by a swordsman. After more conspirators and some who had nothing to do with it were dispatched, and Lorenzo had again appealed for calm, the bloodbath gradually subsided.

News of what became known as the Pazzi Conspiracy spread through Italy like wildfire. When Pope Sixtus IV heard of its failure and the execution of Salviati in his archbishop's robes, he was outraged. Not caring that his actions betrayed him, the pope immediately excommunicated the whole Florentine republic, forbidding mass, the sacraments of baptism, marriage and burial. Medici supporters were undismayed, for it quickly became clear that Sixtus had been deeply involved in the plot, and that it had been a long time brewing.

Girolamo Riario, another 'nephew' widely believed to be the pope's eldest son, had wanted his holy father to buy the town of Imola for him. It lay between Bologna and Forlì and seemed well placed to become the centre of a lordship in the Romagna, part of the Papal States. As bankers to the Vatican, the Medici were asked in the summer of 1476 for a loan of 40,000 ducats to purchase the town from the Duke of Milan. Lorenzo stalled. Imola was also attractive to Florence, strategically important, and he did not want to see it in potentially hostile hands. Sixtus did not hesitate. The wealthy

Pazzi family would advance the cash and were also very happy to replace the Medici as the pope's bankers. Sides were being taken, the elements of a conspiracy beginning to assemble.

Archbishop Salviati had never forgotten the slights he had suffered at the hands of Lorenzo de' Medici, and the Pazzi family longed to see him removed from power. With the murder of Galeazzo Maria Sforza, the Duke of Milan, in 1470, an opportunity presented itself. Sforza was the son of a former *condottiere*, his name means 'force', and he was a powerful ally of the de' Medici. After his death Milan was in turmoil and Lorenzo appeared isolated.

In the early weeks of 1477 three men met secretly in Rome. Francesco Salviati, Francesco de' Pazzi and Girolamo Riario, the Lord of Imola, all had their reasons for wishing to move against Florence. But there were serious objections. Jacopo de' Pazzi, the head of the family, thought the chances of success minimal and would at first have nothing to do with Francesco and his dangerous talk. When Gian Battista da Montesecco was first approached, he too was sceptical: 'My lords,' he warned, 'beware of what you do. Florence is a big affair.'

Behind all of this chatter loomed the mighty shadow of Sixtus IV. If he could only be won over then all things became possible. When Salviati and Riario arranged an audience in Rome, Montesecco went to hear what the Holy Father had to say. The conversation was later recorded, possibly after torture. After confirming that yes, he did want to see the Medici control of Florence removed, the pope was pressed by Montesecco: 'But this matter, Holy Father, may turn out ill without the death of Giuliano and Lorenzo, and perhaps of others.'

'I do not wish the death of anyone on any account since it does not accord with our office to consent to such a thing. Though Lorenzo is a villain, and behaves ill towards us, yet we do not on any account desire his death, but only a change in the government.'

Girolamo interjected: 'All that we can do shall be done to see that Lorenzo does not die. But should he die, will your Holiness pardon him who did it?'

Sixtus IV replied like an impatient father: 'You are an oaf. I tell you I do not want anyone killed, just a change in the government. And I repeat to you, Gian Battista, that I strongly desire this change and that Lorenzo, who is a villain and a rogue, does not esteem us.'

Once he is out of Florence we could do whatever we like with the republic and that would be very pleasing to us.'

'Your Holiness speaks true. Be content, therefore, that we shall do everything possible to bring this about.'

'Go, and do what you wish, provided there be no killing.'

Salviati needed more reassurance, but asked a coded question: 'Holy Father, are you content that we steer this ship? And that we will steer it well?'

'I am content.'

That was enough. Tacit approval of murder by the Vatican in the fifteenth century was scarcely surprising, but Montesecco in particular needed to know that the risks of this uncertain venture had been substantially reduced by papal support. He was a professional soldier.

Now the conspirators could begin to put their plans into action. Montesecco went to see Jacopo de' Pazzi. When the cautious old man heard of Sixtus IV's backing, he warmed to the proposal, offering suggestions. Lorenzo and Giuliano would have to be murdered simultaneously, as far as was possible, and it would be much easier if they could be separated.

Without being told anything of the plot, young Raffaele Riario was encouraged to write to Lorenzo de' Medici, asking if he might come to see some of the treasures in the collections at the Palazzo Medici. Perhaps a Sunday would be best, after mass at Santa Maria del Fiore?

In the murderous confusion after the assassination of Giuliano, Lorenzo sent men to the cathedral to find Raffaele and bring him back to the safety of the Palazzo Medici. When the mob had at last dispersed, the young cardinal stole out of the city in disguise and rode quickly down the road for Rome, travelling with an escort sent by Lorenzo.

Alessandro di Mariano di Vanni Filipepi was summoned. Much better known as Botticelli, the 'Little Barrel' (perhaps a reference to his substantial physique), he had been invited to come and live at the Palazzo Medici by Lucrezia, the wife of Piero the Gouty. Having been apprenticed to the tumultuous Filippo Lippi, the young man had matured into a truly great painter. In his *Adoration of the Magi*, now in the Uffizi Gallery in Florence, he repaid Medici patronage with a series of vivid portraits of Cosimo, Piero, Lorenzo and Giuliano. On the right of the picture, staring insouciantly out at the viewer, is a portrait of a bulky young man swathed in the folds of a voluminous gown. It is Botticelli, the 'Little Barrel'.

In the aftermath of the Pazzi Conspiracy, Lorenzo wanted more portraits painted. On the wall of the Bargello, Botticelli was to paint life-size portraits of all the conspirators. Each should have a noose around his neck to remind passers-by that they had died as traitors, lawfully executed by the Signoria. Botticelli worked fast, finishing the figures in only seven weeks. No-one was to be allowed to forget the events of 26 April 1478, and who was responsible. And beside Jacopo and Francesco de' Pazzi, Montesecco and the others was His Grace the Archbishop of Pisa, Francesco Salviati, splendid in his purple robes, a constant reminder of the involvement of the Church and of Sixtus IV in the plot.

When the pope excommunicated the entire Florentine republic, the reaction was vigorous. Florence excommunicated the pope, and it did so in a very significant way. After a meeting in the Duomo, a document denouncing Sixtus IV was drawn up, and then it was printed on the first press to be set up in Florence, at the shop of Bernardo Cennini. That meant a much wider circulation than anything copied by hand or repeated from pulpits.

Printing had been pioneered in Germany with the publication of the Bible in Mainz by Johannes Gutenberg in 1454–55. The new technology reached Florence in 1477 but it was not immediately adopted by the literate middle classes. They preferred hand-copied manuscripts, seeing printing as an inky, messy business. There is a hint of this in the writings of Giorgio Vasari, the early sixteenth-century art historian, when he wrote his life of Botticelli. After the painter returned from Rome, where he had worked on the early frescoes in the Sistine Chapel (named after Sixtus IV), 'he completed and printed a commentary on a part of Dante's *Divine Comedy*, illustrating the "Inferno". He wasted a great deal of time on this, neglecting his work and thoroughly disrupting his life.'

Despite this sort of disdain, the Florentine Renaissance had a profound influence both on and through printing. When Poggio Bracciolini rediscovered classical manuscripts for Cosimo de' Medici, he immediately copied them. To save space on precious vellum or even paper, many early scribes used various versions of shorthand, and Poggio needed to decipher these so that others could read the manuscripts. For further clarity, he developed a script based on that originally used at the court of the Emperor Charlemagne, what became known as 'Carolingian minuscule'. When Cosimo de' Medici saw this new style of writing, he was so impressed that he decided to have his whole collection of manuscripts re-copied in the same hand. In this way Poggio's script became a standard, and to achieve both credibility and legibility, the first printers in Florence adopted it when they cast the lead fonts for their presses. This became known as 'Roman type' and was much easier to read than the dark, blocky Gothic script used by Gutenberg. It is still the most common typeface in current use.

Niccolò Niccoli was more impatient than Poggio. So that his scribes could copy manuscripts faster, he encouraged a more cursive hand which sloped to the right and allowed the pen to travel more quickly across the page. This became known as 'italic', as distinct from Roman, and it was first used by the pioneering Venetian printer, Aldus Manutius in 1500.

Vasari's sniffy dismissal of Botticelli's stooping so low as to work on a book was surprising. A great eulogiser of all things Tuscan, the art historian missed the importance of what the painter was doing. Since Dante was the first major author writing in Italian (as opposed to Latin) to be printed, he began the process of establishing Tuscan as a standard. Editions of Petrarch and Boccaccio soon followed, and by the sixteenth century Tuscan was widely accepted as the basis for Italian by most literate people.

As relations between the papacy and Florence deteriorated, the printing presses grew busy. When Sixtus IV declared war and induced King Ferrante of Naples to join him, events moved quickly. The Duke of Calabria invaded the republic and took the town and territory of Montepulciano. When he sent a message from Sixtus to Florence, the reply was both eloquent and elegantly threatening:

You say that Lorenzo is a tyrant and command us to expel him. But most Florentines call him their defender . . . Remember your high office as the Vicar of Christ. Remember that the Keys of St Peter were not given to you to abuse in such a way . . . Florence will resolutely defend her liberties, trusting in Christ who knows the justice of her cause, and does not desert those who believe in Him; trusting in her allies who regard her cause as their own; especially trusting in the most Christian King, Louis of France, who had ever been the patron and protector of the Florentine State.

Both sides knew that the possibility of French intervention was remote, and that Milan could offer little help. The *condottieri* hired by the Signoria were at odds with each other, and were in any case outnumbered by the Neapolitan army. The economy was in decline, plague had broken out in the city and by late 1479 the situation had become desperate. Lorenzo took what at first seemed both a tremendously courageous and foolhardy decision. Here is his letter to the *gonfaloniere*, Tommaso Soderini:

> In the dangerous circumstances in which our city is placed, the time for deliberation is past. Action must be taken . . . I have decided, with your approval, to sail for Naples immediately, believing that as I am the person against whom the activities of our enemies are chiefly directed, I may, perhaps, by delivering myself into their hands, be the means of restoring peace to our fellow-citizens . . . As I have had more honour and responsibility among you than any private citizen had had in our day, I am more bound than any other person to serve our country, even at the risk of my life. With this intention I go now. Perhaps God wills that this war, which began in the blood of my brother and myself, should be ended by my means. My desire is that by my life or my death, my misfortune or my prosperity, I may contribute to the welfare of our city . . . I go full of hope, praying to God to give me grace to perform what every citizen should at all times be ready to perform for his country. I commend myself humbly to your Excellencies of the Signoria, Lorenzo de' Medici.

It was certainly a brave tactic, but perhaps a little less reckless than it looked. The Neapolitan king sent a ship to Pisa to bring Lorenzo south, and when he landed in Naples, Ferrante's son, Federigo, greeted him warmly. There were other connections. The Duchess of Calabria was Ippolita Sforza from the ruling family of Milan, and someone who Lorenzo knew well. And a member of the royal council, Diomede Carafa, was another acquaintance. A collector of classical antiques, he had been the grateful recipient of gifts from Florence on more than one occasion. Far from being alone in the lions' den, de' Medici had come to Naples on a diplomatic mission. But the self-sacrificing tone of his letter would magnify any success enormously.

King Ferrante made Lorenzo sweat. During a ten-week stay, he had spent a vast sum – 60,000 florins – in gifts and bribes, throwing money around in an attempt to oil the wheels of negotiation. It seemed to have little effect. Discussions faltered, stalled and seemed to go nowhere. Finally, Lorenzo announced that enough was enough and began to make arrangements for his return to Florence. Surprisingly, for what had been portrayed as a journey into mortal danger, where he would be a virtual hostage, de' Medici was allowed to leave without hindrance. At that exact moment Ferrante finally made up his mind and the terms of a peace treaty followed Lorenzo out of the city. Reparations were to be paid to the Duke of Calabria, Pazzi prisoners were to be released and Pope Sixtus insisted that Botticelli's painting of Archbishop Salviati be erased from the wall of the Bargello. Despite these onerous conditions, it was a workable settlement in that Florence drew closer to Naples and the pope appeared isolated. Lorenzo duly returned home in triumph.

The cost of the Pazzi War had been high and the republic's finances were not robust. Unlike Giovanni di Bicci or Cosimo, Lorenzo was not interested in banking and refused to become involved in the family business. It seems that he also made little distinction between the finances of Florence and those of the Medici family – probably because he correctly saw that their fortunes were indivisible.

Tax used to be raised in the city by means of the *estimo*, a percentage of annual income, and most citizens worked hard to conceal what they really earned. It also meant that landowners paid much less than merchants, bankers or craftsmen. After the conclusion of a very expensive war with Milan in 1427, it was decided to abandon the *estimo* and introduce a new tax on all forms of wealth, possessions as well as income. Known as the *catasto*, a public register of property which is still maintained in Tuscany, it raised more cash and was supported by Giovanni di Bicci. Part of his enthusiasm stemmed from the Medici habit of using taxation as a political tool. As the most wealthy family, the Medici paid most, but their allies paid much less and their enemies more or less, depending on their conduct.

Like all modern governments, Florence operated on credit, on loans advanced against future tax yields. By the time Lorenzo came to power, an alternative source of both cash and credit was available.

Il Monte delle Doti, 'The Dowry Bank', had become popular and well-funded. On the birth of their daughters many Florentine fathers opened savings accounts so that cash might accumulate and make up an adequate dowry by the time the girls were of marriagable age. By 1470 the interest owed on these deposits was huge – 197,000 florins.

Dowries were a social necessity. Maidens would not get a husband without one, and the tradition was based on the notion that women earned nothing and required to be paid for throughout their married lives. Moreover, dowries were only payable on the consummation of a marriage, which is why these private occasions used to be the subject of open discussion. Sometimes lurid demonstrations of proof of the loss of virginity were required. These arrangements also laid a financial imperative on young women to retain their virginity. If it was discovered in the marriage bed that they had not, then a father could lose an entire dowry and with the annulment of the contract even have a twice deflowered daughter on his hands for the rest of his life.

Other conditions were observed by the Monte delle Doti. If a daughter died or entered a convent before she reached fifteen, half of the sum invested was forfeit. Infant mortality in the fifteenth century was sufficiently high for this to be a regular source of funds for the bank.

Lorenzo de' Medici almost certainly raided the funds of the Dowry Bank to pay for the Pazzi war, and by the beginning of 1480, it was unable to pay out dowries in full. The economic climate was inclement and savings had to be made. Changing values and tastes have obscured the contraction of Medici patronage. Known as 'the Magnificent', a talented poet in his own right and the cultivator of great painters like Botticelli, Leonardo da Vinci, Filippino Lippi, Antonio Pollaiuolo and Domenico Ghirlandaio, Lorenzo in fact spent much less on commissioning works of art than Piero, Cosimo or even the prudent Giovanni di Bicci. An inventory of the family collections made at the end of the fifteenth century is very revealing.

The most expensive outlay was for architecture and sculpture cast in bronze, and Lorenzo did little of either. He ignored the pleas of the abbot of the monastery in Florence known as the Badia. The new church had been commissioned by Cosimo and consecrated in the time of Piero, but it was nevertheless unfinished. A letter barely conceals the abbot's impatience: 'We easily believe and trust that you have long desired the same [that the church be completed] . . . but we have seen that the times and circumstance stood against your promise. But now when the greatest prosperity favours you . . . set to work and complete our building under a beneficent star and with the aid of our benefactor, Jesus Christ.'

The inventory valued the Medici collection of engraved gems at between 400 and 1,000 florins each and various Roman and Greek antiques were thought to be likely to attract much higher prices. A bowl known as the Tazza Farnese was listed as being worth 10,000 florins. At the other end of the scale were paintings. Work by great masters such as Lippi, Botticelli and Pollaiuolo was valued between 50 and 100 florins, depending on its size. Because these paintings are now seen as either priceless or, when they very occasionally come on the market, worth tens of millions of pounds, modern assumptions tend to cloud an appreciation of Lorenzo's patronage. Paintings were cheap, and de' Medici was often close to insolvency.

Where money had to be spent, and lavishly, was on public festivals. Florence had a European reputation for the originality and splendour of its feast days, tournaments and parades. And it was a matter of Medici policy to underwrite these civic occasions and thereby keep the Popolo Minuto, the mass of ordinary citizens, well disposed towards their rulers. The Pazzi conspiracy had failed because of the depth of popular support for the de' Medici and Lorenzo never forgot that.

There were many public holidays, very nearly one each week, and they took a variety of forms. Religious processions were colourful, musical and occasions for merriment as well as reverence. Often food and wine were distributed, and the crowds could watch as biblical scenes, such as the crucifixion on Good Friday, were re-enacted on moving floats or in the major public spaces around the city. On Easter Day the Scoppio del Carro, literally the 'Explosion of the Cart', is still held. A cartload of spectacular fireworks is pulled from the Porta al Prato to the Piazza Duomo where, during midday mass, it is ignited. The trigger is an effigy of a dove sliding down a wire and, remarkably, it represents the Holy Spirit. This highly popular show was originally paid for and organised by the Pazzi family – until 1478. Then the Signoria took it over.

The timeless spring festival of Calendimaggio on May Day was very attractive. Before dawn young men ran around the streets and piazzas decorating them with boughs of blossom and leaving small gifts of nuts and sweets at the doors of women they liked. Formal dances were held in the Piazza Santa Trinità (like the maypole in Britain – and the old English song 'Here we go gathering nuts in May' is explicable by a comparison with Florence. There are no nuts in May. The original meaning was 'knot', not nut, and a reference to bundles of spring blossom which used to decorate the streets of English towns and villages) and a tradition of singing to young ladies. Masked men were allowed to accost women and sing a very old and formal song to them.

Lorenzo de' Medici loved the rituals of Calendimaggio and he wrote new songs which could be sung in the streets to bashful ladies. And men could also wear fancy dress as well as masks. The atmosphere became more courtly, more elaborate.

Much encouraged by his friend and fellow poet, Angelo Poliziano, Lorenzo developed into one of the most accomplished and inventive writers of the age – or indeed any age, according to some critics. Considering how intensely his concentration had to be on affairs of state, often matters of life and death, de' Medici's poetry is an amazing achievement. His best work has a refreshing simplicity, and his most famous poem begins:

> *Quant' e bella giovinezza*
> *Che si fugge tuttavia.*
> *Chi vuol esser lieto, sia*
> *Di doman non c'e certezza.*

> How youth is beautiful
> Yet also so ephemeral.
> Waste not time on sorrow
> For there's no certain tomorrow.

The use of Tuscan Italian to talk of higher emotion, even a certain courtly refinement, continued into another form used to great effect by Lorenzo and Poliziano. They became interested in developing an old tradition known as the *canzoni a ballo*, the dancing songs. In what seems now like an awkward and somewhat twee format sometimes seen at festivals or celebrations, music struck up and as a singer embarked on what was generally a love song of some sort, men and women danced. They were drawn up in ranks and danced in a formal series of little more than a set of steps, hops and skips.

Boccaccio, Dante and Petrarch wrote *canzoni a ballo* and they were performed at the likes of Calendimaggio and Midsummer's Day. Lorenzo and Poliziano advanced matters by giving their songs some structure and treating the dance as a very simple narrative, usually about the stirrings of love, about courtship and adoration, and sometimes about the pain of rejection. Lorenzo again:

> *Io non credevo al tuo falso sembiante,*
> *E ben ti conoscevo in altre cose:*
> *Ma de' begli occhi lo splendor prestante*
> *E le fattezze si belle e vezzose,*
> *Fecion che l'alma mia speranza pose*
> *In tue promesse; e morte n'acquistai.*

> I never did belive in your false face,
> I knew you well in every other thing,
> But your fine eyes shone with so bright a grace,
> Your features were so sweet and cozening,
> That to your promises my hopes would cling;
> My soul believed in them; and for this I die.

While these dramatic episodes may seem slight, the *canzoni a ballo* proved a fertile ground. Both ballet and opera had their origins in late fifteenth-century Tuscany, especially amongst Lorenzo and the circles of intellectuals living in Florence at the time. When Catherine de' Medici, Lorenzo's great-granddaughter, became queen of France in 1533, she took with her an Italian who acquired a French name, Balthazar de Beaujoyeux, as a musician and arranger of dances. He created the first true ballet, *Le Ballet des Polonais*, and by the end of the seventeenth century professional dancers were performing to large audiences.

Opera also emerged from the Medici court and the classical scholars who enjoyed its patronage. Their interest lay in the music of ancient Greece, and they believed that the great dramas of Aeschylus, Sophocles and Euripides were originally sung or chanted. Allied to the development of the *canzoni a ballo* by Lorenzo and Poliziano, the idea of plays conveyed in music and song began to evolve. By the end of the sixteenth century two Florentine singers, Jacopo Peri and Giulio Caccini, were writing recognisable opera.

Lorenzo de' Medici and his brother Giuliano were also keen footballers. *Calcio* is the Italian word for football, but more precisely it means a 'kick'. What Lorenzo and Giuliano played was a version of primitive rugby, a game which allowed handling of the ball as well as kicking. Teams were large, sometimes more than 100 each side, depending on the size of the pitch. If the Piazza Santa Croce or the Piazza della Signoria were used, then whoever wanted to could play. Goals were scored by getting the ball, somehow, to a designated area. Perhaps into the Arno.

Florence was divided into four quarters: Santa Croce, San Giovanni, Santa Maria Novella, and for the district south of the river, Santo Spirito. Now known as the Calcio Storico, these fixtures are played on 24 June and the week following in the Piazza Santa Croce. It is the date of the feast of St John the Baptist, Florence's patron. Teams are restricted to twenty-eight a side, and wearing bright colours, blue, red, green and white, they play each other in a simple league system. The trophy is a calf which is spit-roasted in the winning quarter.

Cruelty was an important ingredient in some of these festivals, or at least practices which seem cruel to modern observers. A riderless horse race was run from the Porta al Prato through the centre of the city and as far as the Porta alla Croce. The animals were encouraged to gallop faster and faster by iron balls bristling with spikes which were hung at their flanks. As each horse moved, the balls drove the spikes into them, and as their instincts dictated, they tried to run away from the pain.

For other festivals the entrances to the Piazza della Signoria were blocked and the square converted into a version of the Colosseum. Wild boars were let loose and chased and killed by riders with spears. Florence's lions (maintained at the expense of the Signoria and seen as living symbols of the city) were sometimes uncaged and goaded into attacking and killing dogs. And regular public executions were often carried out in a carnival atmosphere.

The de' Medici spared no expense when civic spectacle and the interests of the family coincided. When Lorenzo was nineteen a bride was sought, and for the first time a bride from outside the leading Florentine families. Lucrezia, Lorenzo's influential mother, went to

Rome to inspect the sixteen-year-old Clarice Orsini, the daughter of Roman aristocrats and the likely supplier of a useful dowry:

> She is fairly tall and fair-skinned. She is gentle in manner without the sophistication of a Florentine, but she should be easy to train ... Her face is on the round side, but pleasant enough ... I could not judge her breasts, for the Romans keep theirs covered, but they appeared to be well formed ... She appears above average, but cannot be compared to our daughters.

In order to pave the way for the arrival of Clarice Orsini and pacify any objections amongst the leading families, a sumptuous spectacle was organised. Costing more than 10,000 florins, a faux-medieval tournament was to take place in the Piazza Santa Croce. Following fashions set at the courts of France and Burgundy, there was to be jousting, heraldry, pages, knights and all the imagined flummery of the great age of European chivalry. The Queen of the Tournament was Lucrezia Donati, thought to be the most beautiful woman in Florence, and at the conclusion of all that prancing and dressing up, her role was to award the first prize to Lorenzo, which she duly did.

In Pistoia and Arezzo relics of these tournaments still continue. Beginning in the early fourteenth century, held on the feast day of Santa Francesca Romana, the Giostra del Orso takes place in Pistoia. The symbolism is obscure; twelve knights representing the city, its guilds and the villages of the *contado* used to attack a bear dressed in Pistoia's coat of arms. Now they ride in pairs and tilt at dummy bears with their lances. At Arezzo, the origins of the Giostra del Saraceno are much clearer. When eight knights drive their lances at a figure known as Buratto, King of the Indies, they remember an event at least 1,000 years old. Arab pirates managed to penetrate deep inland, as far as Arezzo, perhaps as early as the tenth century, and the city repulsed them.

Lorenzo and Clarice appeared to co-exist amicably enough to produce the necessary children. Piero was born in 1470 and from his earliest years was groomed to succeed. His time would come faster than anyone thought.

By 1492 Lorenzo was becoming increasingly infirm, even though he was only forty-two. Already suffering from the family ailment of gout, he seems to have contracted something else, something very serious. There were suspicions of slow-acting poison. On 21 March 1492, Lorenzo asked to be taken to the Medici villa at Careggi. It was the place where his grandfather, Cosimo, had spent his last days. Two weeks later, on 8 April, Lorenzo died.

9

Botticelli's Tears

At the beginning of Lent, forty days of fasting and prayer offered
in imitation of Christ's time in the desert and the long precursor
to the most holy festival of Easter, carpenters were hard at work
in the Piazza della Signoria building a scaffold. But as beams were
trimmed and hammers clattered and thudded, passers-by could see
that no hanging, burning or decapitation could take place on the
curious pyramid-shaped structure which rose in front of the Palazzo
Vecchio. This was no platform for a public execution, but instead
the framework for a huge bonfire which would become known as the
'Bonfire of the Vanities'.

Processions of children dressed in white tunics, carrying olive
branches and red crosses, had been scouring Florence, searching out
vanities. Singing hymns, escorted by armed guards to encourage piety,
they walked the streets and called for the citizens to give up all that
was sinful and profane, whatever could be contrary to God's Eternal
Law. From the doors of the palazzi and the houses of the merchants
and middle classes, these blessed bands of innocents gathered wigs,
mirrors, bottles of perfume and pots of make-up, jewellery, fans,
expensive clothes, especially low-cut dresses, profane drawings and
books, chessboards and dice games, and luxuries of every kind. When
the children could carry no more, they brought Florence's vanities to
the wooden pyramid in the Piazza della Signoria. Around the base all
the godless frippery and finery were placed. Profane and pagan books
were piled on top, the works of Plato, Aristotle, Cicero and more
recent poems and prose by Boccaccio, Petrarch and Angelo Poliziano.

Last to be heaped on the bonfire were paintings and effigies,
representations of pagan mythology, lascivious portraits of naked
men and women, and the false gods of the Greeks and Romans.
Penitent painters themselves brought their sinful works to the piazza

and watched as men climbed ladders to set them near the top. Lorenzo di Credi and Fra Bartolommeo willingly saw the error of their ways and would be glad to see their profanities burn in the cleansing fire. None wept more sincerely than Sandro Botticelli, the painter of beguiling nakedness in the *Birth of Venus* and of pagan nymphs in the *Primavera*. He had seen the light and become 'so ardent a partisan that he was thereby induced to desert his painting, and, having no income to live on, fell into very great distress. For this reason, persisting in his attachment to that party, and becoming a *piagnone*, he abandoned his work.' The *piagnoni* were the weepers, the mourners, some called them the snivellers, the followers of Fra Girolamo Savonarola.

It was Shrove Tuesday 1497 when the black-clad Dominican friar watched the bonfire catch and the flames leap up to engulf the vanities. The crowd sang the Te Deum as the books burned and the paintings blistered. So many beautiful works by famous masters, so much jewellery and other fine and valuable objects had been set on the pyre that a Venetian merchant had offered 22,000 ducats for the lot. Fortunate not to be cast into the fire by the *piagnoni*, an effigy of Satan at its top was said to have been made in his likeness.

Girolamo Savonarola was forty-five years old in 1497, in his towering and terrifying prime, his powers at their peak, his dominance of Florence at its zenith. Born in Ferrara, the son of a minor official at the d'Este court, he was a solitary, inward child much influenced by his grandfather. In contrast to the so-called enlightenment and sinful sparkle of the intellectual and artistic life over the far side of the Apennines at Florence, the old man stuck to the stolid virtues of the medieval past. And he drummed into Girolamo the terrors of damnation and how the modern world was bound for Hell and eternal torment. Sodomites and pagans – the Florentines would burn in the deepest pits. The boy was inevitably drawn to the Church and in 1475 wrote to his father:

> For God has given you a son and has deemed him worthy to become His militant knight. Do you not think it a great grace to have a son who is a cavalier of Jesus Christ? . . . I was unable any longer to endure the evildoing of the heedless people of Italy . . . I too am made of flesh and blood, and as the instincts of the body

are repugnant to reason I must fight with all my strength to stop
the Devil from jumping on to my shoulders.

The tone suggests that father did not approve, and may have had a
military career in mind for him.

Having been initiated into the Dominican order of friars, Savonarola
began the life of an itinerant preacher. By his own admission, he was
at first entirely ineffective. A small and painfully thin ascetic with a
large, hooked nose, thick lips and a tendency to mumble, Girolamo
appears to have lacked confidence and later said that he did not know
'how to move a hen'. His delivery was poor and his gestures clumsy
and overdone.

Notwithstanding his obvious piety, all of this presented the young
friar with a real difficulty. Preaching was the point and purpose of
the Dominican order, and if he could not master its techniques, then
how could God be served? As the flames of the Bonfire of the Vanities
crackled through the pages of Aristotle, Plato and Cicero, it probably
did not occur to a man of such iron conviction that he owed these
classical authors almost everything he had achieved.

The Dominicans quickly realised that the basis of persuasive
preaching lay in the lost arts of memory. Voice projection, inflection
and gesture were straightforward skills and could be easily taught
and learned but what supported all of the power of the Word of
God was an unfailing ability to remember it. Even though they often
quoted scripture, preachers rarely had a text in front of them, and in
any case the Bible only existed in Latin and Greek.

The mysteries of the mass and the formal rites of the Church
would remain in Latin for many centuries to come, but the preaching
orders spoke in Italian, the language of the people, translating or
paraphrasing scripture when they needed to. A powerful sermon,
colourful language and telling simile could all be composed at leisure,
but if it could be recalled instantly and precisely in front of a large
congregation, then the fine words would have their effect. The
Dominicans knew that perfect recall gave preachers great confidence.

Aristotle, Cicero and an anonymous text composed around 83–82
BC known as the *Ad Herennium* were the most common classical
sources for the art of memory. Advocates in Roman courts of law and
politicians standing in front of an assembly needed excellent recall to
make their cases and they developed sophisticated techniques to hone

their memories. They had no notes or typescripts. When Savonarola attacked pagan authors in his fiery sermons, he used many of the devices they had invented to make his points against them.

Two Tuscan Dominicans wrote handbooks designed to train young preachers and Savonarola would certainly have used them. Fra Giovanni di San Gimignano summarised his method:

> There are four things which help a man to remember well.
> The first is that he should dispose those things which he wishes to remember in a certain order.
> The second is that he should adhere to them with affection.
> The third is that he should reduce them to unusual similitudes.
> The fourth is that he should repeat them with frequent meditation.

Fra Bartolommeo da San Concordio was a Pisan writing in the first half of the fourteenth century and his *Ammaestramenti degli Antichi* developed Giovanni's simple techniques. Using a section of the *Ad Herennium* (at second hand, via the work of St Thomas Aquinas), Bartolomeo emphasised the importance of making a clear list or order of things to be remembered and used physical objects or places as an aid. Later writers built a house of memory in which ideas or stories could be found in different rooms. These were visited in a logical order, as though the front door were opened and each room looked at in turn, all the way up to the attic.

Opposites were also helpful and for the Dominicans this usually meant the contrast between virtues and vices, sins and good works. Graphic images could electrify a congregation: Savonarola ranted against prostitutes as 'lumps of meat with eyes'. But the images also helped a preacher stay on track and recall the next part. Sometimes opposites could be memorably joined. When Savonarola attacked Florentine painters he accused them of making the very image of purity, the Virgin Mary, look like a harlot.

In 1485 God at last spoke. Savonarola was preaching in San Gimignano and he had a vision: 'to reveal the Word of God as it spoke through him, to warn the world of the horrors that lay in store for the wicked.' Gathering up all the techniques he had learned, Girolamo now felt the power of the Lord light him up. Observers said that his voice may not have been attractive and his manner still remained awkward, but there was no mistaking the passion, the fire which flashed in his eyes. Savonarola's sermons began to attract huge crowds and the Dominican order quickly brought him to Florence, recognising a rising star and setting him before a larger and more influential audience. But the friar appears to have disconcerted his superiors and within only a few months he was packed off to Bologna and a teaching job.

Lorenzo de' Medici came to his aid. In a fateful twist he brought the fiery friar back to San Marco to teach his son, Giovanni. The boy would become a cardinal and through him the de' Medici were determined to use all their influence to gain a foothold in the Church. Some of Savonarola's simple piety might rub off on Giovanni which, for the sake of appearances, would be no bad thing.

What Lorenzo failed to see was the potential political power of preaching. By 1491 Savonarola had been appointed Prior of San Marco, with the agreement of the de' Medici, and he began to attract a cadre of passionately pious, even fanatical, young men to the monastery. The huge congregations for his sermons overflowed into the streets and permission was sought from Lorenzo to use the cathedral of Santa Maria del Fiore. It was a fatal misjudgement. At last the stage was equal to the performance and dire warnings of doom began to boom across the city.

Savonarola saw himself as a prophet and constantly claimed that he was no more than a mouthpiece for the Word of God. Elijah, Elisha and the ancient firebrands of the Old Testament were his models and increasingly the de' Medici became his targets. As the sermons grew ever more political, coupling predictions of disaster for Florence, the 'Sword of the Lord' hanging amongst storm clouds over the city, with condemnations of tyrants, the influence of Savonarola rippled far beyond the cloistered walls of San Marco and the doors of the cathedral. The power of his preaching caused men to pause and ponder the consequences of their own sinfulness, and also set a question mark over the government of their city. The pageantry, the lavish feast days, the outward show so beloved of the de' Medici – were these things godly? Did they obey the Eternal Laws of the Lord? The tyrants at the Palazzo Medici suffered biblical comparison with Nebuchadnezzar and historical comparison with the dissolute Emperor Nero. 'Repent, O Florence, while there is still time!', thundered the Dominican prophet from the pulpit of the Duomo, 'Clothe thyself in the white garments of purification. Wait no longer, for there may be no further time for repentance!'

Apocalyptic predictions poured out of Santa Maria. Kings, popes and tyrants would die and foreign enemies cross the Alps and descend upon Italy. 'The Lord has placed me here,' Savonarola revealed, 'and He has said to me "I have put you here as a watchman in the centre of Italy that you may hear my words and announce them to the people."'

Despite the fact that the prophecies were more like informed judgements – Pope Innocent VIII and King Ferrante of Naples were both very old and everyone knew that Lorenzo was gravely ill – the friar grew more powerful. In the intense atmosphere of a densely packed city, his influence waxed as Lorenzo's health waned. When it was clear that the end would not be long in coming, Savonarola was summoned to Careggi. What was probably intended as an attempt at diplomacy, an attempt to reconcile the Dominican and his followers to the de' Medici succession, turned into a humiliation.

Standing over Lorenzo, clad in his black robes, the friar made demands. After the formulae of the last rites, asking the dying man if he believed in God and repented his sins, Savonarola immediately assumed a political posture, behaving like a representative of the people. He demanded to know if Lorenzo would give up all the de' Medici wealth and insisted he 'restore the liberty of the citizens of Florence'. When no response came, the cold-hearted friar stood in silence, made the sign of the cross, gave a hasty absolution and turned to leave.

The only consolation for Lorenzo was that it seemed his son, Piero, would succeed unopposed. Savonarola was probably seen as a temporary problem, a flash in the pan. Charismatic preachers had held cities in thrall before. San Bernardino of Siena had even held a Bonfire of the Vanities in the Campo. But an unrelieved diet of damnation was not a strategy for long-term popularity. A man like Savonarola acted like a purgative on the body politic, and after a time his influence would subside.

What mattered to Piero was money, or the lack of it. After years of indifference, the Medici bank was no longer as profitable as it had once been and the levels of cash needed to lubricate the party machine were running dangerously low. In fact other branches of the Medici family had become more wealthy. Piero's cousins, Giovanni and Lorenzo di Pierfrancesco de' Medici had made a fortune as grain dealers and enmities were beginning to fester. At a spring ball in one of the city's palazzi, there was an explosive and boyish dispute between Piero and Giovanni di Pierfranceso over a glamorous dancing partner. Piero stunned the guests by slapping his cousin in public. If the de' Medici were at odds with each other, what did that say about the stability of the government of Florence?

In 1494 another of Savonarola's prophecies came to pass, and the Sword of the Lord threatened to fall on the city. More precisely the sword of Charles VIII, King of France, was raised against Naples. After the death of King Ferrante, the French revived their claim to his throne and began to assemble a huge expeditionary army. Behind fluttering banners of white silk embroidered with the arms of Charles and the motto *Voluntas Dei*, the 'Will of God', 30,000 soldiers marched through the alpine passes and down into Lombardy.

Not since Hannibal had such a vast army invaded Italy and, like the Carthaginians, they seemed invincible. In the French ranks marched Europe's most feared soldiers, thousands of Swiss pikemen. Wielding 12- to 16-foot pikes, these heavily armoured infantry had defeated the forces of Duke Charles the Bold of Burgundy in 1475–77 and thereby established the independence of the Swiss cantons. As poor, upland regions, they needed cash and mercenary soldiering helped to cement their new freedoms. And an enduring French proverb was coined: *point d'argent, point de Suisses*, 'no money, no Swiss'.

As companies of fighting men who knew each other well, the Swiss enjoyed high morale and were ferocious in battle. Not for them the endless manoeuvring of the Italian *condottieri*, the taking of prisoners, the tactical withdrawals, the preservation of expensive soldiers. The Swiss gave no quarter and expected none. They were also highly trained, exercising great discipline, and they were quite unlike any other forces of pikemen. Infantry had developed the long pike essentially as a defensive weapon used in 'bristling', block-formations against charging heavy cavalry. The Swiss took matters a stage further and they charged with their pikes levelled at the enemy. It must have taken immense upper body strength to execute this manoeuvre effectively, but they did it again and again in the war with Burgundy. Backed by crossbowmen or hand gunners, the Swiss pikemen could be devastating.

Charles VIII also brought artillery across the Alps. Drawn by horses and not slow oxen, his limbers were highly adaptable, capable of being set up and ready to fire in short order. Against the new tactic of firing in volleys, when all guns shot at once, the walls of the Italian cities and opposing ranks of troops were very vulnerable. Volleys did not allow defenders to concentrate their men in any one place, but forced them to cover a much wider area.

Writing in the 1520s the Florentine historian, Francesco Guicciardini, believed that the French invasion changed warfare radically:

> Before the year 1494, wars were protracted, battles bloodless, the methods followed in besieging towns slow and uncertain; and although artillery was already in use, it was managed with such a lack of skill that it caused little hurt. Hence it came about that the ruler of a state could hardly be dispossessed. But the French, in their invasion of Italy, infused so much liveliness into our wars that, up to the present . . . whenever the open country was lost, the state was lost with it.

And later, Guicciardini observed that the French guns 'were planted against the walls of a town with such speed, the space between the shots was so little, and the balls flew so quick and were impelled with such force, that as much execution was done in a few hours as formerly, in Italy, in the like number of days'.

Even if Piero de' Medici had been able to afford them, no Italian *condottiere* could have withstood the French army of 1494. Florence eventually declared itself neutral, but as Charles waited on the northern borders of the republic for permission to cross its territory, Piero dithered. Frustration saw the French massacre the Florentine garrison at Fivizzano in the western Apennines.

Savonarola saw himself entirely vindicated. The prophesied enemy had crossed the Alps and the sword had fallen. Feeding on the anxiety of Florentines, he thundered from the pulpit of the Duomo. Piero was forced to act. Hurrying west along the Arno, he made his way to the French camp at Sarzanello. Believing himself virtually powerless, he appears not to have negotiated with Charles VIII, and he conceded every demand. If he had hoped to emulate his father and the success of his journey to Naples, Piero was to be sorely disappointed. When he rode back through the streets of Florence with an armed band at his back, and arrived at the gates of the Palazzo Vecchio, the Signoria refused to see him. As his horses circled and clattered on the paving stones of the piazza, the de' Medici supporters uncertain what to do, the Vacca began to toll, its base tones sounding over the rooftops. It was no time to linger and risk confrontation with an angry mob. Piero rode quickly back to his palazzo, his brother Giovanni removed as many of the Medici treasures as could be carried for safe-keeping at San Marco, and at dead of night the rulers of Florence stole out of the city.

The hostile Signoria sent soldiers to plunder the Palazzo Medici, the Pazzi and Soderini families were invited back from exile, and as a recognition of his growing status, Fra Savonarola became involved in government. When a Florentine embassy set out to meet King Charles VIII, the friar was a leading member. And more remarkably, when the embassy reached the French camp at Pisa, Savonarola took the initiative. Flattering Charles VIII as the instrument of God's punishment of sinful Florence, he preached a sermon, full of opposites and in classic rhetorical style:

You have come as the Minister of God, the Minister of Justice. We receive you with joyful hearts and a glad countenance ... We hope that through you God will abase the pride of the proud, will exalt the humility of the humble, will crush vice, exalt virtue, make straight all that is crooked, renew the old and reform all that is deformed. Come then, glad, secure, triumphant, since He who sent you triumphed on the cross for our salvation.

But then the tone changed abruptly – no doubt to the consternation of the other ambassadors. If Charles dared to harm the city of Florence, God would not hesitate to punish him. Using all his power, Savonarola succeeded in convincing the French that God spoke through him. It was a case of one 'Instrument of God' speaking directly to another. And it worked.

Charles VIII gave assurances that the city would not be pillaged but insisted on a triumphal entry. It was as though Florence had been the object of the expedition, and not Naples. But show was important, and before the age of mass communications politics was not reported; it had to be seen to be done.

The French entered the city from the south-west, through the Porta San Frediano. Charles VIII looked like a triumphant Roman general, wearing gilt armour, a cloak of cloth of gold and his crown, and riding under a canopy decorated with the fleur-de-lys of France. His lance was couched in its stirrup holder and it rested on his shoulder. The symbolism was obvious: Florence had already been defeated – but by negotiation rather than spilled blood.

Behind the king on his huge black destrier, about half of his army marched in ceremonial order, the helmet plumes bobbing, armour and weapons glinting, banners fluttering. They entered the Piazza del Duomo by the Via Larga, passing the Palazzo Medici, horseshoes striking sparks off the cobblestones and the crowds shrinking back from the snorting and spooking warhorses. Florentines were in awe, but, typically, one observer recorded what he saw: 'The heavy cavalry presented a hideous appearance, with their horses looking like monsters because their manes and tails were cut quite short. Then came the archers, extraordinary tall men from Scotland and other northern countries, and they looked more like wild beasts than men.'

The Scottish soldiers who so terrified the crowds were almost certainly gallowglasses. These heavily armed infantrymen from the Western Isles and the Highlands began to hire themselves out in companies, mostly from Clan Donald, in the fifteenth century. They wore long mail shirts known as 'jacks', which reached to their knees and the tops of what came to be called 'jackboots'. Shorter mail shirts worn by horsemen were 'jackets'. The gallowglasses were encouraged to seek employment abroad by the Lords of the Isles since their adventures took them far away, and in so doing removed a potentially disruptive element of high-spirited young men anxious to prove themselves. Perhaps they marched through Renaissance Florence behind the bagpipes. It is a pleasing image.

The occupation was surprisingly peaceful, if expensive. The French and their mercenary companies caused little trouble, but refused to pay for their billets or their food and wine. A much more serious disagreement took place during the public ceremonies in the Piazza della Signoria, where Charles VIII and the Signoria were due to attach their seals to the agreed peace treaty.

As the French king sat on a throne (confiscated from the Palazzo Medici), a herald began to read out the terms of the treaty. Until the invasion of Naples and the matter of the succession had been concluded, the French would occupy Pisa and certain Florentine fortresses on their line of march. Charles' knights and soldiers were stationed around the piazza, and while the crowd may have grumbled, they were in no position to argue. Then came the question of money. The French had demanded 150,000 florins but between agreeing to that and the actual ceremony, the Signoria had revised the figure downwards. When the herald read out that Florence would pay 120,000 florins, Charles sprang up from his throne and shouted in a fury that 150,000 had been agreed and nothing less would do.

It was a remarkable episode. How the Signoria expected such a schoolboy ruse to succeed will remain a mystery, but what happened next was even more surprising. When King Charles threatened to order his trumpeters to call his men to arms, the *gonfaloniere*, Piero di Gino Capponi, jumped to his feet. He had been Florentine ambassador to France and had known the king when he was only a little boy. 'If you sound your trumpets, we will ring our bells!' roared Capponi. The Vacca would summon the citizens to the piazza and there would be bloodshed. Seeing that his vast army might not quickly prevail in the narrow streets of an unfamiliar city, Charles relented and agreed to the lower sum. It was a splendid and daring example of Florentine bargaining skills.

Piero di Gino Capponi's courage and the resolve of the Signoria seemed to wither when the French finally left the city at the end of November 1494. They did little to resist the rise of Fra Savonarola. In a sermon delivered a few days before Christmas, he produced a clumsy justification for a priest as governor of Florence:

The wind drives me forward. The Lord forbids my return. I spoke last night with the Lord and said, 'Pity me, O Lord. Lead me back to my haven.' 'It is impossible,' said the Lord. 'See you not that the wind is contrary?' 'I will preach, if so I must, but why need I meddle with the government of Florence?' 'If you would make Florence a holy city, you must establish her on firm foundations and give her a government which favours virtue.'

In effect, Florence became a theocracy. Like the Medici, Savonarola was backed by a mob, probably encouraged by his cadre of fanatical monks at San Marco. And he also ruled by whispering, spying and fear. Children were encouraged to become the guardians of their elders' morals, watching for excessive consumption, too much laughter, too much of anything except piety. Popular support was rewarded and encouraged by a widening of the political franchise, and a quarter of all men over thirty years of age became eligible for government office. Taxation was eased for poorer people and an amnesty declared for those sent into exile during the years of Medici rule.

These were sensible and popular measures, but Savonarola was attempting to create a theocracy and not a democracy. His relentless religious rigidity began to create opposition, both inside the walls of Florence and beyond. Some of the wealthier and braver mercantile families became known as Gli Arrabbiati, 'the Angry Men', and their supporters abused the friar's followers as I Capernostri, 'the Nodders', a reference to heads bowed in prayer. Pope Alexander VI Borgia was quietly approached by representatives of the Arrabbiati, and persuaded to lure Savonarola to Rome with the offer of a cardinal's hat. The friar sneered and insisted he would accept only a hat 'red with blood'. It was perhaps a prophetic remark.

After Charles VIII had marched his army out of Italy, he had broken the promises made to Savonarola and the Signoria. Fortresses were not handed back and were in fact sold to Genoa, Lucca and Siena. Pisa was allowed to seize its independence. Protest in Florence grew bolder. At the friar's sermons drums were beaten to drown out his words and there were two failed assassination attempts. In the summer of 1497 Alexander VI bowed to more pressure from the Arrabbiati and called Savonarola to Rome to explain himself. When excuses were made, a papal bull of excommunication was issued. When it was ignored and Savonarola continued to preach in the Duomo, the Signoria felt strong enough to act. Outraged at the sight of an excommunicated priest desecrating the cathedral, they banned him from entry. Support was beginning to ebb and the end was fast approaching.

After a poor harvest in 1497 and a difficult winter for the Popolo Minuto, the friar's most ardent supporters, few relished the thought of more fire and brimstone sermons at Lent. Opposition took on a monastic character. There had long been a rivalry between the two major orders of mendicant friars, and by early 1498 the Franciscans of Santa Croce had become exasperated by the Dominican dominance of the city and their endlessly repeated claim that God spoke through Fra Savonarola. They challenged him to prove it – by the medieval ritual of ordeal by fire. It turned out to be a crude, highly theatrical and ultimately effective test.

On the Saturday before Palm Sunday (Lazarus Saturday), carts full of brushwood and oiled sticks trundled into the Piazza della Signoria. A pathway measuring 30 yards long and 10 yards wide was laid in front of the Loggia degli Lanzi with sticks heaped along either side. If Fra Savonarola could walk through this crackling inferno and emerge unscathed, then he was indeed touched by the hand of God and should continue to govern Florence unchallenged. In order to legitimise the primitive ritual somehow, a devout Franciscan, Fra Giuliano, would also walk the burning path.

Savonarola refused, but one of his fanatical supporters, Fra Domenico, would undertake the ordeal as his representative. Stands were set up in the Loggia degli Lanzi, and at the appointed hour crowds poured into the Piazza della Signoria. Armed guards had been posted at the entry streets, anticipating disturbances. A hush fell and the approaching voices of the Franciscans could be heard singing hymns as they entered the piazza with Fra Giuliano. They were kept waiting by the brushwood pathway for some time before the Dominicans made their way from San Marco. Singing a psalm and walking in pairs, they led Fra Domenico to his ordeal. He carried a wooden crucifix but the crowds were appalled to see the excommunicated Savonarola walking beside him carrying the Host.

An argument immediately started. The Franciscans objected strongly to the Dominican taking a crucifix into the flames. It would be sacrilegious. And no, he could not take the Host from Savonarola and carry it instead. As tempers frayed, the heavens suddenly opened. A thunderstorm rumbled over Florence and a heavy downpour soaked the brushwood in the piazza. Each side would have interpreted the portents in its own way.

On the following day, Palm Sunday, resentment detonated into a riot. When one of Savonarola's young adherents began to preach in the Duomo, he was shouted down and pursued by a mob incited by the Arrabbiati. They surrounded San Marco, baying for the prior, and the monks fought back what amounted to a siege. A German Dominican fired a hand-gun, and it seems that weapons had been stored in the event of violence. After burning down the monastery doors, the mob burst in. It was 2 a.m. when they finally found Savonarola at prayer in the library. By that time armed guards from the Signoria had arrived on the scene and they dragged the friar through the hissing and spitting crowds to the Palazzo Vecchio, where he was locked for the night in the *alberghetto* in the bell-tower. No doubt he prayed hard, knowing the terrible torments he would have to endure in the morning.

Chained so tightly that he could not walk, Savonarola was carried to the dungeons of the Bargello where he was to suffer the agonies of the *strappado*. Standing directly under a beam with a pulley and rope slung over it, the friar had his hands tied behind his back with leather thongs. The rope was attached to these bonds and pulled tight. The inquisitor put the question – was not Savonarola guilty of heresy? No doubt the reply was at first defiant. But when the jailor and his men pulled the rope and the pulley wheel began to turn as the prisoner was lifted high off the floor, the pain must have been excruciating, unimaginable. And then it got worse. *Strappado* means 'wrench', and when Savonarola was suspended in the air by his hands behind his back, the jailors suddenly released the rope – but jerked it just before his feet touched the floor.

Savonarola survived four drops before confessing. When the rope was taken off he retracted, but then they dropped him until he was too delirious with agony to say anything. Along with his disciples, Fra Domenico and Fra Silvestro, the Prior of San Marco was hanged in chains in the Piazza della Signoria and then a fire set around the scaffold. It was near the place where the Bonfire of the Vanities had blazed. Luca Landucci, an apothecary, was in the watching crowd, and he kept a diary:

> Part of their bodies remaining hanging in the chains, a quantity of stones were thrown to make them fall, as there was a fear of people getting hold of them; and then the hangman and those whose business it was hacked down the post and burned it on the ground, bringing a lot of brushwood, and stirring the fire up over the dead bodies so that the very last piece was consumed. Then they fetched carts, and accompanied by the mace-bearers, carried the last bit of dust to the Arno near the Ponte Vecchio in order that no remains should be found.

Perhaps Botticelli watched and wept as the martyrs burned. Perhaps he was one of those who searched the banks of the river for relics.

10

Illustrious Tuscans

In a corner of the yard of the cathedral workshop, the *opera del duomo*, lay a huge piece of marble. Quarried at Carrara in the ranges of the Apennines known as the Apuan Alps, it was more than 17 feet long and approximately 6 feet square. The cost of transporting such a large block to Florence had been borne by the cloth guild, the Arte della Lana, and it was intended for use by the workshop of Donatello. On each of the buttresses of the cathedral there would stand twelve figures from the Old Testament, sculpted by the great master and his assistants. Donatello was old in 1464, probably in his seventy-eighth year, and his chief assistant, Agostino di Duccio, was given the task of blocking out the figure, the sort of heavy work his master could no longer manage. After a few days the feet, the legs and parts of the torso had been roughed out, but for some forgotten reason Agostino did not continue. Two years later Donatello was dead and the huge block of marble was moved, with great difficulty, to one side. For thirty years it lay untouched.

After the fall of Savonarola, Piero Soderini had eventually been appointed *gonfaloniere*, and to provide some much-needed political stability, he was confirmed in office for life. Florence also needed to recover some civic pride after the military humiliations and extremes of the 1490s, and while no great architectural scheme for the city could possibly be afforded, a new work of sculpture, prominently placed, might have a powerful symbolic effect.

In 1500 the managers of the cathedral workshop, the *operai*, listed 'a certain figure of marble . . . badly blocked out and supine' in their possession. Known as Il Gigante, 'the Giant', it might serve as the raw material for what Gonfalonier Soderini had in mind. The *operai* had the Giant winched upright so that sculptors might examine the condition of the marble and make the necessary measurements. Exposed to the sun, wind and rain for thirty years, the block had shrunk a little and may have been water-damaged. Leonardo da Vinci came to the cathedral yard to have a look and think what might be done, and other artists were consulted. But it was Michelangelo Buonarotti who convinced Soderini and the Operai that he could create something outstanding from the Giant. In Rome he had made a larger-than-life-size marble statue of the Roman god of wine and revelry, Bacchus, and for the French ambassador to the Vatican, a pietà carved from a very awkwardly shaped block. And Michelangelo was a Florentine; he understood well what his native city needed to see. Out of the Giant he would carve a David, the boy who had killed a giant and become a king, a symbol of and inspiration for Florence and her determination to defeat nations and their armies and survive.

Early in the morning of Monday, 13 September 1501, Michelangelo came to the yard of the Operai and, hidden from sight behind a screen of planks and scaffolding, he picked up his mallet and chisel and began work. Inside the mutilated block of beautiful white marble *David* was waiting. And Michelangelo would release him.

Only twenty-six years of age when he began work on the most famous sculpture the world has yet seen, Michelangelo Buonarotti was raised in Florence, the son of a middle-class family which had seen more prosperous times. After the early death of his mother, the boy went to live with the family of a stonecutter in the little town of Settignano, where his father owned a marble quarry and a smallholding. Much later, Michelangelo reflected on his early life with his biographer, the painter Giorgio Vasari: 'If there is some good in me, it is because I was born in the subtle atmosphere of your country of Arezzo. Along with the milk of my nurse I received the knack of handling chisel and hammer, with which I make my figures.'

When his father packed him off to Florence to study in the school set up by the humanist, Francesco da Urbino, it turned out to be a waste of what little money he had. In the late fifteenth century schools taught a curriculum based on a classical model, what were known as the Liberal Arts. Aristotle had listed the likes of rhetoric, grammar, philosophy and dialectic while the Florentines had added a thorough knowledge of Latin, Greek and even Hebrew. These were thought to be subjects suitable for the education of gentlemen. Painting and sculpture were certainly not.

In 1528 Count Baldassare Castiglione wrote the enormously influential *The Courtier*, and it supplied a simple test, the reason why such superficially artistic occupations ought to be excluded from any curriculum of the Liberal Arts. Both painting and sculpture involved manual labour, a very lower-class activity, and artists routinely got dirty while they worked, paint-spattered and covered in dust. No gentleman could possibly be seen lifting a brush or a chisel. Architecture was borderline. Masons executed the work, covered in muck and doing all the heavy lifting, and a good architect needed intellectual skills like mathematics and an understanding of ancient buildings. But, distressingly, many were also painters and sculptors.

When it became clear that Michelangelo was not thriving under the tidy tutelage of Francesco da Urbino, his father swallowed his aspirations and persuaded the renowned painter, Domenico Ghirlandaio, to accept the boy as an apprentice. It was a substantial consolation to Leonardo Buonarotti that contrary to common practice Ghirlandaio agreed to pay the fourteen-year-old rather than charge his father a fee for training him. Michelangelo's skills must have been obvious and immediately saleable. Vasari takes up the story:

The way Michelangelo's talents and character developed astonished Domenico, who saw him doing things quite out of the ordinary . . . On one occasion it happened that one of the young men studying with Domenico copied in ink some draped figures of women from Domenico's own work. Michelangelo took what he had drawn and, using a thicker pen, he went over the contours of one of the figures and brought it to perfection; and it is marvellous to see the difference between the two styles and the superior skill and judgement of a young man so spirited and confident that he had the courage to correct what his teacher had done. This drawing is now kept by me among my treasured possessions. I received it from Granaccio, along with other drawings by Michelangelo, for my book of drawings; and in 1550, when he was in Rome, I showed it to Michelangelo, who recognised it and was delighted to see it again. He said modestly that as a boy he had known how to draw better than he did now as an old man.

In 1489, only a few months after Michelangelo had arrived at Ghirlandaio's studio, Lorenzo de' Medici heard word of the young prodigy. In the garden of the Palazzo Medici there stood a collection of classical sculptures and it was thought that young artists might benefit from copying and drawing them. Lorenzo asked Ghirlandaio to send him his best pupils. It was the beginning of a long and sometimes stormy relationship between Michelangelo and the de' Medici.

It may be that for a short period Leonardo da Vinci, Michelangelo and Sandro Botticelli all lived in the Palazzo Medici at the same time. Lorenzo greatly enjoyed the company of artists and intellectuals and most evenings they ate together and talked, but perhaps not always harmoniously. Vasari does not equivocate: 'Leonardo and Michelangelo strongly disliked each other.' There was a fundamental difference of character and approach to their art. Perhaps with the rigid exclusions of the Liberal Arts at the back of his mind, Leonardo saw himself as a scientist rather than a mere paint-spattered craftsman. Using his eyes rather than text-books, he spent a lifetime attempting to understand nature and natural phenomena. In order to be able to paint human beings, it was necessary to understand how muscles and the senses worked, and to dissect bodies to discover even more. His voluminous notebooks contain studies of every sort. Machines fascinated Leonardo and he devised schemes for irrigation, for canalising the Arno, for building a helicopter, a tank and much else.

Leonardo's obsessive perfectionism prevented him from completing all the work that he began, and even his most famous fresco, the *Last Supper*, took a very long time. It was commissioned by the Dominicans of Santa Maria delle Grazie of Milan, and they knew his reputation. Vasari again:

> It is said that the Prior kept pressing Leonardo, in the most importunate way, to hurry up and finish the work, because he was puzzled by Leonardo's habit of sometimes spending half a day contemplating what he had done so far; if the Prior had had his way, Leonardo would have toiled like one of the labourers hoeing in the garden and never put his brush down for a moment. Not satisfied with this, the Prior then complained to the Duke of Milan ... and so he [Leonardo] talked to the Duke for a long time about the art of painting. He explained that men of genius sometimes accomplish most when they work the least; for, he added, they

are thinking out inventions and forming in their minds the perfect ideas which they subsequently express and reproduce with their hands. Leonardo then said he still had two heads to paint: the head of Christ was one . . . then, he had yet to do the head of Judas, and this troubled him since he did not think he could imagine the features of a man . . . who could so cruelly steel his will to betray his own master . . . However, added Leonardo, he would try to find a model for Judas, and if he did not succeed in doing so, why then he was not without the head of that tactless and importunate Prior. The Duke roared with laughter.

This incident is an illustration of how much the habits of patronage had changed since the early fifteenth century. The price of an ounce of ultramarine and the amount of gold to be used in a painting had become much less important than estimates of an artist's skill. What Leonardo and Michelangelo added was the notion of relative artistic freedom, perhaps even an early sense of genius also at work. Leonardo, and not the fussing friar, would decide when a piece of work was finished, and as it was created, take virtually every important decision about how it was created.

By 1504 Michelangelo's *David* was ready to be moved out of the workshops of the *opera del duomo*. The problem was – where? Because the figure was a nude, an ecclesiastical location was thought to be inappropriate. A committee met. Leonardo, Sandro Botticelli (said to be a sad figure by this time, penniless and hobbling around on crutches), Giuliano da Sangallo and Piero di Cosimo all knew that the marble had many imperfections and was vulnerable to the weather. They wanted to see the *David* placed under the roof of the Loggia degli Lanzi. Soderini and the Signoria took a more robust view. If *David* was the symbol of Florentine independence then he should stand guard outside the western doors of the Palazzo Vecchio. Michelangelo's views are not recorded, but he will have wanted the fruits of his great labour shown off in the most prominent place possible.

Getting it there was not easy. *David* was very tall and very heavy. Giuliano da Sangallo designed a frame of massive beams, and rather than subject the sculpture to being rattled and shoogled through the streets, he had it suspended on stout ropes. When the frame moved, *David* simply swayed gently. Winching him along on rollers, the workmen of the Opera del Duomo took four days to transport *David* the 500 yards from the Piazza Duomo to his plinth in the Piazza della Signoria.

When the 17-foot-high figure had been set up, but before the frame was dismantled, Piero Soderini came to have a look. 'The nose is too thick,' he remarked to Michelangelo. Fighting down his anger, the young sculptor climbed up to the head, picking up his mallet and chisel – and a handful of marble dust on the way. He then turned his back to Soderini and made clinking noises with the tools, dropping a little dust as he did so. But leaving *David*'s nose entirely untouched. When he had finished, Michelangelo moved out of the way and shouted down to Soderini. 'Now look at it.' The *gonfaloniere* replied, 'Ah, that's much better. Now you've really brought it to life.'

In the five centuries since it was made, the *David* has become visual shorthand for great art and high culture, but if Piero Soderini believed it might act as a talisman for Florence's freedom, he was to be disappointed. European politics had shifted, and the city became simply too small and too poor to continue as a significant player in international affairs. Having resolved its internal conflicts, France emerged as an immensely powerful force and Charles VIII would not be the last French king to involve himself in Italy. The Genoese sea captain, Christopher Columbus, had not only discovered the New World but released a flood of gold and silver which flowed directly into the royal treasury of Spain. The wealth of the Aztecs and Incas quickly translated into military clout in Europe.

Perhaps the astute Lorenzo de' Medici had foreseen the waning of Florence; perhaps he recognised that for his family, the Church and the papacy represented the only route to power. When his son, Giovanni, became a cardinal, it would become possible for him to be pope, and for the fragile fortunes of the de' Medici to find a fresh sponsor. Time would tell.

Meanwhile Michelangelo and Leonardo moved away from Florence and Tuscany, to where political power and money would commission great work from them. At the court of Lodovico Sforza, Duke of Milan, Leonardo was at first celebrated for his talents as a musician. Here is Vasari's history:

> Leonardo took with him a lyre that he had made himself, mostly of silver, in the shape of a horse's head (a very strange and novel

design) so that the sound should be more sonorous and resonant. Leonardo's performance was therefore superior to that of all the other musicians who had come to Lodovico's court. Leonardo was also the most talented improviser in verse of his time. Moreover, he was a sparkling conversationalist, and after they had spoken together the duke developed almost boundless love and admiration for his talents.

Vasari also noted that Leonardo was volatile and unstable as a child, but when he had grown into a very good-looking young man, he seems to have sustained a series of long relationships. Giacomo Salai became a completely untrustworthy assistant, described by an exasperated Leonardo as a thief, a liar, pig-headed and a glutton. But he loved him. The boy wore his hair curled in ringlets, which delighted his master, and they never parted. Leonardo had been denounced for sodomy in Florence in 1476 and in theory he faced the mandatory punishment of being burned at the stake. Since it was probably a veiled attack on Lorenzo de' Medici and his party, Leonardo went to live at the Palazzo Medici for his own protection, and the accusation was quietly dropped.

At the same time as Michelangelo was making a fool of Piero Soderini over the thickness of the nose of the most famous statue ever made, Leonardo was working on the world's most famous painting. In 1504 Francesco del Giocondo asked for a portrait of his beautiful wife, Mona Lisa.

More than any other artist, Leonardo understood how people use their eyes, how much and what exactly they see. Too many fifteenth-century painters had produced figures which appeared stiff, like sculpture, frozen in the midst of action of some sort. Sandro Botticelli had tried to solve this problem in his *Primavera* and *The Birth of Venus* by using the wind to impart a sense of movement: flying hair, flying drapery and the figures somehow levitating. With the *Mona Lisa*, a seated figure who in reality would have stayed as still as she could, Leonardo made her look more life-like than any other artist before him. He did it by leaving the viewer something to guess at by blurring outlines and edges and using shadow and colour to create an atmosphere of mystery. Technically he invented a new way of painting called *sfumato*, which in Italian can mean 'faded' or 'mellow'. And knowing that facial expression is largely formed by the eyes and the corners of the mouth, Leonardo left these ambiguous. If a viewer takes a piece of paper and a good print of the painting and then screens the well-lit left-hand side of Mona Lisa's face, she is certainly smiling. But switch sides and look only at the left, and she certainly is not. Her complete expression is elusive, exactly the effect Leonardo wished to create – and what makes her seem so alive.

In the seventeen years he stayed in Milan, Leonardo completed only six paintings and probably judged that none of them was what he had in mind when he picked up a brush. Michelangelo, by contrast, was tremendously productive, and even though Leonardo detested the young man and what he saw as a God-obsessed set of sensibilities constantly at work, he would have reluctantly recognised the output of a great artist. Michelangelo was also able to inject life into his figures. But it was not subtle *sfumato* but a kind of operatic drama, what contemporaries called *terribilità*.

In 1504 Pope Julius II summoned Michelangelo to Rome. He wanted the young sculptor to build him a tomb and adorn it with marble figures. But the project was halted soon after it began. One of the main reasons was that Julius wanted to see St Peter's rebuilt, and since his tomb would naturally be placed inside the new church, it could wait. According to Vasari, Michelangelo saw this as part of a web of plots being spun against him.

In 1504 a young painter from Urbino arrived in Florence. Raffaelo Sanzio, better known as Raphael, was to complete the famous trinity of High Renaissance artists working in Tuscany and Rome at the same time. Apprenticed at the workshop of Pietro Perugino, the young man quickly grasped the new technique of *sfumato*, and allied it to a delightful sense of composition and character. Just as Michelangelo's *David* became a standard for idealised male beauty, so Raphael's Madonnas fixed a perfect image of purity, motherliness and sweetness.

Like many of his contemporaries, Raphael followed money and influence to Rome and by 1508 was painting frescoes in the Vatican. His countryman from Urbino, Donato Bramante, was commissioned by Julius II to design the new basilica of St Peter's, and Michelangelo became convinced that they plotted with papal courtiers to do him down. Their dastardly masterstroke was to provoke the great sculptor into producing a masterpiece.

So that he would be shamed and would suffer by comparison, Michelangelo was commissioned by the pope to work in an unfamiliar medium in an awkward location. The Urbinese, Raphael and Bramante, had whispered, so he thought, that the Florentine ought to be made to lay down his chisel and pick up a brush to paint the ceiling of the out-of-the-way Sistine Chapel. It was to be Julius II's monument to the founder, his uncle, Pope Sixtus IV. Michelanglo at first refused. Vasari again:

> . . . considering the magnitude and difficulty of the task of painting the chapel, and his lack of experience, [Michelangelo] tried in every possible way to shake the burden off his shoulders. But the more he refused, the more determined he made the Pope, who was a wilful man by nature and who again in any case was being prompted by Michelangelo's rivals, and especially Bramante. And finally, being the hot-tempered man he was, his holiness was all ready to fly into a rage.

Just to show them, Michelangelo decided he would do all the work himself. Normally a large fresco cycle would employ many assistants, but once the scaffolding had been erected, no-one but the painter was allowed in to watch the progress of the work. It took four back-breaking years. Contrary to legend and a famous film script, Michelangelo did not work lying on his back, but standing on a high platform supported from the windowsills of the chapel. But he did work with his head constantly tilted backwards, and for months after completing the frescoes, Michelangelo could read letters and look at drawings only by angling his head in the same way. He complained that his chest became like a harpie's and a goitre swelled in his neck. In a sonnet composed during a break on the scaffolding, Michelangelo compared his paint-spotted face to the veined marble pavement down on the floor of the chapel.

The frescoes are a magnificent achievement. Once Michelangelo declared them finished, crowds flocked to the Sistine Chapel. They still do. His image of the creation of Adam is particularly powerful, and the depiction of a white-haired, bearded figure of God the Father ready to animate the first man with the touch of an outstretched finger has also become a standard.

The ceiling was finished in 1512, the same year during which the pope buckled on his armour and went to war again. A French army was fought to a standstill by Spanish and papal troops near Ravenna.

Julius II's protégé, Cardinal Giovanni de' Medici, had ridden up and down the lines before battle, exhorting his men to pray for victory. When the French retreated, the way to Florence was open. De' Medici offered Soderini terms for surrender, which were refused. The Secretary of the Council for War, Niccolò Machiavelli, had organised a citizen militia and prepared the city's defences. *Condottieri* could be neither relied upon nor afforded. Giovanni de' Medici gave the order to march.

After Spanish troops had pillaged Prato, the Florentine militia lost heart and Soderini resigned and fled. Machiavelli was dispatched to the de' Medici camp to inform Cardinal Giovanni that Florence would open her gates to him. On 1 September 1512, after eighteen years in exile, the de' Medici had returned. The cardinal had important business in Rome and he installed his cousin, Giulio de' Medici, as ruler of the city. When a plot against him was discovered, a list of names included Niccolò Machiavelli's. After four drops on the *strappado*, he did not confess to what turned out to be a false accusation. Released back into exile, Machiavelli took to writing and in the same year as he was arrested he produced his treatise on political power, *The Prince*. In it he approves of the use of torture.

What drew Giovanni de' Medici back to Rome was the electrifying news that Pope Julius II was dying. It was vital to take a full part in the conclave of cardinals called to meet and elect a new pope. But there was a substantial problem. Giovanni had grown hugely fat, and months of riding presumably very large and muscular horses had given him an anal fistula. Eating and drinking too much had allowed a stomach ulcer to develop. Even though he was still a young man, Cardinal de' Medici was not at all healthy. Unable any longer to lower his vast and tender backside into the saddle, he was carried in a litter all the way from Florence to Rome, presumably by muscular young men. The result was that Giovanni missed the opening services and ceremonies of the conclave and all the opportunities for preliminary politicking. Even when he finally reached Rome, the pain and unpleasant side-effects of his anal fistula forced him to spend time in bed. His own chances of election did not look promising.

The conclave was a closed meeting of cardinals in a sealed chapel, and tradition and canon law dictated that they were not allowed to leave until a new pope had been chosen. Most of the power-brokers were Italian aristocrats like Giovanni: Cardinal Gonzaga from Mantua,

Cardinal Petrucci from Siena and Cardinal d'Este from Ferrara. The atmosphere of the conclave must have been highly pressured, even feverish; seventy or so men talking in groups, plotting behind hands, making and unmaking alliances, communicating with looks and barely discernible nods. No-one can have been sure of anything at any given time as support ebbed and flowed for candidates whose fortunes rose and fell in a sea of whispers.

Held in a large chapel (after 1846 the Sistine was always used), the closed conclave was designed to produce rapid results. Cardinals had no separate sleeping quarters, only one servant in attendance, and if after three days no ballot had produced a decisive result, their food supply was reduced to one meal a day. If there was still stalemate after five days, only bread and water were laid at the doors.

Despite these incentives for haste, it took five days for Giovanni to work the room to his advantage. Cardinals were not allowed to vote for themselves (Alexander VI Borgia ignored this rule when he cast the deciding vote for himself in 1492) and ballots were constantly being cast and re-cast. In the beginning there had been four each day, two in the morning and two more in the afternoon. Finally the two cardinals with the most votes were pitted against each other and a simple majority would decide. After making a series of promises to his fellow Italians, Giovanni finally emerged as a clear first choice. As Senior Cardinal Deacon, in charge of voting, perhaps taking a more subtle approach than Alexander VI, certainly in a position to see how voting patterns were changing, he had the pleasure of announcing to the conclave that he himself had been elected. White smoke told the crowds that there was a decision and a senior cardinal announced '*Habemus papam!*' 'We have a pope!' 'God has given us the papacy,' said Giovanni to his brother. 'Let us enjoy it.'

Taking the name Leo X, de' Medici quickly secured a tight grip on both Rome and Florence. It was his ambition to create a de' Medici principality in central Italy and he would use the resources of the Holy See ruthlessly to that end. When Giovanni had first become a cardinal, his father, Lorenzo, advised him that 'it will not be difficult for you to aid the city and our house'.

Raphael painted Pope Leo X and two of his cardinals, one of them probably his brother, Giulio. It is not a flattering portrait. Voluminous garments hide the papal corpulence but under a fur-trimmed scarlet cap, a fleshy face stares into the middle distance. In his left hand Leo holds a spyglass, not only for reading the illuminated manuscript opened on the table in front of him, but also as an aid to overcome acute short-sightedness. He cannot have seen much of the detail of the elaborate ceremonies held in Rome to welcome him to the papal throne. But the crowds could clearly see this sweating, fat man riding side-saddle to save his tender backside, and like many of the cardinals who were persuaded to elect him, they may have looked forward to a short reign.

Raphael, by contrast, hoped that Leo would enjoy long life, at least long enough to pay for all the work he commissioned. In addition to the portrait there was an elaborate fresco cycle in the Vatican, and other pieces. At one point debts mounted so steeply that the pope hinted to the painter that he might make him a cardinal to wipe the slate clean. It was a remarkable proposal, a measure of how corrupt the papacy had grown, but evidently a serious one. Not only was Raphael not a priest, nor even remotely religious, his reputation in Rome was well known. Vasari offers details:

> He was indeed a very amorous man with a great fondness for women whom he was always anxious to serve. He was always indulging his sexual appetites; and in this matter his friends were probably more indulgent and tolerant than they should have been. When his close friend Agostino Chigi commissioned him to decorate the first loggia in his palace, Raphael could not give his mind to the work because of his infatuation for his mistress. Agostino was almost in despair when with great difficulty he managed with the help of others to arrange for the woman to go and live with Raphael in the part of the house where he was working; and that was how the painting was finished.

Leo X's chronic lack of funds threatened to inhibit his papacy profoundly. The warlike Julius II had emptied the coffers of the Holy See, and the vast building project of St Peter's was a tremendous drain on what cash there was. But increasing revenues had been coming in from a new source. Julius had promoted the sale of indulgences. These were paper guarantees which limited the time any soul might have to spend in purgatory, and the arrangement was very simple. The more a poor sinner paid, the shorter the sentence. It was a plainly ridiculous practice, no more than a fancy means of donating money to the Church, and it became very popular. Leo X quickly expanded the sales operation and, no doubt for a healthy commission, priests and licensed indulgence sellers plied their trade all over Europe. The initiative was to have unintended and disastrous consequences.

If the proceeds for indulgences had been used for Christian purposes, then the practice might have been tolerated. But all Christendom knew how corrupt the papacy had become, and when humble, poor and credulous people were shamelessly fleeced by the indulgence sellers, resentment grew. In 1517 it boiled over. An outraged Martin Luther hammered a list of 95 proposals or arguments for the reform of the Church to the doors of the castle church in Wittenberg in southern Germany. The demand for change would quickly ignite the Reformation and divide the Church and Europe.

The advent of printing, developing fastest in southern Germany, facilitated unprecedented circulation of Luther's demands, and as he acquired more and more aristocratic support, the movement for reform gained unstoppable momentum. In 1521 Leo excommunicated the troublesome German priest. But before more could be done, the pope suddenly died. From what had been thought no more than a chill, Leo took to his bed and in a matter of days he expired, almost certainly poisoned.

Doctors believed that the pope had caught the fatal chill as he sat at an open window watching the celebrations to mark the victory of the Emperor Charles V over Francis I of France. Leo had every reason to shiver. Charles V was the most powerful European monarch since Charlemagne. In 1519 he had been crowned Holy Roman Emperor at Aachen, the old imperial capital, and was already Count of Flanders, King of Naples and King of Spain. Most importantly, he also ruled over all the sprawling and fabulously lucrative new dominions of the crown in Spanish America. After his defeat of the French, Charles V was virtually irresistible. But popes had confronted mighty emperors before.

When the conclave was called to Rome to elect a new pope, Cardinal Giulio de' Medici was determined to keep the job in the family. But this time resistance was better organised and his cousin's record played against the chances of a de' Medici succession. Leo had alienated the French cardinals (and was probably poisoned on the orders of Francis I) when he withdrew support for the wars with

Charles V, and Cardinal Francesco Soderini, the brother of Piero, former *gonfaloniere* for life, bore ancient grudges and had allied himself with the Roman aristocrat, Cardinal Colonna. And this time there were other strong contenders: Cardinal Thomas Wolsey and Cardinal Alessandro Farnese. As the doors of the chapel were closed and the conclave sealed, Giulio realised that it was going to be far from easy to engineer his election.

As the early ballots whittled down the field to those who were truly *papabili*, worthy and capable of being pope, de' Medici hit on what seemed like an excellent ploy. He and his supporters would back an obscure candidate, someone who could never be thought seriously *papabile*, and this would reflect well on Giulio, showing him to be selfless and ready to do whatever was best for the Church, even sacrifice his own candidacy. A pious, scholarly and unworldly cardinal was found, presumably with some difficulty, and was escorted, blinking, into the limelight. Cardinal Adrian Dedel was a Fleming, had been tutor to Charles V, and to Giulio's amazement he not only enjoyed the limelight but turned out to be an attractive compromise candidate. When the obscure cardinal, previously unknown to most of those who voted for him, was asked by the Senior Deacon if he would accept the papacy, the old man replied that he would. Giulio was appalled.

The crowds waiting outside St Peter's greeted the announcement in stunned silence. Who? A German? A Fleming? A foreigner. It was not long before astonishment soured into resentment, or before the cardinals realised what a dreadful decision they had made. A saintly, scholarly ascetic as pope? Madness.

Taking the name of Adrian VI, Dedel quickly disbanded the papal court, sending the cardinals, archbishops and bishops back to their dioceses to minister to their flocks. Many had never visited them and had only the vaguest idea of where exactly they were bishop of. Pageantry and parades disappeared, and Vasari complained that artists were 'little better than dying of hunger'. As Rome emptied, all of the economic activity around the papacy ground to a halt. Prostitutes, pickpockets, tailors and merchants starved and priests were forced to attend to their sacred duties. It could not last. And it did not. After two long years, Adrian VI succumbed to a mysterious affliction of the kidneys, almost certainly encouraged by poison. He was the last non-Italian pope until 1978.

This time Giulio de' Medici came to the conclave prepared. But it proved extremely difficult to force the right result. After sixty days, the longest conclave in history, with the cardinals practically fading away, news filtered into the chapel that Giulio had the tacit support of Charles V, Henry VIII of England and finally, Francis I. The usual promises were exchanged, deals done, and when the chapel was unlocked de' Medici emerged as Pope Clement VII. He was forty-five years old, and in the next few years would need all of his maturity.

Clement's immediate problem in Tuscany was that the de' Medici were running short of heirs, or at least legitimate children from the two main branches of the family. In the absence of any relatives old enough to do the job, he was forced to appoint Cardinal Passerini to rule Florence and to coach two young and illegitimate de' Medici boys. Apparently it was a poor choice. Alessandro (almost certainly Clement's son) and Ippolito found themselves under the tutelage of 'a eunuch who spent the whole day in idle chatter and neglected important things'. The historian, Francesco Guicciardini, did not mince his words when he spoke to Clement VII about the situation in Florence.

Raphael and Leonardo had died within a year of each other. By 1519, da Vinci was in France, at the self-consciously Renaissance court of Francis I, in receipt of a generous pension and great admiration. Leonardo was seen as more than a great artist. The original meaning of genius was related to a sense of being productive and contemporaries complained that Leonardo was never that. But it also came to carry connotations of uniqueness, and no-one who knew the great man would have quarrelled with that definition. When he died in 1519 there was genuine grief at the loss of a remarkable man. One historian has described Leonardo neatly as 'more admired than understood.'

Raphael was also touched by genius, but tremendously productive. Despite an early death in 1520, aged thirty-seven, he maintained an output sufficient to make him very wealthy, and to establish a large workshop staffed by several talented assistants. Vasari wrote that Raphael 'lived more like a prince than a painter'.

It was Michelangelo who did most to change the status of artists. In a long and busy life, surviving until he was eighty-nine, he constantly insisted on his integrity, defying popes and princes. What gave Michelangelo the power to be so independent-minded was his genius. Because he was seen as a truly great artist, popes and princes knew that if he accepted a commission from them, it would confer immortality. And they were right. So conscious did Michelangelo become of his enhanced social status that as a grouchy old man of seventy-seven, he rebuked one of his correspondents:

> Tell him not to address his letters to the sculptor Michelangelo, for here I am known only as Michelangelo Buonarotti . . . I have never been a painter or a sculptor, in the sense of having kept a shop . . . although I have served the popes; but this I did under compulsion.

For his last significant commission, the cupola on the dome of St Peter's, the grand old man refused payment. Michelangelo Buonarotti had made the crowning glory of the greatest church in the world, and that was payment enough.

Great talent was increasingly accompanied by eccentricity. Especially in his later years, Michelangleo rarely washed, often slept in his clothes and was very fond of a pair of dogskin breeches which urgently needed repair or replacement. In Florence Leonardo was seen as strange for several reasons, but one which endears him was his habit of buying caged birds in the markets and then setting them free. But few artists behaved as eccentrically as Jacopo Pontormo. Commissioned by the de' Medici to decorate their villas and the old church at Certosa, he was seen as a great master of the 1520s and 1530s. Pontormo kept a diary in which he chronicled almost every ailment, no matter how minor, that afflicted him. Kidney disorders, erratic bowel movement, scratches – nothing was too trivial. Unable to tolerate the company of other people, he lived in an attic in Florence. It was only reachable by a ladder, which the painter pulled up behind him. And to substitute for intolerable live models, Pontormo was said to keep corpses in a large tub. Apparently his neighbours objected strenuously.

Two years after the crowning of Giulio de' Medici as Pope Clement VII, the world changed again. In 1525 the armies of the Emperor Charles V joined papal forces and defeated Francis I at Pavia, near Milan. Like de' Medici rulers before him, Clement attempted to maintain his independence by playing off one foreign power against another. But his calculations began to look misconceived. Charles V had grown far too powerful. In 1526 the pope joined the League of Cognac with France, Venice, Florence and Milan against the might of the emperor. The effect was delayed, but devastating.

By 1527 Charles had turned his attention to Italy and mustered an invasion army. Many of his soldiers were mercenaries from those German principalities which had supported Martin Luther and the movement to reform the Church. Rome, the seat of the corrupt papacy, was about to be assailed by an army of Protestants.

They swept all before them, and by 6 May, had arrived below the walls of Rome. The Florentine goldsmith and sculptor, Benvenuto Cellini, was on the ramparts:

> When we got up onto the city walls we could see below the formidable massed ranks of the Duke of Bourbon's army, which were battling their utmost to break into the city. The fighting was particularly bitter where we were, and already many young men had been killed by the attackers. The whole place was covered in the thickest fog and the fighting was desperate.

Soon the defenders were beaten back to the papal fortress of Castel Sant' Angelo, what had once been the tomb of the Emperor Hadrian. It was almost impregnable, but around it the city of Rome was being torn apart by bands of German mercenaries. Nothing like this had happened since the days of the barbarian invasions after the fall of the Roman Empire in the west. Martin Luther believed that the corruption of the papacy was being purged by the agents of God's fury. Others saw the Sack of Rome as an episode of unbridled and shocking savagery.

After five weeks, the siege of Castel Sant'Angelo was lifted, and Clement forced to sign a humiliating peace treaty, ceding a great deal of territory in central Italy. In December 1527, six months after the demonic Germans charged out of the mist, the pope was allowed to escape. But he could not flee north to take refuge behind the walls of Florence. The useless Cardinal Passerini and the de' Medici boys had fled, and Niccolò Capponi was appointed *gonfaloniere*. He was the son of Piero Capponi, the man who warned Charles VIII that Florence would ring her bells if he called his men to arms. In another moment of symbolism, rioters had broken into the Palazzo Vecchio and thrown a wooden bench out of one of the windows. It struck Michelangelo's *David* and broke off the left arm. Young Giorgio Vasari, only sixteen years old, gathered up the shattered pieces and took them to a nearby church. Those who look closely can still make out the marks of repair.

It was only thirty years since the death of Savonarola, and the fires of democracy and piety still burned in the hearts of his old supporters. A council was formed and it voted immediately to extend voting rights to most citizens. Once again books were banned, vanities frowned upon, and in a Tuscan echo of some of the reforming notions in the north, Jesus Christ was proclaimed King of the Florentines. The spirit of Savonarola hovered over the Piazza della Signoria. Carnivals and parades were outlawed and, united behind the cross, the Florentine republic sang hymns and offered prayers on its march into oblivion.

Christendom, by contrast, seemed irreparably broken. There had been schisms and heretics before, but no movement of dissent on such a wide scale and with real political clout behind it. The antics and machinations of the most outrageous of the fifteenth-century popes had left an indelible stain. By 1529 the Protestant German princes had evolved a doctrine known by its alliterative Latin shorthand, *cuius regio, eius religio*, whatever was the religion of the ruler, that was the religion of the state. Christendom had fractured on a broadly north/south axis, and Clement VII, the papacy, and the power of Rome were diminished.

In order to buttress a weakened pope, Florence and its new republican government were about to be humbled. Charles V had agreed the Treaty of Cambrai in 1529 with Francis I and the emperor had ordered a Spanish army of 40,000 troops to besiege Florence and restore it to the de' Medici. For such a massive and professional force, it should have been a simple operation, relatively easily achieved.

The Florentines knew what was coming, and for once were well prepared. They also knew that their republican independence was seriously threatened, and the leading families realised that they were in all probability fighting for their political survival. Michelangelo was in Florence in 1529, sent by Clement VII to work on the de' Medici chapel in the family church of San Lorenzo. The Signoria ordered him to lay down his chisels and take up the post of Supervisor of the City Walls. If Leonardo could design war machines and new sorts of fortification, so could his great rival.

Artillery was now seen as central to the success of any siege, and to the south of Florence lay hilly country offering good elevated sites for batteries of enemy cannon. Michelangelo immediately realised that the closest of these hills, where the old church of San Miniato al Monte stood, would have to become part of the defences and well protected. Built in 1015 over a much earlier church, San Miniato was much loved by the Florentines, and the Calimala, the Cloth Merchants' Guild, had lavished money and care on it over many centuries. The interior is filled with treasures: terracotta and medallions by Luca Della Robbia, a chapel designed by Michelozzo, and paintings by Piero de' Pollaiuolo.

Michelangelo ringed the church with a series of bastions, creating a small but robust fortress. Its walls were canted back and thick so that they could absorb cannon fire, and each bastion projected at the corners to permit enfilading fire along the line of the walls to cut down any attackers who got close. To protect the green, black and white marble of the bell-tower, Michelangelo had palliasses stuffed with straw suspended from the windows down all four sides and strapped into place. These proved very effective.

At night the Supervisor of the City Walls took refuge from the Spanish bombardment in the Medici tombs at San Lorenzo. But instead of cowering and clapping his hands over his ears, Michelangelo later claimed that he was working on the sculpture commissioned by Clement VII. Uncharitable historians have accused the great man of keeping all his political options open.

Giorgio Vasari painted a panorama of the great siege of 1529, and the Spanish army is shown encamped to the south of Florence, its tents and gun emplacements carpeting the hills. San Miniato al Monte and its bastions are clearly visible on the right of the picture. Just to the south of the church, a Spanish battery is firing into the city, but patriotically, Vasari paints several puffs of gun smoke coming from the heavily defended gates of Florence.

At first the Spanish could only dent the defences and it became clear that preparations for a long resistance had been well made. With the onset of winter, besiegers and besieged settled down for a drawn-out affair. In the rain, the cold and the shortening days, it was unlikely that any decisive move could be made. The deadlock was occasionally broken by the dash and daring of Francesco Ferrucci, one of the city's militia captains. He knew the ground around the walls, its swales and blind spots, much better than did the Spaniards, and under cover of darkness he and a company of troopers often spurred their ponies out of one of the city gates and broke through the enemy lines. Wherever the secret rendezvous had been arranged, Ferrucci and his men found cartloads of supplies waiting and rushed them back into the hungry city. The defence held through the spring of 1530 and on into the summer.

Nevertheless, Florence was beginning to suffer. Plague had been festering and the starving Popolo Minuto grew ever more restive. Ferrucci hatched a bold plan. With a large troop of soldiers at his back, he pierced the Spanish perimeter once again, but this time he was looking for men, not food. In the valley of the Arno and its towns there was no love for the plundering Spanish. Ferrucci began to recruit soldiers and cavalry and a substantial army started to form. Intelligence reached the prince of Orange, the Spanish commander, and he quickly set out in pursuit. In the hills near Pistoia, Ferrucci's volunteers were cut to pieces by Orange's grim veterans. And when news of the death of their dashing captain reached the city, morale collapsed. Ferrucci's desperate gamble had been a last throw of the dice.

Inside the walls, it became clear to the council that its mercenary captain, Malatesta Baglioni, had quietly done a deal with the Spanish. When the outraged citizens attempted to have the treacherous Baglioni arrested, he smiled and threatened to have his gunners turn their artillery on the city. The fight was lost; there seemed nothing else to do but negotiate the best terms possible for surrender.

Clement VII had asked that there be no massacre and as few recriminations as were sensible. He wanted his son, Alessandro, to rule a city and not a charnel house, a population grateful for the bread the de' Medici could provide and not seething with resentment at the brutalities of the Spanish.

Alessandro was not named *gonfaloniere*, and from 1530 onwards that office disappeared into history. He was known simply as Head of the Florentine Republic. After a time, the Signoria was dissolved, and in 1532 a band of de' Medici supporters climbed up the stairs to the top of the bell-tower of the Palazzo Vecchio. After cutting its thick ropes and pulling it over to the sill of the western window, they hurled the old city bell, the Vacca, down to the piazza below. It smashed into smithereens, which were then gathered up to be cast into medals commemorating the de' Medici. It was not just a turning moment in the glittering history of Florence. All over Tuscany the age of the communes was drawing to a close.

11

Grand Tuscany

Galileo Galilei was broke, embittered and desperate. By 1609 he was forty-five years old, the originator of scientific method, the inventor of several useful and important devices, a former university professor and, admittedly by his own measure, an entirely original thinker, a genius greater even than Leonardo da Vinci. And yet he was penniless, his inventions were exploited by others and his radical theories discredited by second-rate members of an outdated academic establishment.

When the servants of Christina, the Grand Duchess of Tuscany, contacted Galileo, his gloom lifted, the outlook suddenly brightening. De' Medici patronage had come to his rescue before. The Grand Duke, Ferdinando I, had employed Galileo as a tutor for his young son and heir, the fifteen-year-old Cosimo. The great astronomer hurried through the streets of Florence, crossed the Arno and presented himself at the Pitti Palace to learn what new commission awaited.

Unfortunately, Grand Duchess Christina had not fully grasped exactly what it was that Galileo was expert at. It turned out that she was under the unshakable impression that he was a skilled astrologer rather than an astronomer. Perhaps none of her staff had had the gumption to point out the difference. What mattered was that Duke Ferdinando was gravely ill and his wife wanted his horoscope cast. And without delay. Would he recover? What did the future hold? Galileo no doubt bit his tongue. With a mistress and three children to support, he needed money badly. If the grand duchess wanted a horoscope, she would get one.

Having quickly discovered what he needed to do, Galileo drew together a series of predictions based on the positions of the planets and the stars, and their conjunctions. It all looked promising, he declared; the future seemed assured, the grand duke would survive.

The duchess was reassured. All was well. And Ferdinando died a week later.

Galileo would have been both appalled and sad. The de' Medici had long been very important in his life and work. Born in Pisa and enrolled as a student at the university, his curiosity was awakened by a series of lectures given by Ostillion Ricci. He was the court mathematician appointed by Grand Duke Cosimo I and his appearance in Pisa the consequence of an insistence that the de' Medici dukes move out of Florence for part of the year. Wishing to unite Tuscany into a sovereign state and set aside the historic rivalries between its cities, Cosimo I in particular was anxious to show that his family were more than mere Florentines.

Lorenzo de' Medici had been at pains to revive the ancient university at Pisa and encouraged attendance from all over the republic. But his own humanist studies and innovative thinking had failed to percolate down the Arno. Mired in the ruts of the past, the University of Pisa was a stolid bastion of tradition, teaching the works of Aristotle in the medieval manner, insisting on rote-learning, unwilling to admit much that was new. When Galileo heard Ostillio Ricci talk about mathematics and abstract calculation, it was like a revelation, as if a whirlwind had blown away all the Aristotelian cobwebs.

The young student persuaded Ricci to introduce him to the work of Euclid and Archimedes, to help him understand how they had used a process of proof to establish a clear understanding of natural phenomena. At Pisa University the rigid old schoolmen clung to the simple and comforting truth that whatever Aristotle asserted was correct – because Aristotle asserted it. Galileo abandoned his studies and took himself off to Florence to continue to work with Ricci. And after a time, when a few favours had been brokered, the young contrarian managed to get himself appointed to the vacant chair of mathematics at Pisa in 1589. It had been vacant for many years for a good reason. The stipend was a miserly 60 florins a year.

It was at the 'Leaning Tower', the campanile of Pisa's great cathedral, that Galileo was said to have conducted one of the world's most famous scientific experiments. When he had an assistant stretch over the parapet and drop two objects of differing weight, his aim was to prove a basic law of motion. Galileo believed that the objects would fall at the same rate and consequently hit the ground at the same time. In fact, they did not, but the slight discrepancy has more to do with a difference in air resistance than weight.

Controversy swirled around Pisa, and when the Aristotelians claimed the results of Galileo's experiment as proof that they were correct, he countered with a conjecture that objects of differing weight would hit the ground at precisely the same moment in a vacuum. And from his experiments Galileo formulated a series of laws of motion; 'when falling, the final velocity of a body is proportionate to the time it has been falling'. What was most significant was this new method of working. Galileo had successfully applied mathematics to enquiries into the natural world. Through observation and experiment, phenomena could be measured in terms of time taken, distance travelled, weight and comparison. This approach produced recorded results and these could be compiled into a body of data, which then allowed general laws to be understood. It was the beginning of modern scientific method.

Far from suffering fools gladly, Galileo appears not to have suffered them at all. He was so forthright in his views and so forceful in presenting them, he quickly alienated his conservative colleagues at Pisa. De' Medici influence came to the rescue and helped him move on to Padua as professor of mathematics. The stipend was 500 florins a year, a great relief.

Galileo began to correspond with other innovative scientists, confiding in the German, Johannes Kepler, that he broadly accepted the theories of Nicolaus Copernicus. Almost a century before, Copernicus had used measurement and experiment to establish that the earth orbited the sun, and not the other way around. This was very dangerous territory.

Medieval astronomy had developed from a series of modifications of the ideas of Ptolemy, a Greek scientist and geographer who lived in the second century AD at Alexandria. He visualised the earth as a sphere suspended in space with the planets and stars revolving around it. This image chimed with biblical notions of the earth as the centre and focus of all creation. Addressing God, Psalm 93 asserts: 'Thou hast fixed the Earth immovable and firm.' And that was that.

As a mathematician, Copernicus could see that the conventional view caused all sorts of problems, and made the observable movements of the planets and stars very difficult to explain. However, if the earth revolved around the sun, then many of these mathematical problems would simply disappear. But Copernicus was well aware of how incendiary his views were, and he stipulated that they could be published only after he was safely dead.

When they did finally emerge, the Catholic Church was predictably outraged, but so too were the Protestants. Martin Luther thundered: 'People give ear to an upstart astrologer who strove to show that the Earth revolves, not the heavens or the firmament, the Sun and the Moon . . . This fool wishes to reverse the entire science of astronomy; but sacred scripture tells us that Joshua commanded the Sun to stand still and not the Earth.' Jean Calvin added: 'Who will venture to place the authority of Copernicus above that of the Holy Spirit?'

Galileo was not to be so cautious as Copernicus. In 1604 he made an astounding discovery. In the night sky he saw a new star. In the fixed cosmos of the conventional wisdom, this was simply impossible. According to Aristotle, and the Church's interpretation of Aristotle, God had created the universe complete in itself: nothing could be added and nothing could be lost. There was only one act of creation. But here was a new star, a nova, the first to be observed since 134 BC.

The discovery was, literally, earth-shattering. Aristotelians understood that their world was made up from four elements: earth, air, fire and water. The heavens were different and separate, composed of a single celestial and stable fifth element, which became known as the 'quintessence'. This simple fact invalidated Copernicus', Kepler's and Galileo's thinking. There could not be a new star: it had been there all the time. In point of fact the Aristotelians were correct, although they could not know it. A nova is a brightening, an existing star made visible by explosion and light travelling across the galaxy.

After he had failed to predict the death of Grand Duke Ferdinando I, Galileo's spirits were lifted by news of an invention developed in Holland by the optician, Hans Lippershey. The Italians christened it the 'Far-looker', the telescope. After he had tinkered with the basic arrangement of two lenses fixed in a tube as a means of magnification, Galileo produced an instrument ten times more powerful than Lippershey's. And on the first cloudless night after that the universe changed.

In the night sky what seemed to be a new solar system came suddenly into focus. The moon had craters, clouds and mountains, and Jupiter had its own orbiting moons, previously invisible to the naked eye. Galileo named them the *Sidera Medicea*, the 'Medici Stars'. Using smoked glass to screen out much of the glare, he could also make out the spots on the sun and what appeared to be storms of exploding gases. But the Church continued to be unimpressed. A German abbot dismissed the discoveries: 'I have read all the works of Aristotle and have found nothing resembling what you describe . . . Your spots on the Sun are defects of your optical instruments or eyes.'

When Galileo published his findings in *The Starry Messenger* in 1610, he announced: 'The astronomical language of the Bible is designed for the comprehension of the ignorant.' Dispute intensified and became very pointed. Galileo and his supporters attacked theologians and alienated many in the Church, especially in the Jesuit Order, who might otherwise have been sympathetic. Cardinal Maffeo Barberini warned the astronomer to confine his researches and views to mathematics and to abstract science. If he persisted in applying his theories to reordering the real world, there would be trouble. The writings of Copernicus were banned and Galileo was told not to promote them.

Under the protection of Grand Duke Cosimo II, the besieged astronomer continued his experiments and measurements. Having established that every projectile moved not in a straight line but a parabola (thereby greatly assisting the developing skills of artillery), Galileo first made the fundamental observation that the natural behaviour of a moving body was in fact to proceed in a straight line, unless it was acted upon by another force. For example gravity and the curvature of the earth compelled arrows and cannonballs to follow a parabola. If several different forces acted on a moving object at the same time, the effect was ultimately the same as if they had acted separately. Allied to this revolutionary idea, Galileo further argued that these and other laws of physics are likely to be the same in any system that is moving at a constant speed in a straight line regardless of velocity or direction. There could be no notion of absolute rest or absolute motion. In constructing these theories, Galileo built the framework both for Isaac Newton's laws of motion and Albert Einstein's general theory of relativity. A truly original and radical thinker, Galileo was a genius by any definition, perhaps the greatest Tuscan of them all.

The Church, on the other hand, believed him to be a heretic. After Cardinal Barberini had warned Galileo to restrict his writing and stay firmly in the abstract, the great astronomer sought and was granted permission to set down the arguments for and against the new ways of thinking about the world. Two characters debated in a new book. In favour of the heliocentric universe and the application of mathematics and physics to the heavens, Sagredo spoke eloquently. Against him, defending the Aristotelian view, was Simplicio. The names said it all, and when *The Dialogue Concerning the Two Chief World Systems* was published, Galileo was summoned to Rome.

In 1633 a jury of cardinals and canon lawyers convened a trial for heresy. It was no ritual set-piece or formula, but a matter of life and death. Only thirty years earlier another prominent intellectual, Giordano Bruno, had been burned at the stake for his espousal of the work and ideas of Hermes Trismegistus and other pagan mystics. Faced with the certainty of torture at the age of sixty-eight, and unwell, Galileo quickly recanted all he had argued with such passion since the 1580s. The sun revolved around the earth after all, and the laws of physics did not apply to the quintessence and the heavens. Supporters said that as he was discharged, Galileo muttered '*Eppur si muove*' ('But it does move'). Such bravery is unlikely.

The old man was sentenced to life imprisonment but this was commuted, on account of his age and infirmity, to house arrest in a villa to the south of Florence. Going blind and failing, Galileo nevertheless managed to design the first pendulum clock. Drawn by his assistant, Vincenzo Viviani, it was to prove much more accurate than its primitive forerunners.

Despite the charge of heresy and his subsequent confinement, Galileo lived long enough to see his ideas spread throughout Europe. Learned academies sprouted in Italy and many adopted his approach and experimental discipline. Before his death in 1642, Galileo's last manuscript was smuggled out of Italy and published in Holland.

The de' Medici were central to these world-changing events. Even if the grand dukes were unable to prevent Galileo being tried for heresy, they used their power to make much else possible – because they could recognise the significance of what he was doing. Having been great patrons of the arts, they became supporters of the scientific revolution. It was an extraordinary achievement for one family, and one which looked extremely unlikely in 1532 when Alessandro de' Medici took over the city of Florence and his thugs smashed its ancient bell.

Alessandro quickly acquired an unsavoury reputation for sexual rapacity, and no woman was safe, married or unmarried. But his rule and his behaviour were underpinned by the looming presence of the Spanish garrison in the Fortezza da Basso and the ease with which its guns could be trained on Florence. But it did not last. In 1537 Alessandro was murdered by his cousin, Lorenzino de' Medici, and the city teetered on the edge of chaos and subjugation. Francesco Guicciardini, the head of the civil service, and Cardinal Cibo knew that the Spanish would not hesitate to impose a severe colonial rule. They had done it elsewhere in Italy. And so they managed to keep Alessandro's murder a secret long enough to install young Cosimo de' Medici as the new duke. This apparent continuity (they were distant cousins) averted an uprising in favour of rival candidates from the other leading families, and kept the Spanish inside the *fortezza*.

Even though his succession was little more than a hurried expedient, the elevation of Cosimo to the dukedom turned out very well. In welcome contrast to the utterly dissolute Alessandro, the young man was something of a puritan and both hard-working and calculating. In order to secure Tuscany for his family, Cosimo knew that the new state had to be well organised and his rule absolutely ruthless. Following the precepts of Machiavelli, he suppressed the ambitions of the Strozzi, the Pazzi and other possible rivals, finally defeating them at the Battle of Montemurlo. Once a standing army had been recruited and a powerful fleet built, there were to be no other challenges to de' Medici power in Tuscany.

The money needed for these military initiatives was produced by an efficient and modern bureaucracy. To house it, Giorgio Vasari was commissioned to build the Uffizi, the 'Offices', between the Palazzo Vecchio and the Arno, and when the Emperor Charles V was at last persuaded (and paid) to withdraw the garrison from the Fortezza da Basso, a new barracks was built nearby. Cosimo hired Swiss Guards, but the Florentines still knew them as the fierce *Landsknechten* of the 1520s. The beautiful Loggia degli Lanzi, which abutted the barracks, recalls the local pronunciation.

Cosimo's wife, Eleanor of Toledo, disliked the draughty old medieval Palazzo Vecchio. Particularly irritating were the neighbours. Florence's famous lions were caged directly behind the palazzo in what is now known as the Via dei Leoni. Their dung must have been ripe enough, but it was their habit of roaring during the night which terrified the duchess. With her own money, she bought the unfinished palazzo across the Arno which belonged to Luca Pitti. When it was completed in 1560 and the gardens laid out behind (land formerly owned by the Bogoli family but now known as the Boboli Gardens for some reason), the ducal family moved in.

But there was an immediate problem. More building work was needed for what would become one of the most remarkable pieces of architecture in Florence, and yet something entirely hidden from sight. Used to living at the centre of civic power in the Palazzo Vecchio, Cosimo I found the location of the Pitti Palace unnerving. The Uffizi, the new seat of government, now lay on the other side of the Arno, some distance away from the ducal palace. Cosimo would have to make the journey most days, exposing himself to the very real risk of assassination or the attentions of an angry mob.

Giorgio Vasari solved the problem. In only five months, he had the Corridoio Vasariano created. A sealed passageway built on top of existing buildings or around them, it crossed the Arno on a new storey above the shops on the Ponte Vecchio and ran on an arcade by the bank of the river before finally connecting with the façade of the Uffizi. Entering from the grounds of the Pitti Palace, the duke could walk unhindered and unseen to his offices, and officials were able to travel in the opposite direction to attend him. Placed at intervals are barred round windows looking down on the streets below. Florentines called them 'Cosimo's eyes'. The millions who crowd around the Uffizi and the Ponte Vecchio each year have no idea what runs above their heads.

After the savagery of the Sack of Rome in 1527, the siege of Florence and the rampages of invading armies, Italy began to recover a little. The population rose and by 1600 Tuscany had become one of the most densely settled and farmed regions of Europe. Travellers noted in their journals that more of the hillsides had been terraced, new rows of vines were being planted and the production of woollen cloth doubled in Florence between 1527 and 1572. Banking also revived and the Florentine and Lucchese houses developed profitable relationships with the French monarchy and nobility.

Duke Cosimo I could afford to flex his economic and military muscles. In 1548 he bought Elba from Genoa not only to expand his territory and exploit the island's mineral resources, but also because he had ambitions to create a powerful navy. Lying so close to the Tuscan coast, Elba had a strategic value and it could no longer be allowed to remain in Genoese hands.

The fishing village of Livorno was developed out of all recognition. Since the Arno had begun to silt up, Pisa had found it increasingly difficult to maintain her role as a major Mediterranean port. Livorno had a coastal harbour and to stimulate its growth quickly the de' Medici dukes advertised a radically new proposal to allow all forms of religion to be tolerated there. Turks, North Africans, even English Roman Catholics set up businesses and made their lives in the new port. The largest Jewish community in Italy, growing to more than 22,000, established itself. By the early seventeenth century there was an English consul in residence and the ridiculous anglicisation of 'Leghorn' was coined. The port also became the centre of the European slave trade.

To the south, Siena had suffered the installation of an imperial garrison by Charles V, and in 1550 plans to build a large fortress in the city had been laid. To pay for construction, even heavier taxation would be levied on the citizens. It was too much to bear and in 1552 Piero Piccolomini arrived below the walls with a French army of liberation behind him. But his version of freedom lasted only two years before Charles V's brutal general, the marquis of Marignano, and his Florentine allies crushed resistance. Filippo Strozzi was amongst the defeated defenders. Three years later came the ultimate humiliation when Philip II of Spain sold Siena to Duke Cosimo, and the old republic was absorbed into the expanding state of Tuscany. But most saw it as final victory for Florence. It was also the moment for a defiant gesture. Two thousand stubborn Sienese marched out of their subjugated city to set up the Republic of Siena at Montalcino. It lasted for four years before history caught up.

By 1700 Siena had dwindled. Some historians reckon its population was as low as 6,000. Only Lucca avoided disappearing into de' Medici Tuscany, its high walls and its insignificance acting as a joint deterrent. In any case, Cosimo I was seeking grandeur by another route. In 1569 he purchased the title of Grand Duke of Tuscany from Pope Pius V. It allowed him to be addressed as *Vostra Altezza*, 'Your Highness', only one notch down from 'Your Royal Highness'. The de' Medici were moving up in the world.

The pretensions were not empty, however. Cosimo's distant cousin, Caterina, became Catherine de Medicis, Queen of France and an enormously influential figure. His granddaughter, Maria, became Marie de Medicis, also queen of France. But unfortunately there was decline closer to home. After 1580 Tuscany began to slide into recession. Both merchant banking and textiles began to fade, and as revenues decreased the shipbuilding programme slowed to a halt. Only the new port at Livorno appeared to flourish, occupying Pisa's old central position at the crossroads of the Mediterranean. Italy as a whole was becoming an exporter of raw materials and a net importer of finished goods – a reversal of the medieval economic traffic. With the continuing exploration and exploitation of the New World, the axis of trade shifted from the Mediterranean to the coast of the Atlantic. As merchants sought new markets in the west and manufacturing declined, Italy began to trade on her past.

When Grand Duke Ferdinando I died in 1609, so inconveniently for Galileo, and Cosimo II succeeded, visitors began to arrive. The papal jubilee of 1600 brought many to Rome, following the Via Francigena through Tuscany, and while the Eternal City would continue to draw pilgrims, those with more than religious motives for undertaking the rigours of travel began to spend time in Florence. The Grand Tour was getting under way.

Elizabethan intellectuals like Sir Philip Sidney in the 1570s and Sir Henry Wooton a decade later were the first to come from England. The Grand Tour was gradually seen as the culmination of a wealthy young gentleman's education. Having studied the classics at school and university, it was considered fitting for them to travel through Europe to Italy, the scene of all that ancient glory. Florence and then Siena became part of the itinerary, and when in 1705 Joseph Addison published his *Remarks on Several Parts of Italy*, a version of a guide book became available.

Grand Tourists began to record their impressions of a society and countryside that seemed preserved in aspic since the Renaissance. Even though many of the more articulate came in the eighteenth century rather than the seventeenth, they described a Tuscany which changed only very slowly. The Scottish writer, Tobias Smollett, watched a procession in Florence which might have walked out of the Middle Ages:

> I had occasion to see a procession, where all the noblesse of the city attended in their coaches, which filled the whole length of the great street called the Corso. It was the anniversary of a charitable institution in favour of poor maidens ... About two hundred of

these virgins walked in procession, two and two together, clothed in violet-coloured wide gowns, with white veils on their heads, and made a very classical appearance. They were preceded and followed by an irregular mob of penitents in sack-cloth, with lighted tapers, and monks carrying crucifixes, bawling and bellowing the litanies: but the great object was a figure of the Virgin Mary, as big as life, standing within a gilt frame, dressed in a gold stuff, with a large hoop, a great quantity of false jewels, her face painted and patched, and her hair frizzled and curled in the very extremity of the fashion. Very little regard had been paid to the image of our Saviour on the cross; but when his lady-mother appeared on the shoulders of three or four lusty friars, the whole populace fell on their knees in the dirt.

With the death of Cosimo II in 1621, the long reign of his son, Ferdinando II, began. He seemed generally uninterested in the business of government, leaving matters of state in the hands of the Dowager Grand Duchess Christina. Devout and gloomy, she allowed Florence to fill up with priests and nuns and encouraged the sort of ceremonies witnessed by Tobias Smollett. But Tuscany in the seventeenth century was at least stable, dominated by the Spanish, who established a military enclave on the coast at Orbetello known as the Presidi.

The de' Medici dynasty was beginning to fail, finding it difficult to produce male heirs. There were good reasons. Ferdinando II's mother was outraged at the degenerate moral tone of Florentine society and brandished a list of all the gay men working in the ducal bureaucracy. Her son took it and calmly added his own name.

Ferdinando appears to have been a cheerful eccentric. Impressed by the use of camels as pack animals, he introduced them to Tuscany and for several generations they were a common sight, plodding along the dusty highways. There is still a herd of 200 kept in a park near Pisa. Ferdinando's brother, Cardinal Leopoldo de' Medici, founded the Accademia del Cimento in 1657, basing its activities on the experimental techniques pioneered by Galileo. This was five years before the Royal Society was set up in London. And one of Galileo's assistants, Evangelista Torricelli, invented the barometer.

When Ferdinando died in 1670, the de' Medici dynasty began slowly to disintegrate. For the following fifty years Tuscany groaned under the rule of a succession of helpless gluttons, depressives,

obsessives and dissolutes kept afloat by the efficient bureaucracy
of the Uffizi. Grand Duke Cosimo III was educated by priests, and
observers noted a marked change in character:

> He is dominated by melancholy to an extraordinary degree, quite
> unlike his father. The Grand Duke is affable with everyone, as
> ready with a laugh as with a joke, whereas the Prince is never seen
> to smile. The people attribute this to an imperious and reserved
> disposition.

An advantageous marriage for Cosimo was seen as vital and
Ferdinando had worked hard to secure the hand of Marguerite-
Louise, the daughter of Gaston, Duke of Orléans, one of the greatest
French noblemen. On paper it looked an excellent dynastic match,
further cementing relations between the de' Medici and the French
royal family. In reality it was a disaster.

Imploring Louis XIV on her knees, Marguerite-Louise begged
not to be sent to Florence, which she saw as little more than an
impoverished backwater. She loved Charles of Lorraine, and was
appalled at the prospect of Cosimo de' Medici. Young Cosimo was
equally unenthusiastic. But eventually forced to it, Marguerite-Louise
arrived in Florence. Sumptuous wedding celebrations took place
around the sullen and unsmiling bride and groom. When they took
to their marriage bed, as they had to, Cosimo complained of illness
and slept. In the surprising way that the frequency and success or
failure of dynastic sex became a matter of public discussion, Princess
Sophia of Hanover evidently knew enough to report:

> He sleeps with his wife but once a week, and then under the
> supervision of a doctor who has him taken out of bed lest he should
> impair his health by staying there overlong.

The Bishop of Béziers was also well informed, noting that Cosimo
had only: 'couched with her three times . . . Every time he does not
go, he sends a valet to tell her not to wait up for him. The French
ladies . . . are much embarrassed because she is always sad . . . She
finds life here very strange.'

With the help of her French ladies, Marguerite-Louise took to
sleeping in different bedrooms in the vast Pitti Palace. If Cosimo felt

amorous, he first had to find his bride. To everyone's amazement, he appears to have caught up with her at least once and Marguerite-Louise became pregnant. Anna Maria Luisa was born in 1667, then a son, Ferdinando, and finally a spare heir in the shape of Gian Gastone in 1671. The grand duchess had gritted her teeth and done her dynastic duty, and soon after her last delivery she wrote to her husband: 'I declare that I can live with you no longer. I am the source of your unhappiness as you are the source of mine.'

In 1674 Marguerite-Louise was allowed to return to France and enter a convent near Paris. Apparently she had a riotous time, drinking and gambling. Still needing the financial support of Cosimo, she wrote demanding money. In one letter she added: 'There is not an hour or a day when I do not wish someone would hang you.'

The grand duke sank into a mire of misery and self-gratification. He ate vast meals, was often at prayer and began to take his unhappiness out on his fellow Tuscans. Capital punishment became common and was carried out in public; there were 2,000 executions in Florence in a single year. Anti-Semitism reared its head and the Jewish population of Livorno began to flee, further impoverishing the ducal exchequer. By 1700 the population of Florence had shrivelled to 42,000. There were derelict, half-ruined houses in many streets, and even outside the palazzi of the gentry, the signs of an economy in recession were obvious. Here is an observation from the English traveller, Samuel Sharp:

> At all the houses of the Nobles in Florence, you see an empty flask hanging out, to denote they sell wine by retail: this custom shocks an Englishman, as a practice very derogatory from their dignity, and he cannot but speak of it with surprise . . . The truth is that through all Italy, a great part of the rent for estates is paid in kind, which, joined with a certain exemption from the import on wine, granted to the nobles in Florence, has led them, I believe, into this seeming littleness . . .
>
> The Nobles are numerous and poor; indeed, for the same reason; that is to say, because all the children are noble, and because it is a fashion to divide their estates equally amongst them: This custom had a very good effect, when it was honourable to be engaged in commerce, as was the case when the trade of Europe was in a manner carried on by the Nobles of Florence, Venice and

Lombardy: Every son, by this article, improved his fortune, and enriched his country; but the discovery of the passage to the Indies, by the Cape of Good Hope, putting an end to this monopoly, and to the exorbitant gains attending it, commerce, by degrees, became contemptible, as it grew less profitable; and the Nobility, finding no resources beyond their pitiful incomes, became wretched, at least the greater part of them.

While Cosimo III guzzled his enormous meals in the Pitti Palace, the de' Medici spirit flickered briefly once more in his first-born son. In 1701 Ferdinando organised an exhibition of paintings, the first ever to be held in Florence, perhaps anywhere, at the Cloister of Santissima Annunziata. And he clearly had an eye for high quality, buying small pictures by great artists and preserving the work of Raphael and Fra Bartolommeo. A room in the Uffizi, La Tribuna, was decorated and hung with some of the best of the de' Medici collection. Classical sculpture was also displayed. But Ferdinando was destined to be another dynastic blind alley. A gay man with a long-term partner (a castrato known as Cecchino), he died young, before his father.

Tuscany was beginning to make a little money from visitors. Ferdinando's Tribune Gallery became a favourite destination in itself, but English travellers sometimes found the culture which had produced such great art rather uncongenial. Here are the impressions of Mrs Hester Thrale, a close friend of the equally irascible Dr Johnson:

> The clatter made here in the Piazza del Duomo – where you sit in your carriage at a coffee-house door and chat with your friends according to Italian custom, while one eats ice and another calls for lemonade, to while away the time after dinner – the noise made then and there, I say, is beyond endurance.
>
> Our Florentines have nothing on earth to do; yet a dozen fellows crying 'ciambelli' [little cakes] about the square, assisted by beggars, who lie upon the church steps and pray, or, rather, promise to pray, as loud as their lungs will let them, for the 'anime sante di purgatorio'; ballad singers meantime endeavouring to drown these clamours on their own, and gentlemen's servants disputing at the doors whose master shall first be served, ripping up the pedigrees of each to prove superior claims for a biscuit or macaroon – do

make such an intolerable clatter among them, that one cannot for one's life hear one another speak.

Meanwhile Cosimo III worried about the future of the de' Medici. Not only had Ferdinando died young, his sister, Anna Maria Luisa, had married a German prince with chronic syphilis. Gian Gastone was the only hope. But sadly, a forlorn one. Hugely obese, alcoholic and reclusive, he too turned out to be gay.

Undeterred, or perhaps unable to be deterred, Cosimo III sought a bride for his second son. Anna Maria Francesca of Saxe-Lauenberg was perfect, or at least available. A contemporary offered an unfortunate description: 'of enormous weight, immense self-will and no personal attractions.' The first meeting of the betrothed couple may only be imagined. After ten hilariously miserable years in his wife's draughty castle near Prague, Gian Gastone was allowed to return, heirless, to Florence. Cosimo III prayed hard for a miracle: '[He] had a machine in his own apartment whereon were fixed little images in silver of every saint in the calendar. The machine was made to turn so as to present in front the saint of the day, before which he continually performed his offices . . . He visited five or six churches every day.'

Despite all that mechanical devotion, Gian Gastone became grand duke in 1723. There was no alternative, heaven-sent or otherwise. After an initial burst of activity, he retreated to the Pitti Palace to lead a reclusive life of singular corruption. Spending many of his waking hours in bed, the grand duke surrounded himself with a large group of good-looking young men from the leading Florentine families, almost all of whom were by now impoverished. With some of these boys in bed beside him, Gian Gastone encouraged the others to dress up and have sex with each other for his titillation. As these squalid spectacles took place, he roared obscenities before falling noisily asleep. The young men were known as the Ruspanti, after the *ruspi*, the coins paid to them.

As the grand duke descended into ever more lurid depravities, and spent almost all his time in bed, Florentines began to believe he was dead. To scotch the rumours, Gian Gastone was heaved upright and into outdoor clothes. But as the carriage taking him through the city street and showing him to the populace began to rock a little, the grand duke started to vomit out of the windows. When it reached the

Porta del Prato, the location of the horse races, Gian Gastone had roused himself to watch; he revived and took to shouting obscene remarks to the gentry seated in the stands beside him. After a while and to general relief, he subsided into sleep and had to be carried back to the Pitti Palace in a litter. It was 1729, and eight long years later, Tuscany, Florence and Gian Gastone were at last put out of their misery when he died.

It was a sad end for the de' Medici and all that this remarkable family had achieved. But their legacy would in large part be preserved by the astuteness of the very last of the line. Anna Maria Luisa's will contained a crucial clause. On her death in 1743 she bequeathed 'the galleries, paintings, statues, libraries, jewels and other precious things . . . for the benefit of the people and for the inducement of the curiosity of foreigners, nothing shall be alienated or taken away from the capital or from the territories of the grand duchy'. This would be the saving and the making of Florence and Tuscany. The curiosity of foreigners was to become an industry, and Anna Maria Luisa's foresight a last but vital example of de' Medici acumen.

12

La Bella Toscana

The King and Queen of Great Britain and Ireland lived in Florence for ten years. Between 1774 and 1784, they held court in the Palazzo Guadagni, not far from the Pitti Palace. So popular was the queen that her many admirers knew her as the 'Queen of Hearts'. Her German accent may have grated a little, but her beauty and vitality charmed all who came to court. Sadly, the king grew increasingly unwell and on 30 January 1788, he died. As he lay in state, dressed in sumptuous royal robes, a crown on his head, a sceptre in one hand and a sword of state in the other, the king's brother said a requiem mass. He then declared to the mourners that he himself was now King of England, Scotland and Ireland. Cardinal Henry Stuart was now to be addressed as King Henry IX. God save the King!

All of these things happened. After his flight from the failed Jacobite rebellion in Britain in 1746, the man known to history as Bonnie Prince Charlie came to Rome, to the Palazzo Muti. As a Catholic prince, his best hope of support against the Hanoverian usurpers was from the pope and the kings of France and Spain. After the death of his father in 1766, Bonnie Prince Charlie became King Charles III. Despite the fact that his brother, Henry Stuart, was a cardinal, the exiled king could find little help in Rome. Forced to endure insults such as the pope's insistence that the royal arms of Britain be removed from above the gates of the Palazzo Muti, King Charles and his German queen, Louise de Stolberg-Gedern, left for Florence in 1774.

The British ambassador in Italy, Sir Horace Mann, was delighted. He lived in Florence, only a short distance from the Stuart court at the Palazzo Guadagni. He deployed his spies immediately. What the British government feared most was the establishment of a dynasty in exile, and if Charles III and Queen Louise were to have children, it meant that any opposition to the Hanoverians could readily find an alternative monarch. Servants were bribed by Mann's agents to rummage through the laundry baskets at the Palazzo Guadagni to report on whether or not Queen Louise was still menstruating.

She was. The royal couple loathed each other. In the embittered and febrile atmosphere of his court in exile, Charles had taken to drink, becoming an alcoholic. Like the appalling Gian Gastone, had also grown obese, becoming a belching, farting embarassment. Inevitably the young Queen Louise took lovers, and that worried Sir Horace Mann. A child by another man would almost certainly be presented as a legitimate Stuart heir. It had happened often enough with other dynasties. But the spies sorting through the laundry continued to report that all was well.

On 30 November 1780, the Palazzo Guadagni was the scene of an incendiary royal row. Having drunk even more than usual, King Charles was telling the great tale of his year as the Rebel Prince in Scotland and England. No doubt for the thousandth time. Perhaps Queen Louise passed a cutting remark, perhaps she interrupted at a dramatic moment. In any event, King Charles suddenly flew at her, attacking violently, trying to rape her, some said afterwards. A terrified Louise fled for sanctuary to a convent in the Via del Mandorlo. The King of Britain and Ireland was enraged, banged on the door and demanded to be let in to see his wife. The abbess refused, and Charles III stood in the street, screaming abuse.

It was all very embarrassing, and very sad. The grand duke had already called the Palazzo Guadagni a house of scandal and discouraged the Florentine nobility from having anything to do with the Stuart exiles. The charismatic young prince who had raised the clans at Glenfinnan, defeated one government army after another and reached within 100 miles of London had become an obese, violent drunkard shouting obscenities in the street. He left Florence and died soon after in Rome. Queen Louise and her lover, Count Alfieri of Piedmont, visited England and lived in Paris for a time. But by 1803 she was back in Florence, insisting on being addressed as 'Majesty' and that her servants leave the royal presence by walking backwards.

The eighteenth century saw many exotic visitors to Tuscany, and most were to pass through without much incident. Gone were the convulsions of the early sixteenth century, the divine rages of Michelangelo; gone was the independent spirit of the Florentines, and long gone was the ambition of its rulers and citizens. Tuscany began to doze in the late afternoon of its distinguished history. Even its destiny did not concern those who governed it.

When it became clear that the obscene Gian Gastone would father no heirs, a conference was convened in Vienna in 1731 to decide who would succeed. The grand duke was not invited nor were his views sought. The dominant European powers being France and Spain, the fate of Tuscany would be a matter for them. After a false start, Francis of Lorraine would be named as grand duke on Gian Gastone's death. Confusingly, this man with a French title was in the Austrian camp since he was betrothed to the great Maria Theresa, the heiress to the Habsburg dominions. Tuscany was to become part of the patchwork of European power politics, little more than a southern province of the Austrian Empire.

Soldiers known to the Florentines as 'Lorrainers', in reality Austrians, marched into the city in 1737 to replace the Spaniards. Based in the looming Fortezza da Basso, the Austrians began to take over Tuscany, systematically occupying key roles in the grand duchy's administration and showing scant respect for tradition. Most of the special holidays associated with the achievements of the de' Medici family were banned.

Grand Duke Francis I had little time for Tuscany. Having married Maria Theresa in 1736, he himself became Holy Roman Emperor in 1745. His remarkable wife was Archduchess of Austria, Queen of Hungary, Queen of Bohemia and the ruler of a scatter of lesser territories. The most powerful woman in Europe, energetic, ambitious and intelligent, she set about reforming the Austrian bureaucracy and army, laying the foundations of the Austro-Hungarian Empire. Francis I was said, by contrast, to be affable but idle, content to leave the affairs of state to his wife.

Tuscany required attention. After generations of de' Medici torpor, the grand duchy was badly in need of reorganisation. The legal system remained medieval in its labyrinthine intricacies; Florence alone had more than forty separate jurisdictions and courts, fourteen of which were still run by the major craft guilds even though several were defunct. These chaotic and confusing relics made policing and the pursuit of justice so difficult as to be almost impossible. Even if identified and accused, criminals still had the right of sanctuary on ecclesiastical property, and thousands sought it regularly. That meant churches were the habitual haunts of thieves and murderers rather than a place of resort and solace for their victims.

The Austrians at first paid little attention. Francis I sent Prince Craon to rule Tuscany in his stead, and society continued much as it had done: mannered, privileged and mired in its petty rituals. Here is Sir Horace Mann's description of a bizarre visit to the theatre in Florence in 1747:

> . . . went to the opera with the Princess Craon last night . . . I wish I could give you a description of her setting forth . . . When we thought all was ready to march, she sent Tozzoni into her room for twenty things. Amongst others, he brought her half a hood to hang over her whole face, to keep the air from striking it, and a monstrous fan, or little screen, made of linen, with a long handle, for a servant to carry at some distance before her, to prevent the air coming with too much force against the covering to her face. I was put into the coach with her, and was vastly afraid of hurting her, or squeezing her. I was heartily glad when we got to the theatre where, you know, she takes great precautions to arrive as the curtain draws up, as she pleases herself with the notion that it is done to do her honour . . .

On the death of Francis I in 1765, Tuscany at last attracted a talented grand duke. After an initial and frustrating five years of regency when his mother's powerful ministers ran the government, Leopold I set to work. Well and widely read, he was much influenced by the ideas of the European Enlightenment and aimed to put some of them into practice.

As a matter of urgency, the system of taxation was radically reformed and the privileges and exemptions enjoyed by the nobility and the Church were either abolished or reduced. Leopold had ambitious public works in mind and needed to find the money to pay for them. Protected by the blanket security of the Austrian Empire, he could save money by having no army or navy and he squeezed as much as he could out of the Church. Common land was sold off with the aim of making it more productive in private hands. And the craft guilds in all the Tuscan cities were simply abolished, thereby allowing much greater freedom and creating an unfettered urban labour market.

Talented administrators trained at the University of Pisa occupied the Uffizi and as the pace of reform quickened, the ramshackle fiscal system was much simplified. When local autonomies were systematically broken down, Tuscany began to emerge as a unified modern state. Under government sponsorship, irrigation schemes were dug, and especially in the Val di Chiana, drainage brought much more land into cultivation.

Where Leopold's reforms faltered was in the failure to improve the central institution of Tuscan farming, the *mezzadria*. A version of sharecropping, it developed in the Middle Ages and by the eighteenth century was common throughout Tuscany. In essence, a landowner rented a farm to a tenant not for cash but in return for half of the crops. As landlords spent more time at court in Florence or as absentees in the other cities, middlemen such as estate agents (in the original meaning of the term) became involved and the *mezzadria* grew increasingly corrupt and unattractive to both partners. That led to a drop in productivity and an unwillingness to improve the land, the barns, stables and houses on it. But the *mezzadria* was tenacious and it clung on in Tuscany until the middle of the twentieth century. It is the reason why the countryside looks so traditional even now. Small fields, old farm buildings and hedges, copses and dense woodland still remain, untouched by the gigantic machinery which has torn apart the landscape of many other European countries. The anachronism of the *mezzadria* has kept Tuscany beautiful.

While Leopold failed to reduce significantly the power and wealth of the Church and claw back some of the effects of all that de' Medici devotion and obsession, he did produce one enduring reform. Helped by the talented Lombard lawyer, Cesare Beccaria, the administrators in the Uffizi created a new legal system for Tuscany which was one of the most advanced in the world. Consistency and rationalism, proper rules of evidence, guidance for judges and much else were enshrined. And Tuscany was the first state to abolish the death penalty and the use of torture.

When Leopold's brother, Joseph, died in 1790, the throne of the Holy Roman Empire fell vacant and the grand duke also became an emperor. One of his first difficulties arose in France. In the aftermath of the revolution in 1789, Leopold's sister, Marie Antoinette, and her feckless husband, Louis XVI, found themselves in mortal danger. But before he could move to protect them, the new emperor himself died in 1792.

Ferdinando III had succeeded his father in 1790. The new grand duke was twenty-one, in no need of a regent, but like most of his family, more interested in matters Austro-Hungarian. In common with most major European dynasts, his gaze was firmly fixed on the epoch-changing events taking place in France. In 1796 Napoleon crossed the Alps at the head of the French Army of Italy, and marched into history. His dazzling talents and energy had a profound effect on Tuscany, and on one part of it in particular.

With a characteristically sweeping disregard for tradition, Napoleon dissolved the grand duchy and in 1801 created the kingdom of Etruria. In a round of dynastic musical chairs, the heir to the Bourbon duchy of Parma, Louis, was installed as king with a royal court in Florence, and the outgoing Ferdinando III was compensated with the territories of the archbishopric of Salzburg. When King Louis, or perhaps Luigi, of Etruria inconveniently died in 1803, Maria Louisa of Spain became queen regent in favour of their young son, Charles Louis. Four years later, the music stopped once more when Napoleon abolished the kingdom of Etruria and promised its rulers a new nation, the kingdom of Northern Lusitania, a bit of Portugal. Etruria was incorporated into France as three *departements*: Arno, Ombrone and Mediterranée. For the Tuscan farmworkers in the olive groves and vineyards, the men and women who planted each spring and harvested in the autumn, nothing much changed as the Emperor of France invented countries and his armies rumbled across the landscape of central Europe – well to the north.

When Napoleon was at last forced to abdicate in 1814, life did change for 11,380 Tuscans. It changed abruptly and radically for all of the inhabitants of the island of Elba when the deposed emperor landed in a British warship at Porto Ferraio in early May 1814. The terms of surrender had included the outright gift of the sovereignty of this part of Tuscany and also allowed Napoleon to bring with him 600 of his hard-bitten Old Guard and eighty faithful Polish cavalrymen. An annual pension of 2 million francs was promised but seems never to have been paid. On disembarkation, Napoleon was taken to his palace, and it was not Fontainebleau, the Tuileries, or Versailles but a dilapidated house known as the Old Mill.

If thoughts of *sic transit gloria* occurred to the man who had governed most of Europe only a year before, they were not permitted to linger. In a whirlwind of activity, Elba was utterly transformed, over a matter of months dragged from the Middle Ages into the modern world. Security was the first priority. Fearing assassination or kidnap, Napoleon commandeered a small makeshift fleet, seized and garrisoned the small neighbouring island of Pianosa, and 1,000 soldiers were deployed around Elba. Somewhat farcically, a cabinet of ministers was appointed, including General Drouot as Minister of War. Uniforms were ordered and a new flag run up. Its stripes were red and white, the colours of the de' Medici.

A brilliant administrator in the habit of dictating to a dozen secretaries at a time, sending out a stream of directives, requests and plans at an astonishing speed, Napoleon insisted on a completely new infrastructure for Elba; new roads were built, sewers and cesspits dug and streets swept and lit. The detail is awe-inspiring; where the seafront at Porto Ferraio afforded good views, benches should be placed. Elba had long depended on the extraction of her mineral resources, and to raise revenue quickly, Napoleon pre-sold the production of ore for 1815 in August 1814. Alternative industries were badly needed and 500 mulberry bushes were imported to feed silkworms and stimulate textile production. Schools, hospitals, a new cemetery and a theatre were built. The islanders must have gasped at the scale and speed of change.

Perhaps it was all a blind, rather than the reflex of a man driven by adrenalin and unable to live without such intensity. For all the time he was issuing decrees on Elba, the emperor was listening to reports from France. Refugees arrived on Elba every week and they told him how unpopular – and incompetent – Louis XVIII was and how badly army veterans were being treated – men who had fought for years for France. Disaffection was growing, and many hankered after the glory days of the recent past.

The British had posted a commissioner-keeper on Elba. Colonel Neil Campbell was instructed to keep an eye on Napoleon, intercept messages and letters and report on visitors. Still only forty-four years old, the deposed emperor was dangerous, still a threat. When Colonel Campbell made the mistake of taking a holiday, sailing to Livorno to spend time with his mistress, Napoleon did not hesitate. With only a thousand men and two cannon, he sailed for France to begin the extraordinary hundred days that would lead to Waterloo. Elba must have heaved a great sigh of relief.

After the fall of Napoleon and the Treaty of Vienna, the status quo was restored, at least nominally. Grand Duke Ferdinando III returned to Florence and, supported by the Austrians, resumed his rule of Tuscany. But in reality the ground had shifted under Europe's monarchies and aristocracies. The French Revolution and the convulsions which followed showed how the power of the popular will, interpreted and led by the middle classes, could turn the status quo on its head and allow Napoleon, a man from nowhere, to lead victorious armies right across Europe.

The political revolutions of the nineteenth century were fed and guided by industrial revolution. Led by the inventors and entrepreneurs of Britain, Europe began to change from an agrarian society, dispersed and traditionally conservative, to an urban culture, concentrated and often radical. In Italy the pace of industrialisation was slower. Landowners doggedly maintained the *mezzadria* system, believing it encouraged social cohesion, and the migration to the cities was most marked in Lombardy. By 1840 Britain had laid 2,390 kilometres of railway while Italy had managed only 20. Nobody was going anywhere fast. Nevertheless, the impulse for change began to grow, but just before it sparked political consequences, Tuscany became the scene of a quintessentially romantic episode, one which coloured how it is seen in the English-speaking world.

Percy Shelley eloped with the sixteen-year-old Mary Wollstonecraft Godwin in 1814 and spent most of his brief life with her in Tuscany. When the couple arrived in Florence in 1818, the great romantic poet was captivated:

> . . . the most beautiful city I ever saw. It is surrounded with cultivated hills and from the bridge which crosses the broad channel of the Arno, the view is the most animated and elegant I ever saw. You see three or four bridges – one apparently supported by Corinthian pillars, and see the white sails of the boats relieved by the deep green of the forest which comes to the water's edge, and the sloping hills covered with bright villas on every side. Domes and steeples rise on all sides, and the cleanliness is remarkably great.

Often unwell, Shelley was advised by his Pisan doctor to move to the countryside and he rented a beautiful woodland villa near Bagno di Lucca. Poems flowed, 'Ode to the West Wind', *Prometheus Unbound*, 'To a Skylark' and much else. And Mary Shelley was also inspired. Taking the stirring tale of Lucca's hero, Castruccio Castracani, she wrote a historical novel to add to her timeless classic, *Frankenstein*. In 1820 they moved to Pisa, where they were joined by George Gordon, Lord Byron and James Leigh-Hunt. When the noble lord dared to suggest that Venice was a more beautiful city, Shelley recorded his reply: 'Stand on the marble bridge, cast your eye if you are not dazzled on its river glowing as with fire, then follow the graceful curve of the palaces on the Lung' Arno till the arch is naved by the massy dungeon tower, forming in dark relief, and tell me if anything can surpass a sunset at Pisa.'

His passion for Pisa was short-lived and in 1822 Shelley and his family moved to an isolated house on the beach in the bay of Lerici in the Gulf of La Spezia, just to the north of the Tuscan border. They used a small schooner, the *Ariel*, to visit friends, and on a return trip from seeing Byron and Leigh-Hunt in Livorno, it sank in a sharp summer squall. Shelley, his friend Edward Williams and a young English boy were all drowned.

More than a week after the tragedy, the three bodies were washed ashore. In Shelley's pocket a copy of Keats' poems was found. Quarantine laws forbade burial in the English cemetery in Rome and Byron, Leigh-Hunt and Edward Trelawny built a pyre on the beach near Livorno. With offerings of salt, oil, wine and frankincense and the book of Keats' poems, they cremated Shelley. After the ceremony Byron dived into the sea and swam for many miles. Trelawny raked out the poet's heart and gave it to Mary. The romance and tragedy of it all fixed Tuscany as a near-sacred place for writers. Wordsworth came, then Tennyson. Dickens enjoyed Siena and Florence and 'the whole sweet valley of the Arno'.

Two years after Shelley's death, Leopold II succeeded to the grand duchy on the death of his father, Ferdinando III. His government appeared more tolerant; political as well as poetic exiles were allowed to settle in Tuscany and the press were permitted to publish without heavy censorship. Austrian military muscle remained, for the moment, in the background.

While it is essential to avoid the temptation to read history backwards, Leopold's relative liberalism looked to be too little and too late. Many middle-class intellectuals had begun to believe that a united Italy was not only a desirable political goal, but also achievable. Thousands joined a secret society known as the Carbonari, the 'Charcoal-burners', which was organised along the lines of freemasonry and inspired by the ideals of the French Revolution. In 1830 Giuseppe Mazzini joined a Tuscan cell of the Carbonari, and in the same year several uprisings flared in Modena, Parma and the Papal States. Their leaders planned to create the United Italian Provinces, but the pope had other ideas, not hesitating to invite urgent Austrian intervention. The powerful chancellor, Franz Metternich, dismissed the aspirations of the Carbonari, remarking that Italy was nothing more than 'a geographical expression'. Austrian dragoons ruthlessly crushed the insurrections.

Mazzini fled to Marseilles, where he lived in the apartments of Giudetta Bellerio Sidoli, a beautiful Modenese widow who became his lover and steadfast supporter. With the suppression of the Carbonari, Mazzini founded La Giovine Italia, 'The Young Italy', and showed tremendous skill in publicising and idealising the new movement. By 1833 Young Italy may have recruited as many as 60,000 members. One of these was an absolutely remarkable man. In 1833 a sea-captain called Giuseppe Garibaldi pledged his life to the cause of Italian unification, and after several false starts and reverses, he, more than any other, succeeded in bringing it about.

Only one other figure could credibly claim to match Garibaldi in his efforts at unity. But Camillo Benso (Count Cavour, the Prime Minister of Piedmont) and Garibaldi came to loathe each other. Alone amongst the Italian states, the kingdom of Piedmont, Savoy and Sardinia had escaped Austrian domination, and Cavour brilliantly deployed his international connections as well as his country's geographical position between France and Austria to negotiate support for his policies. But in one phase of diplomacy he handed over Nice to the French in return for concessions in Lombardy. Nice/Nizza, had been a thoroughly Italian city and the birthplace of Garibaldi. He never forgave Cavour.

In the early 1840s Grand Duke Leopold sensed the rumblings of discontent. Demands for a constitution and a widening of the franchise grew louder in Tuscany. Dissent spilled onto the streets of Livorno in the summer of 1845 and there was serious rioting, and again in 1846. Leopold reacted with a programme of reforms, but the more dynamic impulse for change was the election of Pope

Pius IX, thought to be a progressive. In the same year, 1847, Barone Bettino Ricasoli founded a pro-unification journal in Florence, *La Patria*, and used it as a vehicle for arguing for more far-reaching measures. A colourful, creative figure, Ricasoli accepted the revived office of *gonfaloniere*, but later resigned when the grand duke refused to devolve more power.

Across Europe, 1848 saw major revolutions and rapid constitutional change elsewhere. A flood-tide seemed to be running. The grand duke granted Tuscany a written constitution and the Marchese Cosimo Ridolfi was appointed prime minister. On 26 June the first Tuscan parliament was convened in the Palazzo Vecchio – and events began quickly to spiral out of control. Troops had been sent to support the Piedmontese army in Lombardy as they confronted the Austrians, and when news of defeat reached Florence, there were serious disturbances. Ridolfi resigned, but riots continued to break out in Livorno. The more radical democratic party came to power under Francesco Guerazzi and Domenico Montanelli. Proposals for a central Italian kingdom to be ruled by Leopold failed to reassure the grand duke, and as power ebbed away he panicked. Having fled first to Siena, then to Porto San Stefano and finally to Gaeta, near Naples, he covertly contacted the Austrians.

After they had occupied Livorno and Lucca, Leopold thought it safe to return to Florence. In 1850 he agreed to an indefinite occupation by 10,000 Austrian troops and two years later revoked the Tuscan constitution. It was all in vain. Events would quickly catch up with Grand Duke Leopold.

The 1850s saw an uneasy peace. Count Cavour realised that the Piedmontese could not expel the Austrians from Italy without the help of powerful external allies. He courted the French and the British, even to the extent of sending soldiers to fight in the Crimean War in 1855. But Piedmont was ignored, and while rioting flared sporadically in the cities in the centre and north and Mazzini plotted and wrote from exile in London, there seemed to be political stalemate.

As often, a random act by an individual changed the landscape. In early 1858 an Italian nationalist, Felice Orsini, attempted to assassinate Napoleon III, the French emperor. But instead of pleading for mercy from his prison cell, Orsini wrote an impassioned letter to his intended victim, urging him to help Italy gain its freedom. Perhaps Orsini knew that the emperor had been a member of the

Carbonari as a young man; perhaps he was very eloquent. In any event, Napoleon became convinced that he should ally France with Piedmont against the Austrians. Cavour seized the opportunity and an agreement was struck.

At the battles of Magenta and Solferino (both commemorated by street names in a thousand Italian towns and cities), the allies triumphed and northern Italy was suddenly there for the taking. And then Napoleon III promptly double-crossed Cavour and negotiated a separate peace with the Austrians. This was a turning moment. The Piedmontese knew that the popular will for unification was strong in the central Italian states, including Tuscany, and Cavour and his king, Victor Emmanuel II, decided to press on alone. And they succeeded. By December 1859 Parma, Modena, many of the northern and eastern cities of the Papal States and Tuscany had all joined the United Provinces of Central Italy. Plebiscites had been held and overwhelming majorities recorded everywhere. As Tuscan Minister of the Interior, Barone Ricasoli had been a key player in this dramatic sweep, even engineering the bloodless exit of Grand Duke Leopold. He fled to Bologna and then to Austria. Abdicating in favour of his son, Ferdinando IV, he hoped to see his family restored to the Pitti Palace after all this unpleasantness had died down. But Ferdinando was never to reign.

The brief war of 1859 left Italy divided in four: Venice was still in the hands of the Austrians, there was the new kingdom under Victor Emmanuel, the Papal States under an intransigent pope and the kingdom of Naples and Sicily in the south. There could have been deadlock unless the momentum of unification were maintained. Mazzini saw the Papal States as the most stubborn blockage and advocated simply marching south to overrun them and establish the capital of Italy in Rome. But Cavour knew that worldwide Catholic opinion might mobilise behind the pope and oppose the disappearance of the ancient Patrimony of St Peter. Enter Giuseppe Garibaldi.

Having spent many years fighting in the liberation struggles of South America, he was both battle-hardened and a charismatic leader. Cavour was nervous. With a cadre of a thousand volunteers and as deputy for Nice/Nizza in the Piedmontese parliament, Garibaldi was desperate to win back his native city for the new nation. Cavour knew that France could not be alienated if he wanted them to turn a blind eye to the takeover of the Papal States. Why not a bold stroke? Cavour suggested that Garibaldi and his volunteers mount an expedition to Sicily. There had been riots in Messina and Palermo and if Garibaldi could harness public sentiment, he might sweep the Neapolitan monarchy aside and bring the south into Italy. The strength of public sentiment was debatable. Some Sicilians had little idea of what Italy might mean exactly, some thought La Talia was the name of the Queen of Piedmont. Somehow Garibaldi was persuaded. Perhaps the scale and daring of the expedition appealed. Garibaldi was a romantic, eccentric figure. To take his seat amongst the sober and frock-coated fellow deputies at the Piedmontese parliament he had turned up in a poncho and a sombrero.

With only a small corps of volunteers, Garibaldi set sail, and was immediately successful. His 'Thousand', I Mille, faced a well dug-in force of 1,500 on the hill of Calatafimi in the west of Sicily. Garibaldi is said to have turned to his lieutenant, *'Nino Bixio, qui si fa L'Italia o si muore'*, 'Nino Bixio, here we will either make Italy or die'. Charging uphill with bayonets fixed, they made it, overrunning the small Sicilian force and beginning an extraordinary campaign, winning a string of victories as they marched through Sicily, crossed the Straits of Messina and made their way north. The army of liberation had swollen to 24,000 and Garibaldi was determined to take Rome. Cavour was anxious that he did not, and to forestall the juggernaut, he engineered an epoch-making meeting.

The Piedmontese army, led by King Victor Emmanuel, hurriedly marched south, annexing most of the rest of the Papal States but carefully avoiding Rome. At Teano, north of Naples, his men met Garibaldi's volunteers. The masters of the north linked with the masters of the south. When the Piedmontese approached, no-one knew what would happen. Garibaldi spurred his horse. And when this remarkable soldier and genuine patriot met Victor Emmanuel II, he addressed him as the King of Italy and they shook hands. With that greeting, all of the dramatic conquests in the south were passed to the new king. On 7 November 1860 the two men rode into Naples side by side and in triumph. Garibaldi refused to accept any reward, office or title for his services and immediately retired to the rocky island of Caprera in the Tyrrhenian Sea to become a farmer. Italy was born, and the grand duchy of Tuscany had ceased to exist.

The first parliament of the incomplete state met in Turin, the Piedmontese capital, on 18 February 1861 and a week later formally proclaimed Victor Emmanuel II as king. Garibaldi's handshake had made a monarch and his kingdom. But it was a bitter-sweet moment. The other principal architect of unification was dying. Camillo Benso, Count Cavour, had only three months to live, but at least he saw his life's work rewarded. At the end he is said to have said: 'Italy is made. All is safe.'

Barone Bettino Ricasoli became in effect the first Prime Minister of Italy, the first to be elected and endorsed by the new parliament. Rome had been declared the capital city of the kingdom but it still remained outside it, in the stubborn hands of Pius IX, and there was a large French garrison at Civitavecchia on hand to see that it stayed there. Ricasoli began negotiations, offering a substantial cash settlement for the appropriation of church lands, and later, a convention to agree the fate of other properties. The pope was not interested.

Only a year after his appointment, Ricasoli began a long and frustrating Italian tradition of short terms of political office by resigning. Urbano Rattazzi had been plotting against the aristocratic Tuscan, who appears to have seen the dirty business of political survival as somewhat beneath his dignity. As the *barone* made his way home to Castel di Brolio in the Chianti hills, another melancholy traveller was leaving Tuscany behind for the last time.

Robert Browning had eloped to Pisa and then moved to Florence in 1846 with his sickly wife, Elizabeth Barrett Browning. The tyrannical Mr Barrett had refused to allow any of his children to marry and the lovers were forced to flee abroad just as Percy and Mary Shelley had done. Elizabeth's health improved immediately and Robert remarked that a glass or two of good Chianti was a much more effective balm than a draught of laudanum, and his wife adored their new home:

> The city lies along the ample vale,
> Cathedral, tower and palace, piazza and street,
> The river trailing like a silver cord
> Through all.

Elizabeth's poetry was highly regarded in Britain and on the death of Wordsworth in 1850, it was probably only gender which prevented her from becoming the next poet laureate. Both Brownings were popular writers and back home their life in Tuscany became a famous idyll. Elizabeth was a fervent supporter of Italian unification and her collection of poems named after their house in Florence, *Casa Guidi Windows*, was occasionally unequivocally political. But her most fluent and pungent passages celebrated the beauties of the city and the landscape:

> I found a house at Florence on the hill
> Of Bellosguardo. 'Tis a tower which keeps
> A post of double observation o'er
> The valley of the Arno (holding as a hand
> The outspread city) straight towards Fiesole
> And Mount Morello and the setting sun,
> The Vallombrosan mountains opposite,
> Which sunrise fills as full as crystal cups
> Turned red to the brim because their wine is red.
> No sun could die nor yet be born unseen
> By dwellers at my villa.

Florentines understood something of the effect well-known writers could have and with the coming of the railways (eventually Italy built some) and a new ease of travel, tourism began to develop significantly amongst the better-off. Tuscany became an attractive destination. When Elizabeth died in 1861, the Commune of Florence erected an affectionate plaque on the Casa Guidi:

> Here wrote and died
> Elizabeth Barrett Browning
> who in her woman's heart blended
> learning and the spirit of poetry
> and made of her verse a ring of gold
> joining together Italy and England.
> This memorial was placed here
> by grateful Florence
> 1861.

The question of the annexation of papal Rome rumbled on through the 1860s, and when Barone Ricasoli became prime minister for the second time, at least he could negotiate in more familiar surroundings. In 1866 Florence's hour of pre-eminence arrived when the capital of Italy was moved there and the parliament sat in the Palazzo Vecchio.

Turin was not pleased, and as the king hurriedly left the city there was rioting.

Further to the east there was war. Italian soldiers were marching into battle with the Austrians. It was a scrappy campaign. Giuseppe Garibaldi came back from retirement, led his romantically named 'Hunters of the Alps' towards Trento to remove the area from the clutches of the enemy, and scored the only Italian success. But defeat elsewhere did not prevent the absorption of Venice into the new kingdom. Once again external factors weighed in Italy's favour. The Austrians were also at war with Prussia and overstretch caused them to lose their grip on the Veneto. There was a plebiscite when, apparently, only sixty-nine Venetians were recorded as voting against the extinction of their ancient republic. Perhaps there was a little ballot-rigging, perhaps some coercion, almost certainly some questionable arithmetic.

Barone Ricasoli resigned yet again, his premiership lasting less than a year, and was once more supplanted by Urbano Rattazzi. But European events were overtaking domestic political squabbles. When the Franco-Prussian War began in 1870 and the French suffered a calamitous defeat at Sedan, the temporal independence of the papacy and the protection of the Patrimony of St Peter fell far down the list of priorities. The French garrison was withdrawn and Rome lay almost defenceless. Even at that point Pius IX still insisted in deploying his tiny force of papal troops to defy the approaching Italian army. Before he was forced to concede the inevitable, on 20 September, fifty-three Italian soldiers and nineteen men from the papal forces had to be killed. It was a disgraceful episode. After a plebiscite had been held on 9 October, Rome and Lazio became part of the kingdom of Italy. In 1871 the parliament moved from Florence, and Italy at last extended approximately to its modern frontiers.

A central difficulty for the new kingdom was that so few of its subjects spoke Italian. It has been estimated that only 2.5 per cent spoke the language in 1860 and almost all of those were concentrated in Tuscany and Rome. The vast majority either spoke dialects related to Italian or different languages entirely. Many Piedmontese, including King Victor Emmanuel II, had French or Provençal as a first language. In the south, Greek had survived in large pockets since the Byzantine invasions of the eighth century, and Sardinian was not intelligible to Italians. When Count Cavour rose to speak in the first parliament of 1861, it was said that his command of Italian was hesitant.

These wide regional differences have survived into the twenty-first century. Dialect and ancient local allegiances are closely linked. Venetians have been Venetians much longer than they have been Italians and their language (many would see the use of the word 'dialect' as an insult) of Veneziano is a daily reminder of local pride and a distinguished and independent history. The same could be said for Milanese, Torinese, Calabrese and many other groups.

In his excellent history of Italy, Christopher Duggan produced a list of variations on two everyday words to show that these regional differences are not mere variations:

	Thursday	*Boy/Child*
Italian	Giovedì	Raggazo/Bambino
Tuscan	Zovedi	Bimbo
Piedmont	Gioves	Cit
Liguria	Zogia	Matotu
Lombardy	Giuedi	Bagai
Veneto	Zioba	Putelo
Friuli	Ioibe	Frut
Emilia Romagna	Zobia	Puten
Lazio	Giovedi	Regazzino
Abruzzo	Giuveddi	Quatraro
Campania	Iueri	Guaglione
Calabria	Iovi	Pedi
Sicily	Ioviri	Carusu/Picciottu
Sardinia	Iovia	Pizzinnu

As in Germany, Italian politicians longed to incorporate all communities who spoke a version of Italian or who thought of themselves historically as Italians. Known as Italia Irredenta, 'Unredeemed Italy', these included Nice, Malta, parts of the Dalmatian coast, Corsica and the Istrian peninsula.

Not every Italian politician dreamed of expansion. After Barone Bettino Ricasoli had resigned for a second time, he was rarely seen in parliament, speaking on only a handful of occasions between 1866 and his death in 1880. He preferred to spend most of his time at the beautiful Castel di Brolio in the Chianti hills. And he was not wasting it.

To many, Chianti means not hills but wine, and the image is of a pot-bellied, dark green bottle with its bottom half wrapped in a straw covering. This was largely the invention of Barone Ricasoli. Chianti wine had existed long before and been the subject of a grand ducal decree. In 1716 Cosimo III made history by defining the first-ever area of production for a particular wine. Chianti Storico included only the vineyards around the towns of Greve, Gaiole, Radda and Castellina in Chianti. Wine made outside the designated area could not be called Chianti. Ricasoli not only expanded production but made the wine world-famous.

After a period of pleasant experimentation, the Barone hit on the classic Chianti mix of grape types: 70 per cent Sangiovese, 15 per cent Canaiolo and 15 per cent Malvasia Bianca, an aromatic white grape of Greek origin. He also made mandatory the traditional *governo* method of wine-making. This involves some grapes being kept back from the harvest and allowed to dry and sweeten a little before being added to the main body of the wine when fermentation has finished. It imparts a softer and rounder finish and allows Chianti to be drunk young.

Ricasoli was also inspired when it came to marketing. Once the formula for the wine was right, he concentrated on presentation, something entirely new in Italy. Local women from Castel di Brolio wove straw liners to fit around the *strapeso*, the dark green bottle, to make it look somehow authentic and pleasingly rustic. Ricasoli then took his newly packaged product to the great Paris Exhibition of 1878, where it created a sensation. And an industry was born.

In 1924 the defined production area of Chianti Storico was doubled to create Chianti Classico and the symbol of the *gallo nero*, the 'black cockerel', first appeared on the neck of the bottles. It had been the badge of the medieval Chianti League, a string of Florentine fortresses at Radda, Castellina and Gaiole which guarded the frontier with Siena. The straw liner has mostly passed into cliché and history, but the wine remains wonderful, especially at Castel di Brolio, and is best drunk on a summer's evening in the Chianti hills.

Francesco Crispi had refused to join Barone Ricasoli's cabinet in 1866. A deputy elected in the south, from an Albanian-speaking family (a dialect known as Arberesh) and one of Garibaldi's Thousand, he became a dominant figure in Italian politics in the last quarter of the nineteenth century. It was an immensely difficult time, a tortured and unhappy birth for the new nation. As Minister of the Interior, Foreign Minister and Prime Minister, Crispi had constantly to contend with the antagonism of the papacy and the fact that Pius IX had forbidden any Catholic involvement in the politics of a state he considered to be illegitimate. Catholics made up the vast majority and they were not allowed to vote or stand for election. Many ignored the pope, but voter turnout was chronically low and there persisted a strong sense that the new state could not be fully representative. Banking scandals and the involvement of corrupt deputies in fiscal legislation passing through the national parliament quickly devalued much that Garibaldi and Cavour had achieved.

Francesco Crispi was tainted by the scandals and banking collapses but refused to resign. And he even managed to survive an astonishing challenge to the validity of his marriage. Parliamentary opponents had discovered that he was a bigamist: he had married in 1878 while his wife from a previous marriage in 1853 was still alive. A convoluted process of extrication and dubious interpretation of the law (something which has become all too familiar in Italian politics) began. In a hilarious judgement, the courts revealed that Crispi had in fact been a serial bigamist, but that that actually had the effect of exonerating him from the most recent charges. It appeared that when he married in 1853, he was at that time actually married to another woman. That meant that the second marriage was invalid – because Crispi was a bigamist, at that time. But by 1878, when he married his third wife, his very first wife had died and that therefore meant that he was not a married man. So, technically, he was a bigamist in 1853 but not in 1878.

Italian politics was less complicated but equally contradictory, and uncertain. Crispi believed that if Italy could fight a successful war, win an empire, be seen to act on the world stage as a modern nation amongst other nations, then that would foster unity and a sense of common identity at home. In the nineteenth-century scramble to grab territory in Africa, Italy had belatedly claimed Eritrea and Somalia. Bordering both colonies to the west was the huge and independent empire of Abyssinia. Crispi negotiated a treaty relationship and a document was drafted and signed by the Emperor Menelik II which would designate Abyssinia as an Italian protectorate. Without the inconvenience and expense of military conquest, a large swathe of Africa could be coloured Italian and stand comparison with the British and French colonies. Except that it didn't work. Because of a mistranslation in the text of the treaty, Emperor Menelik did not in fact sign over his country into Italy's keeping. Crispi felt humiliated, and when an opportunity arose, he vowed to redress the embarrassment.

It arose in 1896. Led by General Oreste Baratieri, 18,000 Italian soldiers invaded Abyssinia and sought to sweep away the medieval host summoned by the Emperor Menelik. Fully armed and with fifty-six artillery pieces, three brigades confronted approximately 100,000 Abyssinian tribesmen, most of whom carried spears. They met at Adwa, and after a series of charges, the Italian army was routed. More than 7,000 were killed, another 1,000 wounded and the rest fled eastwards in headlong retreat. The shame was almost unendurable as the world first gasped and then laughed, and the defeat at Adwa spelled the end of Francesco Crispi's career.

The year 1896 also ushered in an age of growth and achievement for the Italian economy. The date is of course coincidental, but between the botched expedition to Abyssinia and 1914, prosperity began to blossom, especially in northern Italy. Famous companies and brands such as Fiat, Lancia, Alfa, Olivetti and Pirelli were founded, most of them in Lombardy. In the south the agrarian economy ground on eternally and most people continued to hover around the margins of subsistence. In Tuscany the *mezzadria* ensured stability, even tranquility, but by the 1880s Florence had conceded her pre-eminence in banking to Milan.

Tuscany's cultural role remained undiminished. In 1858, in Lucca, Giacomo Puccini was born. His family was steeped in music and its traditions, having been virtually hereditary organists at the Lucchese cathedral of San Martino, and Puccini showed signs of early talent, in at least two directions. Finding himself short of cash, the young man stole and sold several organ pipes from the village church where he accompanied the services but was a good enough musician to alter the harmonies so that no-one would notice that they were missing. Described as 'possibly the least likeable of all the major composers', Giacomo seemed to his contemparies a self-centred and amoral man.

After leaving the Milan Conservatoire, the young Puccini entered a competition for new one-act operas. Because the score was illegible, his entry, a piece called *Le Villi*, 'The Witches', did not win, but when he played the music at a party, a very important person was listening. Giulio Ricordi ran a hugely successful music publishing business which owned the rights to most of the output of the best of Italian composers: Rossini, Donizetti, Bellini and Verdi. When he heard Puccini play his own work on the piano, Ricordi immediately recognised a great talent in the making and offered to pay him a monthly retainer (as a loan) until his first success came – which took nine years. It was an act of extraordinary faith and one which repaid Ricordi many times over.

Premiered in 1889, *Edgar* repaid no-one. Although it was a flop, his first full-length opera taught Puccini a vital lesson. Almost as much as the quality of the music, a good and credible libretto mattered very much. For most of the rest of his career, he took great care to find the most suitable stories around which he could write memorable scores. In fact, almost all of his great operas had already existed as popular theatre, sometimes with the same title.

Meanwhile Puccini was busy making his life the stuff of melodrama. He seduced Elvira, the wife of a school friend, and they lived together for many years, before marrying in 1904. Puccini was often unfaithful and Elvira became pathologically jealous. Suspecting their maid, Doria Manfredi, of having an affair with her husband, she drove her out of the house, calling her a tart, a slut and a whore. Not content with that, Elvira hounded Doria around her village until the sixteen-year-old was finally driven to take poison. Her brother was determined to clear her name and there followed a scandalous trial and sensational publicity. Puccini fled to Paris and a judge sentenced his wife to a prison term. As the case went to appeal, Elvira bought some time and her husband finally persuaded her that Doria's family should be bought off. Tuscany had long been tolerant of the behaviour of its greatest artists and Puccini's popularity was undimmed.

What promoted a settlement in this sordid affair was *Manon Lescaut*. Puccini's second opera was a huge and very lucrative success. It opened in 1893 and established a familiar pattern. The critics panned the opera while the audiences loved it. And unlike many other composers, Puccini had repeated commercial triumphs: *La Bohème*, *Tosca*, *Madama Butterfly*, *La Fanciulla del West* and *Turandot*. The critics hated them all. At the Paris premiere of *Tosca* in 1903, the French composer Fauré wrote:

At the very beginning of September there will be an important premiere at the Opera-Comique; important because of the personality of Sardou, the librettist, and the bizarre school of music to which the composer of the music belongs, Puccini. They consist of three or four fellows who have conjured up a neo-Italian art which is easily the most miserable thing in existence; a kind of soup, where every style from every country gets all mixed up. And everywhere, alas! they are welcomed with open arms.

All of Puccini's operas were distressingly popular, partly because all contain memorable arias, all of which have kept their appeal through successive generations.

During his lifetime Puccini made a great deal of money and lived like a playboy. But one biographer has detected a fundamental sadness behind all the conspicuous consumption: '[his] melancholia demanded relief in violent sex, slaughtering birds and driving high-powered cars at reckless speed'.

Puccini died in 1924, having failed to complete his last work, *Turandot*. Diagnosed with throat cancer after a lifetime of chain-smoking, and knowing he might die, he asked his friend, Arturo Toscanini, the great conductor, to make sure it was finished by another composer. For the premiere at La Scala in Milan, Franco Alfano had written the last duet – but it was not played. At exactly the place where Puccini had been forced to stop work, Toscanini ended the performance, laid down his baton and turned to the audience: 'The opera ends here because at this point the maestro died.'

The memorial service was held in the Duomo in Milan. Toscanini conducted the orchestra of La Scala and the funeral oration was given by 'Il Duce', Benito Mussolini, the recently appointed Prime Minister of Italy. His rise had been meteoric.

After the departure of Crispi in 1896, Italian politics had been dominated by Giovanni Giolitti, and while the economy surged in concert with the rest of Europe and America, he found it difficult to control domestic turbulence. In 1900 King Umberto I had been assassinated by an anarchist and several cities suffered chronic bouts of rioting. Italy had seen a significant rise in very welcome foreign earnings from tourism, especially in Rome and Tuscany and these regular disturbances were bad for business. Florence itself became the centre for a new and vigorous version of nationalism. Through articles in newspapers and journals, a group of young Tuscans began to attack the growth of socialism in Italy, asserting that the nation needed to make itself strong through individual sacrifice. War would achieve this, and at a conference held in Florence in 1910, many advocated victory in war as a means of galvanising the new nation. These impulses would in time nourish the growth of Fascism.

In 1915 Italy entered the First World War on the side of Britain and France. One of the most vocal advocates of involvement had been Benito Mussolini, at that time a newspaper editor in Milan. 'How could Italians be inert spectators of this tremendous drama?' he argued. Five million young men were conscripted and more than 600,000 perished in the fighting against the Austrians in the northeast. Discipline was extremely harsh, with execution by decimation carried out when general insubordination arose. Between 1915 and 1919, 300,000 soldiers were court-martialled. And yet, in difficult terrain, badly equipped and badly led, they held on. Arthur Conan-Doyle visited the Italian front in 1916 and sent back this analysis:

> From first to last the Alpini have had the ascendancy in the hill fighting. The spirit in the ranks is something marvellous. There have been occasions when every officer has fallen and yet the men have pushed on, have taken a position and then waited for official directions.
>
> But if that is so, you will ask, why is it that they have not made more impression upon the enemy's position? The answer lies in the strategical position of Italy. The Alps form such a bar across the north that there are only two points where serious operations are possible. One is the Trentino Salient, where Austria can always threaten and invade Italy. She lies in the mountains with the plains beneath her. She can always invade the plain, but the Italians cannot seriously invade the mountains, since the passes would only lead to other mountains beyond.
>
> Therefore, the only possible policy is to hold the Austrians back. This they have successfully done, and though the Austrians with the aid of shattering heavy artillery have recently made some advance, they can never really carry out any serious invasion. The Italians, then, have done all that could be done in this quarter.

It seems that Conan-Doyle saw what he wanted to see, and in 1917 what he judged to be impossible came to pass. At Caporetto, the

Austrians broke through, the Veneto was overrun and 300,000 Italians taken prisoner.

Despite their defeats and the relative success of the Austrians, Italian politicians expected to do well out of the post-war settlement. In 1915 the Treaty of London, signed by the Western Allies, agreed that not only would Trentino, the south Tyrol (with 250,000 German speakers) and Trieste go to Italy, they could also incorporate a stretch of the Dalmatian coast, a port in Albania and most of the Dodecanese islands (those which had been Genoese and Venetian possessions centuries before) off the coast of Turkey.

After their poor showing in the north-east and despite Conan-Doyle's puffery, the Italians had lost a great deal of respect amongst the Allies and as the Treaty of Versailles carved up post-war Europe, much of the London agreement was ultimately ignored. The British Ambassador in Paris summed up the prevailing attitude to Italy: '[it] has been one of supreme contempt up to now and now it is one of extreme annoyance. They all say that the signal for an armistice was the signal for Italy to begin to fight.'

When it became clear that the Dalmatian territories and the Dodecanese would not become Italian, there was great resentment. The government in Rome was made to appear very weak in its conduct of foreign affairs, and domestically seemed unable to keep order. The Partito Socialista Italiano grew very powerful, the red flag flew over many cities and strikes were frequently called. In 1919 Benito Mussolini founded the Fasci di Combattimento in Milan and adopted what he hoped would prove a popular programme: the abolition of the Senate, grants of land to peasant farmers, a more democratic parliament and the confiscation of excessive wartime profits made by industrialists and producers. The new party barely registered. No Fascist deputies were elected and even in his home-town of Predappio in Romagna, Mussolini did not attract a single vote.

In a dizzying series of policy reversals, motivated by nothing more than a hunger for power, Mussolini swung away from the left to the far right in a matter of months. The catalyst was the appearance of the *squadri*. These were groups of paramilitary thugs often led by demobbed junior officers and supported by local landowners and businessmen, and they began to impose order of sorts and violently to oppose the PSI, the Italian Socialist Party. Having been a fertile ground for nationalism, Tuscany spawned many *squadri*, sometimes exporting them to Umbria and Lazio. Mussolini allied himself to the black-shirted *squadristi* and they in turn acknowledged him as a national figurehead. Local bosses, the *ras*, were in effect more immediately dominant, but they saw the eloquent, theatrical, publicity-savvy former newspaper editor as a valuable asset. The *squadristi* often enjoyed more than tacit support from the police and the army. A deadly momentum was building.

At Livorno in 1921, the national conference of the PSI made the rise of Fascism significantly easier. Led by Antonio Gramsci, a faction walked out to form the PCI, the Partito Communista d'Italia. The forces opposing the thugs of the *squadri* were now divided.

By 1922 the Fascist Party had become a popular movement with more than 300,000 members. At a mass rally in Naples, 40,000 roared for a coup d'état. Like Garibaldi, the 'blackshirts' should march on Rome. The parliament in Rome trembled and Mussolini swore: 'a solemn oath that either the government of the country must be given peaceably to the Fascisti or we will take it by force'.

King Victor Emmanuele III was indecisive and badly advised, the government chronically weak, and at the end of October 1922 squads of Fascists entered Rome and seized railway stations, telephone exchanges and post offices and whatever else seemed important. There appears to have been no clear plan, and Mussolini was hedging his bets. As his supporters made their move on Rome, he went to the theatre in Milan with his wife, Rachele, and during the performance whispered: 'The news has got out that the Fascists have mobilised, we must pretend to know nothing about anything.' But it worked. The king refused to sanction action against the *squadristi*, fearing civil war, and would not sign an order imposing martial law. Mussolini arrived on the overnight train from Milan and went to the Quirinale Palace to see the king who promptly appointed him prime minister. And then began a remarkable period in Italian history.

The new regime was conjured out of nothing more substantial than slogans, mysticism, wildly exaggerated propaganda, the machismo cult of Mussolini himself, Il Duce, and it was all backed not by a parliamentary majority but by vicious gangsterism. The *squadristi* purged opposition, committing a series of particularly brutal murders in Florence. Policy was extrapolated out of phrases. 'Better to live one day as a lion than a hundred years as a sheep,' said Mussolini, and foreign policy followed. Perhaps the absurdity is best summed up by Il Duce's office in the Palazzo Venezia in Rome. It was so vast, larger than a ballroom, that civil servants who entered at one end had to communicate with Mussolini by using hand signals. His desk was the sole piece of furniture and it took so long for his ministers to approach it that they were instructed to run the last 20 metres.

The cult of Il Duce was quickly developed by his brother, Arnaldo, and by 1925 he had become something close to a secular god. Posters carrying the words 'Mussolini is always right' were plastered everywhere. Supremely conscious of image and anxious to exploit the new medium of cinema, Il Duce behaved like an actor, going in for a great deal of strutting and attitude-striking, jaw jutting and pouting, scowling and eye-rolling. Comparisons with actors in silent films are entirely apt. But what looks ridiculous now appears to have hypnotised Italy. Driving fast cars, riding fast horses, Il Duce's masculinity was constantly advertised. And only thinly veiled were the stories of his magnetism for women. Apparently hundreds, maybe thousands, found themselves succumbing to his manly urges, on the floor of his vast office, in his private apartments, anywhere his irrepressible virility demanded. It is said he rarely removed his trousers, or his shoes, and was not in the habit of bathing frequently.

Nevertheless, despite all this cavorting and play-acting, the Fascist regime did change the face of large areas of Tuscany. The flatlands to the north and south of Grosseto are known as the Maremma, and in the time of the Etruscans they had been fertile and productive. But from the Roman occupation onwards the drainage systems had been allowed to decay and the fields and pastures reverted to marshland. Malaria mosquitoes thrived and the Maremma could be a dangerous place, especially for those who liked to hunt its wild land. Grand Duke Leopoldo encouraged efforts to revive the Maremma in 1828 but real progress in rebuilding the drainage canals was only made under Mussolini. By 1950 malarial mosquitoes were extinct.

Another of Mussolini's genuine achievements was an accommodation with the papacy. In 1929 the Vatican City became a sovereign state, complete with its own colourful army of Swiss Guards. The concordat settled a generous sum as compensation for the annexation of the Papal States and religious education was formally enshrined in school curricula. The pope went so far as to describe Il Duce as 'this man sent by providence'.

Adolf Hitler saw him as an inspiration, declaring: 'The brown shirt would probably not have existed without the black shirt.' But the relationship was soon inverted. After Mussolini visited Germany in 1937, he seemed to be diminished and began to imitate Hitler. The introduction of the anti-semitic Racial Laws in 1938 ran against the grain of Italian Fascism, and were at first widely ignored. When deportations began many communities successfully hid their Jews. Outside Rome, one of the largest ghettos was in Pitigliano, in southern Tuscany, and even sixty-five years later, old men still boast that not one Jew was found.

In the late 1930s Mussolini suffered from various illnesses and seems to have been in near-constant pain. When Hitler's armies invaded Poland, Il Duce claimed surprise and great disappointment that he had not been consulted or even informed. In fact Hitler probably did tell Mussolini of his plans when they met in the summer of 1939 but was, literally, not understood. The Italian leader's prodigious powers apparently included a mastery of many languages and he liked to claim fluency in German, refusing interpreters at his meetings with Hitler. When the plans to attack Poland were explained, Il Duce probably smiled and nodded, having no clear idea of what was being said to him.

In 1940 Italy entered the Second World War. Once again badly equipped and badly led (there were only light tanks available to the army because Il Duce believed that they were more in keeping with the Italian character), Italian forces were routed in Greece and North Africa. When the Allies landed in Sicily, they met very little opposition. With the Americans in the war, many Italians believed that defeat was inevitable. Plots swirled around Mussolini, and only a fortnight after the invasion of Sicily he was forced to resign and promptly arrested. Even after being rescued by German special forces and set up in the north as the dictator of the Republic of Salò, Mussolini was a spent force, little more than a symbol. German reinforcements had poured through the alpine passes and they began a brilliant fighting retreat, engaging the Allies south of Naples. Throughout the winter of 1943–44 war crept ever closer to Tuscany.

Iris Origo, the author of the *Merchant of Prato*, the fascinating biography of Francesco Datini, had married a Tuscan nobleman, Marchese Antonio Origo. They lived in a large villa at La Foce, in the centre of their farming estate near Montepulciano. Marchesa Origo

kept a diary, later published as *War in Val d'Orcia*. In vivid detail
it records how world war rumbled over the Tuscan landscape, how
its people fared and how the soldiers, prisoners and fugitives of both
sides behaved.

It was a very dangerous business, keeping a war diary, and each
morning Marchesa Origo hid her manuscript in the garden behind
their house. She and her husband also took in refugee children from
the Italian cities and helped escaped Allied prisoners as they attempted
to penetrate German lines and rejoin their comrades in the advance
through Italy. Every day for a year they risked discovery and death,
and Marchesa Origo recorded this extraordinary period without any
sense of drama or fuss. Her diary is surely one of the most valuable
documents to emerge from the chaos of the Second World War.

In September 1943 the Germans billeted a small group of British
prisoners of war at La Foce and the Origos did their best to look after
them:

September 18th 1943.
Antonio is sent for by the German lieutenant who has been left
in command at Chiusi. When Antonio mentions his address,
'Ah, you're the man who has got the British prisoners!' says the
lieutenant. 'I can't spare any men now to take charge of them, but I
could perhaps send up a Carabiniere'. 'Sorry, I can't spare any men
either,' says the captain of the Carabinieri. 'Well, then,' says the
German to Antonio, 'I'll give you a couple of rifles, and you can see
to the guard.' Antonio begins to laugh. 'No, I really can't do that.'
'Well, then – you really think these men won't make any trouble
now?' 'Certainly not.' 'You'd better be responsible for them. And
we'll leave it at that.' Surely a very odd conversation.

In the afternoon we walk down to the prisoners' farm and tell
them of this arrangement, but warn them to continue to keep a
sharp look-out, in case the situation should suddenly change. We
also tell them the war news, which today is better, advance parties
of the Eighth Army having joined up with the Fifth at Eboli.

In the evening we turn on the radio and suddenly hear Mussolini's
voice – 'once', as he remarks, 'well known to you.' After relating
the dramatic circumstances of his capture and of his release he
proceeds to a violent attack upon the King – and ends with an
appeal to Italians to unite once again under his leadership to form

the new Republican Fascist Party. But nothing will come of all this. Too profound a disillusion, too violent a revulsion, is associated for all Italians with Mussolini's name – and now no emotion is left but a weary passivity. That spring is broken.

A constant theme in the diary is confusion. Reliable news of how the war was unfolding in Europe and the Far East was difficult to find, and it was risky to listen to the BBC broadcasts. And even within a short distance of La Foce, the picture was often far from clear. Occasionally a visitor (whose identity is deliberately concealed) arrived with an eye-witness account:

September 26th 1943.
V. arrives to beg us to give shelter to his son, who has left his regiment and is hiding in Rome. Some of his companions are trying to get through to the Allied forces with papers provided by the Vatican, bearing a forged stamp of the German Command. V's account of Rome is grim. Conte Calvi has been arrested and sent to a concentration camp and the 'Piave' Division which he commands has been disbanded. The S.S. rule over the city. Seven German soldiers have been killed by the population and now six thousand hostages have been demanded by the Germans. Sealed trucks leave daily for Germany by rail, carrying Italian soldiers to labour camps. There are frequent rumours, as yet without foundation, of Allied landings . . . .
    New orders issued by General Kesselring award the death penalty for the possession of firearms, for sabotage, or for sheltering or in any way assisting members of enemy forces. The Fascist Government also issues a proclamation awarding the death penalty to those who give help to prisoners of war.

Kesselring's orders left the Origos in no doubt about the potentially dire consequences of what they did almost every day. But to a degree they found themselves less vulnerable than those in the cities still controlled by Fascist officials:

November 5th 1943.
A friend returning from Florence brings accounts of fresh arrests in the provinces of Florence and Pisa: mostly innocuous old Senators whose only crime is that they are known to be loyal Monarchists . . .

In Florence the Prefect is a fanatic, and has issued most inconvenient orders. One of the most unpopular is that ordering all employers to give a gift of a thousand lire to each of their employees, to celebrate the 28 Ottobre [the date of the March on Rome].

Events at La Foce often took place in a dangerously farcical sequence. Escaped Allied prisoners hid in the woods behind the house and the estate and its owners had become widely known as a resort of help and information. Marchesa Origo worried constantly that if Allied soldiers on the run knew about La Foce then it was only a matter of time before the Germans knew too and arrested her and her husband. Sometimes the two sides almost met:

December 28th 1943.
Coming downstairs this morning, I am greeted by the by now familiar information: 'There are some Germans in the fattoria courtyard – and an English prisoner in the garden.' I hastily put the latter into the little room by the garden door where I do the flowers and (while Antonio is dealing with the Germans) listen to his story. He was originally, he says, in a camp near Trento, and has already twice been recaptured: the first time by the Germans, from whom he escaped near Trento; the second time by the Fascist militia who put him in the barracks at Arezzo – from which he escaped during an air-raid. He then found refuge with a family near Sinalunga – but yesterday someone gave him away, the police turned up, and the friend who was with him was arrested, while he himself only got away by the skin of his teeth. 'They were father and mother to me,' he said of the family which had sheltered him, and his chief anxiety was lest they should now be in danger. It was difficult to know what to advise him, since many men who have tried it have told us it is now impossible to get through the German lines, and that in the mountains south of Rome many prisoners have been rounded up. But he was determined to attempt it and, after consulting a map, he wearily set out.

Acts of individual courage became almost commonplace, and when the Germans began rounding up the Jews in Tuscany, many escaped the deadly net, some with the help of the Church:

The Archbishop of Florence, Cardinal della Costa, has taken a courageous stand. When some of his nuns were arrested, in consequence of having given shelter to some Jewish women in their convent, the Cardinal, putting on his full panoply, went straight to the German Command. 'I have come to you,' he said, 'because I believe you, as soldiers, to be people who recognise authority and hierarchy – and who do not make subordinates responsible for merely carrying out orders. The order to give shelter to those unfortunate Jewish women was given by me: therefore I request you to free the nuns, who have merely carried out orders, and to arrest me in their stead.' The German immediately gave orders for the nuns to be freed, but permitted himself to state his surprise that a man like the Cardinal should take under his protection such people as the Jews, the scum of Europe, responsible for all the evils of the present day. The Cardinal did not enter upon the controversy. 'I look upon them,' he said, 'merely as persecuted human beings; as such it is my Christian duty to help and defend them. One day,' he gave himself the pleasure of adding, 'perhaps not far off, you will be persecuted and then I shall defend you.'

As the front edged closer and closer to La Foce, the countryside was overrun by retreating German soldiers. Looting was widespread, and many farm-workers found their storehouses emptied as their hams, cheeses and even grain were stolen. When the Germans retreated, they did not hesitate to destroy Tuscany's history:

June 28th 1944 [Montepulciano].
In the afternoon the Germans blow up some houses inside the town, to obstruct the inner road, and also, alas, destroy the magnificent Medicean gateway at the foot of the town. Antonio tries in vain to save it, but does succeed in saving the fine fourteenth-century arcades of the old hospital. The Germans say that we must expect some shelling here tomorrow, but that that should be the last day.
  'You want der Tommy: well, by Friday you'll have him!'
  The Montepulcanesi, however, as the end draws near, are more and more jumpy. When I went out this evening, they were standing about in little knots, looking at the ruins of their gateway, and finding some comfort in the fact that the image of the Madonna, which stood in the upper part of the arch, is miraculously intact.

Little family parties with prams and bundles were making their way to the shelters for the night.

The evening news brings little change. The guns go on rumbling, and we go to bed expecting the bridge to be blown up during the night.

On 29 June 1944 the moment of liberation at last arrived. The Origos had temporarily abandoned La Foce, fearing fierce fighting around the estate, and had sought refuge in Montepulciano. In the late evening the British arrived:

Well, they have come – at last! All day the partisans have been watching the roads, and at four p.m. the first news reached us: 'They are coming!' The news coincided with a burst of German shelling, but meet them we must, so we hurried along the narrow streets, climbing over the rubble and dodging into doorways until we reached the Bersaglio, the Bracci's stretch of hillside garden overlooking the road to Villa Bianca. And at last, scrambling up the steep grassy hillside, we saw the first British helmet! Beneath it was the round, flushed face of a very young subaltern, who (as we afterwards were told) had no business to be there at all, but had set out on a little reconnoitring party of his own. He was followed by an officer in the R.E, (who wanted to find out about the bridge) and by four or five men. We came forward and greeted them with tears in our eyes – we all shook hands – the peasants brought out glasses of wine. A young partisan sprang up out of nowhere and demanded a gun, to fight by their side. Remembering, however, that twenty Germans were still just above our heads . . . I went straight to the point. 'How many of you are there?' But the young officer, in addition to breathlessness, had a severe stutter: 'B-b-b--barely t-t-two d-d-d-dozen!' he brought out with maddening slowness, and I found myself replying crossly, 'It isn't nearly enough!' The young man's actions, however, were less hesitant than his speech, and as soon as the partisan was able to tell him in what part of the town the Germans were, he and his men set off there at once. We then hurried back, and under the arch of the old gateway of the town we met the other platoon. Very strange it seemed, to see them marching up the Montepulciano street – and oh, what a welcome sight! In every doorway there were beaming faces to greet them . . .

I heard one old man saying, as tears streamed down his cheeks, 'I don't mind dying, now that I've seen them arrive!'

The liberation was not an unmixed blessing. French North African troops known as Goums formed part of the Fifth Army and their behaviour was barbaric. Iris Origo reported that they looted, and raped girls, young women and even an old lady of eighty. There was privation everywhere as people tried to find enough of the shattered remnants of their old lives to patch them together again. Water, food, shelter were all in short supply. Often the most urgent task was to re-roof bombed buildings to keep out the weather and allow children and old people a dry place to sleep. But after all that they had been through, the countless risks they had taken, Marchesa Origo found time to write a fitting last entry in her remarkable diary:

> Nevertheless, for the future I am hopeful. The whirlwind has passed, and now, whatever destruction it may have left, we can begin to build again. And it is here that the deepest qualities of the Italian people will have a chance to show themselves. To speak of the patience and endurance, the industry and resourcefulness of the Italian workman has become almost a commonplace. But, like other commonplaces, it is true, and sometimes, in times of crisis, these qualities reach a degree that is almost heroic. Time and suffering have engraved them in the lines of the peasant-women's faces – a sorrow too deep for complaint, a patience that has something sculptural, eternal. Resigned and laborious, they and their men-folk turn back from the fresh graves and the wreckage of their homes to their accustomed daily toil. It is they who will bring the land to life again.
>
> The Fascist and German menaces are receding. The day will come when at last the boys will return to their ploughs, and the dusty clay-hills of the Val d'Orcia will again 'blossom like the rose'. Destruction and death have visited us, but now – there is hope in the air.

The whirlwind passed on through Tuscany and four days after Marchesa Origo met the red-faced subaltern at Montepulciano, the Allies reached Siena. General Yves Montsambert, commanding the French Expeditionary Force and an American division, surrounded the city and then issued a surprising order: anyone who fired a shell into Siena 'would be shot'. Mercifully the token garrison surrendered without a fight and the medieval city survived intact. Other Tuscan towns and cities were less fortunate: Poggibonsi suffered badly and Pisa and Livorno were shelled. Apart from its sixteenth-century walls, Grosseto had to be largely rebuilt.

Allied commanders like General Montsambert appear to have done what was possible to avoid needless destruction, and their consideration was by no means one-sided. When the front line reached Florence, the Fascist defenders exploited any hesitation and delayed the capture of the city for as long as possible. Many medieval and renaissance buildings on the southern bank of the Arno were destroyed and every bridge blown, except for the Ponte Vecchio. With Mussolini as his guide, Hitler, the failed painter, had visited Florence in 1938, and it was said that express orders from Berlin forbade the removal of the Ponte Vecchio. It was to prove a significant strategic and untypically sentimental misjudgement. To get across the Arno, partisans secured the northern exit of the Corridoio Vasariano and like the grand dukes before them, Allied assault troops entered it at the Pitti Palace and stole across the river, unseen, to the Uffizi.

Once a bridgehead had been established in the centre of the city, German troops appear to have retreated rather than risk a very damaging street fight. Panzer tanks did not rumble into the Piazza del Duomo and mortar shells did not punch holes in the façade of Santa Maria del Fiore. But shooting continued. Florence was a city of surprising loyalties. Die-hard Fascists fired from the rooftops on advancing Allied columns before disappearing into the warren of medieval lanes. The German consul, Gerhard Wolf, had risked his life again and again to protect Florence and Florentines from the excesses of Nazism, while the director of the British School had been strongly pro-Fascist. And the fanatical Prefect noted by Iris Origo did as much damage as possible before fleeing the city.

After the liberation of Florence in August 1944, and the onset of autumn and winter, the Allied advance gradually ground to a halt. The Germans had dug in in the Apennine passes. Tuscany had survived better than most places, and as the Allies fought their way across the north European plain in early 1945 and Nazi Germany ultimately collapsed, the Second World War in Europe shuddered to a close.

The overwhelming instinct of most Italians was to put fascism behind them as quickly as possible, and to make a clean break with the excesses and the horrors of the past. The first casualty of the post-war period was to be the monarchy. King Victor Emmanuel III had hesitated fatally after the march on Rome in 1922, and when Mussolini was removed twenty years later, he blundered once more. In 1943 he fled Rome and the German occupation for Brindisi in what looked more like a panicky act of cowardice than the strong leadership Italy badly needed at that moment. In an attempt to preserve the institution of the monarchy, Victor Emmanuel abdicated in May 1946 in favour of his son, Umberto. But it proved little more than a parting gesture. A referendum result declared Italy a republic, and few regions were more emphatic in their rejection than Tuscany. More than 70 per cent voted to remove the king and reconstitute Italy as a modern nation. It was time to move on.

After the failure of the punitive settlement of 1919 and 1920, the Allies took a radically different approach at the close of the Second World War. The best bulwark against fascism – and communism – was regeneration. After a devastating war, Europe would be rebuilt. Italy took full advantage, and between 1943 and 1948 American aid amounted to a massive \$3.5 billion. The north industrialised, and in Tuscany smaller businesses were established around the cities. At 44 per cent of the workforce, the proportion still in agriculture in 1945 remained very high, but as jobs were created, the exodus into the cities began.

The post-war settlement also radically realigned Italian politics. Supported by the Vatican, the Christian Democrats came to power in 1948, led by a genuine statesman in Alcide de Gaspari. Having been persecuted and imprisoned by the Fascists before the war, de Gaspari was given sanctuary by the papacy, working in the Vatican Library as a cataloguer for thirteen years. Nevertheless, when he at last took office as prime minister, he attempted to distance himself and his party from the Church. He could see that Italy's future lay with her European neighbours, and he was one of the founding fathers of the EEC. The Treaty of Rome was signed in 1957 by the original six members of the European Community: France, Germany, Belgium, The Netherlands, Luxembourg and Italy.

There were immediate benefits. Production of factory goods soared and within a generation, Italy changed from a predominantly peasant society to one driven by industry and the needs of urban life. In a series of coalitions with smaller parties, the Christian Democrats oversaw these seismic societal changes. On the surface politics appeared to be as turbulent as ever, with fifty governments in the fifty years since the Second World War. It developed into a defamatory cliché that the Italians demanded constant and chaotic political change, a revolving door for prime ministers and governments. Instability appeared to be the norm.

In fact, the opposite was the case. Between 1948 and 1992 the Christian Democrats were never out of government, always dominant partners in various combinations of coalition. The real problem was not constant change but a stultifying continuity. One of the central goals of the Christian Democrat hegemony was to keep the Italian Communist Party out of power. Many of the partisans helped by Marchesa Origo were Communists and that sustained resistance to Fascism brought them tremendous esteem, especially in Tuscany, Umbria and Emilia-Romagna, the central regions of Italy. At its height the PCI had 1.7 million members, but with the covert help of the Americans, the Christian Democrats plotted successfully to maintain themselves in power.

Political frustration began to build. In the late 1960s and early '70s protest turned into terrorism, perpetrated by both ends of the political spectrum. A bomb in the Piazza Fontana in Milan killed sixteen people in 1969. In 1978 the president of the Christian Democrats and former prime minister, Aldo Moro, was kidnapped by the Red Brigades and killed, and two years later a bomb planted by neo-Fascists in Bologna station slaughtered eighty-five. But the terrorists never ignited any mass unrest or sustained realignment. Part of the reason was that in the same period Italy was enjoying economic success and rising living standards. Industrial wages doubled between 1968 and 1973, and a settlement which pegged them to the rate of inflation was enshrined in law.

There was genuine mass frustration at the obvious abuses and inefficiencies of the public sector. Controlled for so long by one political party, the state had become largely corrupt. Government departments behaved like independent fiefdoms held together by complex obligations between individuals. Surveys showed popular dissatisfaction at between 70 per cent and 80 per cent. Central government became widely discredited and often ignored.

Amidst all of this unhappiness, however, Italy became fashionable. A generation of film directors and fashion designers lifted the image of Italy out of the ruins of wartime. Glamorous and voluptuous actresses and sophisticated actors spoke of a new nation. Fashion flourished in Tuscany. World-famous names such as Guccio Gucci, Salvatore Ferragamo and Emilio Pucci established reputations and profitable businesses, their shops continuing an ancient Tuscan tradition in textiles.

As foreign travel became possible and then cheaper, with package holidays particularly popular, Tuscany's tourist economy began to prosper, and Florence and all the glories of the Renaissance were seen as unmissable attractions. The sun shone and the future seemed assured.

At the end of September 1966, it began to rain. In a biblical cycle, it carried on raining for forty days, and on 2 and 3 November, more than half a metre fell on Tuscany. The Arno roiled with brown floodwater but the embankments on the Lungarno streets of Florence were holding. Upstream, however, there was danger. A huge reservoir had filled alarmingly and the pressure threatened to burst the retaining dam. It was decided to open the sluices to relieve it and release vast volumes of water into the Arno, but remarkably, no-one thought to warn the authorities downstream in Florence.

The first warning came from a nightwatchman. He was employed to patrol the jewellers' shops on the Ponte Vecchio. In the early hours of the morning of 4 November he telephoned his employers to tell them that the old bridge was shaking. When shopkeepers arrived to remove their stock, watching policemen were asked why they had not alerted the houses on the riverbank or any of the rescue services. 'We have no orders.'

It was only a matter of an hour before the raging Arno poured over the embankments and into the city. Half a million tonnes of water engulfed Florence, gushing into churches, houses, museums and shops. Lying near the Ponte Vecchio, the Uffizi was immediately inundated. It happened so quickly that people were drowned in the underpass at Santa Maria Novella Station, and in all thirty-five Florentines lost their lives. Many thousands of works of art were badly damaged; some destroyed by a lethal cocktail of water and heating oil from burst basement tanks. A crucifixion painted by Cimabue was washed into the central flow of the raging river and only rescued by brave men in a motorboat.

Without being asked, Florentines mobilised an impromptu rescue force. Paintings were taken down, even fallen or floating fragments of paint from frescoes or panels were painstakingly collected and carried to the restorers in plastic bags. Three thousand paintings and dozens of major buildings were badly affected by water, particularly in the lower-lying Santa Croce district. Many pieces were found to be beyond rescue.

In Florence public buildings in the centre of the city carry a memory of the devastation; a small marble plaque fixed, it seems, impossibly high on a wall with '*Livello dell'Arno, 6 xi 1966*' carved above a red line. The rain, and the flood, damaged Florence much more seriously than the Second World War or the Spanish soldiers of the sixteenth-century sieges.

By 1970 the Italian constitution had finally embraced the aspiration of regionalism. Along with nineteen others, the region of Tuscany gained a significant measure of autonomy, and its borders were broadly those of the Grand Duchy. With Umbria and Emilia-Romagna, Tuscany elected a Communist regional government, forming part of the 'Red Belt' of Italy. It seemed that voters who were happy to cast their ballot for the Christian Democrats nationally could easily travel some distance along the political spectrum to vote Communist. And yet the best-selling newspaper in Tuscany is not the Communist *L'Unità* or the left-wing *La Repubblica*, but the right-wing *La Nazione*. The secret is simple, and it plays to another impulse. *La Nazione* publishes a Tuscan edition with many pages of even more local news covering all of the ten provinces inside the region.

The weather struck hard at Tuscany once more in the late twentieth century. In the winter of 1985–86 temperatures plummeted and a hard and sustained frost gripped the land. It was most extreme on the higher ground, up amongst the terraces and the land given over to pasture and olive groves. Many of these gnarled, tough and twisted old trees were hundreds of years old, having survived savage weather and savage pruning. But the frost and ice storms of 1985 were without parallel, and between 50 per cent and 70 per cent of Tuscany's olive trees were killed. It was a disaster, something profoundly upsetting. Tuscans felt that part of their heritage had died.

What lifted spirits was the Sorpasso. In 1986 the Italian economy was reckoned to have grown larger than those of both Great Britain and France. Usually arcane measurements of GDP, net export and import values became a cause for national rejoicing. Perhaps there was a sense of finally shuffling off the weight of the recent past and regaining the old mercantile prowess of the Middle Ages and the Renaissance.

Prowess of a different sort also fed Italian self-esteem. One of the most powerful forces in Italian society is football. The country unites behind the national team and there were wild and lengthy celebrations when Italy won the World Cup in 1982 and again in 2006. But football also colours a vivid patchwork of local allegiances, and in Tuscany passions run especially high. Fiorentina, based at the Stadio Communale in Florence, are the premier team and their history has been operatic: full of glory, scandal and despair.

Known as the Viola, after the colour of their violet strip, the club has been Italian champions, winners of the Italian cup and successful in European competitions. But when in 1990 the owners decided to sell the great Roberto Baggio to the Turin club, Juventus, for what was then a world record figure, the city exploded. Fans rioted in the streets of Florence, protest placards were hung in the Piazza della Repubblica and the directors of the club required police protection. With the arrival of the Argentinian striker, Gabriel Batistuta, Fiorentina began to do well again, winning the Italian cup in 1996 and consistently finishing high in the Serie A, the premier division. Like the great *condottieri*, the Argentinian became a Florentine hero with the nickname Batigol (something like 'Goal-basher'). And when he was transferred to Roma, more mayhem ensued. But worse was to come.

All of the Serie A clubs had borrowed huge sums against the sale of future TV rights, and when these collapsed in 2002, Fiorentina – maintaining a long Florentine tradition – was found to have borrowed more than most. The club went bankrupt. This meant the dissolution of Fiorentina and the relegation of a replacement entity to the lowest division, Serie C2B.

An amazing Fiorentina Renaissance then took place, with the reformed club somehow able to jump two divisions in one season and finding itself restored to the Serie A by 2005. A year later the revelation of match-fixing scandals saw Fiorentina relegated again, but this time only to Serie B. Now, they seem to be on an upward curve, enjoying renewed success in Europe, and seeing fewer riots.

Football in Tuscany, as in most of the rest of Italy, is a way of life, a daily topic of conversation, a soap opera, sometimes only a game but always an art form. After victory, what Italian fans prize most is style. Scorer of many goals in the 1982 World Cup, Paolo Rossi was the embodiment of elegance, poise, skill and speed, the perfect example of a stylish footballer. And he was good-looking, with flowing, jet-black hair. It is not difficult to imagine him amongst the portraits in the corner of Sandro Botticelli's *Adoration of the Magi*. It was said that Lorenzo de' Medici and his brother, Giuliano, played a version of football in the Piazza Santa Croce. There can be no doubt that they would have applauded the grace, *la bella figura*, of Paolo Rossi.

Football even came to have a profound impact on politics. By 1990 voters had become overwhelmingly disenchanted with the political system. Surveys showed high percentages demanding change. In Milan a radical and courageous magistrate, Antonio di Pietro, spearheaded the fight against corruption in the Mani Pulite ('Clean Hands') campaign. The murky inner workings of what was known as Tangentopoli ('Bribesville') were gradually uncovered and most were shocked at its scale. More than 35 per cent of all the deputies in the Italian parliament were involved. Pressure for change became irresistible.

In 1992 there occurred what was popularly known as the end of the First Republic. After referenda, the voting system was changed from proportional representation to something more like the British system. The Christian Democrat party saw no option but to dissolve itself and reform, and what seemed at first like a new party entered the arena. *Forza Italia* is a chant shouted from the football terraces, meaning 'Go, Italy!', but under the leadership of media tycoon and owner of A.C. Milan, Silvio Berlusconi, it became a political party. Drawing heavily on the language and sentiment of football, it seemed to speak directly to the electorate and signal a new departure. Portraying himself as uninvolved in the corrupt politics of the past, Berlusconi swept to power in 1994. But soon it became clear that he was not a man apart, and in fact was suspected of all sorts of self-serving activities, quasi-legal and plain illegal. To many it appeared that the main motivation of the media mogul was to use political office to secure immunity for himself and his business interests. His first government lasted only seven months.

Terrorism in Italy did not cease in 1980 with the Bologna Station bomb. On 27 May 1993 a huge explosion outside the Uffizi in Florence killed five people, demolished a building and tore holes in the walls of the gallery, damaging many paintings. It was a car bomb containing 100kg of TNT, and it had been planted by the Mafia. After the government assault on organised crime began in the early 1990s, centred on Sicily, Mafia bosses decided that Florence and its famous art gallery would be a suitable target for retaliation. They wanted not only to create a climate of fear well beyond their heartlands in the south, but also to damage the cultured image of Italy and terrify and discourage foreign tourists. Where better than Florence?

An episode combining violence, money, the lowest sort of politics and high culture seems a perverse note on which to end this narrative. But a backward glance through this history will quickly reveal the Uffizi bombing of 1993 as only the latest in many such episodes. The story of Tuscany is by turns sublime and inspiring, but almost never saintly and often brutally violent. Above all, it is a tale of human beings and the extremes of which they are capable. And that is at least part of the fascination. The Tuscan landscape and townscape so obviously bear the marks of human activity over millennia that it is impossible to feel remote from even the heightened lives of the great artists, writers and scientists who have peopled this remarkable place. All seems familiar, warm and close. In the streets of Siena and Florence or amongst the evening hills of Chianti, the past everywhere whispers its stories.

Postscript

After the heat begins to ease off the day in the late afternoon, there is often a breath of air in the Piazza della Repubblica. Open to long vistas at each end and with Pitigliano's tufa cliffs dropping away sheer below the parapets, the piazza cools as the westering sun throws the shadow of the Orsini fortress across it. From a table outside the Bar Centrale, it is possible to watch the whole town wake for a second time. Shops, cafés, the bank and the barber's shop on the corner open after the long lunchtime siesta. Old men sit down on the steps of shaded doorways in the Via Roma and old ladies shuffling in their slippers shop for the evening meal. All of them watch intently as their world goes by, again.

History walks past the café tables. Carla Antonini floats over the paving stones, her blond tresses trailing like Botticelli's Venus's as she makes her way to her wine shop. Giuliano, smoking too much, as always, nods to her and watches her walk up the Via Roma with routine interest. He sees her every day, floating. With sallow, hollow cheeks, heavy-lidded eyes and a hook nose, Giuliano looks like Fra Savonarola but certainly does not think like him. La Vedova, 'Sophia the Widow', still dresses in black, the best-cut and most fashionable black, but her evening smile beguiles like Claudia Cardinale's.

They are all still there, those people who made Tuscany. They are still making it. For past the superficial resemblances, the good looks and the eternities of the landscape always glimpsed from the clifftop streets of Pitigliano, the town itself turns out to be the sum of all that experience in one place. The essence of Tuscany is in its towns and cities, what Italians call *civiltà*. A dictionary will list the meaning as 'civilisation', but that does not even approach its Tuscan sense. *Civiltà* is something like townishness, community, a civic sense, pride, identity all wrapped up together with its tangible consequences: the great churches and the paintings and sculpture inside them, the Palio, Dante, Boccaccio, the designs of Guccio Gucci, the convulsions of Fiorentina, and a lip-curling contempt for any other town that is not our town.

On the same page as *civiltà*, *città* is, incidentally, defined as a city but in truth the word is more a mark of status than scale. Even though only a thousand souls live in the medieval quarter of Pitigliano, it is the *centro storico*, the centre of history, and it is most certainly *una città*. *Che bella città!* Tuscans live in the centre of their history, its achievements and sadnesses lie all around them, and they see themselves as its continuators, the lineal descendants of famous men and women, for they walk precisely in their footsteps, every day of their seamless lives.

Tuscan townishness is also built on talk, and sometimes action. When the *città* stirs into life at around 4 p.m., Pitigliano begins to talk to itself. Old men meet at the fountain in the Piazza della Repubblica, people going to work stop to exchange news, even though they met that morning. There is always something more. And this is a world that foreigners without the language cannot enter, for they have nothing to say. The republic of talk requires exactly that, but only that. Those who have some Italian or Pitiglianese are always asked for their news and encouraged even when they struggle. There is a Tuscan saying: 'Keep away from sick doctors, dogs that don't bark, men who don't talk and people who go to mass twice a day.'

Civiltà is from *civis*, the Latin for a city, and a community. Citizens in Pitigliano seem less divided than others. There are no great mansions in the *centro storico*, everyone lives piled on top of everyone else and there is a certain egalitarianism. No doubt the old *signore* at number 98 has a mattress stuffed with banknotes, a matter for endless speculation, but on the surface, the divides are not stark. The republic of talk is therefore more inclusive and knowledge is shared more than in most places. An elegiac example is the habit of death posters. When someone dies in a Tuscan town, their relatives have black-bordered posters printed and fixed on walls where they can be widely seen. The community is diminished, the generations unfurl into their future, the past slips by, bit by bit. Everyone wants to know.

Pitigliano comes chattering to life in the early evening. Much more than *buona sera* is exchanged as *la città* comes out to walk and talk. Women and their daughters or nieces or granddaughters link arms, youthful friends do the same, men stop to shake hands and fail to get any further. Some settle with a glass of cold wine outside the Bar Centrale and the world comes to them.

And what do Tuscans talk about? Anything. Whatever is fresh. Football, the government, the weather, aches and pains, heartaches, scandal, supper, the Sicilian oranges Maria has in her shop, anything will do, nothing is too trivial. And they cannot stop. At mass in the cathedral, women turn and whisper to each other, teenagers dodge into a side chapel to text, and behind the priest there was once an animated argument amongst the choir. All of this endless talk is heaped on the mountain of knowledge every Tuscan has access to and it creates the strongest possible bond between all who live in these remarkable communities.

And it also makes everything possible. Powerful and vibrant communities throughout history – in Athens, London, Paris and New York – they have all produced great art of every sort. When human beings live close to each other in some comfort, creativity flowers. And nowhere did it bloom more beautifully than in Tuscany, *La Bella Toscana*.

Bibliography

Abulafia, David (ed.), *The Mediterranean in History* (London, Thames & Hudson, 2003)

Asprey, Robert B., *The Reign of Napoleon Bonaparte* (New York, Basic Books, 2001)

Balletto, Barbara (ed.), *Insight Guide Tuscany* (London, APA Publications, 1998)

Baránski, Zygmunt G. and West, Rebecca J. (ed.), *The Cambridge Companion to Modern Italian Culture* (Cambridge, Cambridge University Press, 2001)

Baxandall, Michael, *Giotto and the Orators,* Oxford-Warburg Studies (Oxford, Oxford University Press, 1971)

Baxandall, Michael, *Painting and Experience in Fifteenth-Century Italy* (Oxford, Oxford University Press, 1972)

Bentley, James, *A Guide to Tuscany* (London, Penguin, 1987)

Bing, Gertrude (ed.), *Giovanni Rucellai ed Il Suo Zibaldone*, (Warburg Institute, 1960)

Burke, Peter, *Tradition and Innovation in Renaissance Italy* (London, B.T. Batsford Ltd, 1972)

Cellini, Benvenuto, *Autobiography* (London, Penguin Classics, 1956)

David, Elizabeth, *Italian Food* (Barrie and Jenkins, 1954)

Davies, John A., *Italy in the Nineteenth Century* (Oxford, Oxford University Press, 2000)

Duggan, Christopher, *A Concise History of Italy* (Cambridge, Cambridge University Press, 1984)

Facaros, Dana and Pauls, Michael, *Tuscany, Umbria and the Marches* (London, Cadogan, 1989)

Gombrich, E.H., *The Story of Art* (London, Phaidon, 1950)

Hay, Denys, *The Italian Renaissance* (Cambridge, Cambridge University Press, 1968)

Hibbert, Christopher, *The Rise and Fall of the House of Medici* (London, Penguin, 1974)

Hudson, Roger (ed.), *The Grand Tour* (London, The Folio Society, 1993)

Jacob, E.F., *Italian Renaissance Studies* (London, Faber and Faber, 1960)

Kristeller, Paul Oskar, *Renaissance Thought II: Papers on Humanism and the Arts* (London, HarperCollins, 1965)

King, Ross, *Brunelleschi's Dome: the Story of the Great Cathedral in Florence* (London, Vintage, 2008)

Le Goff, Jacques, *The Birth of Europe* (Oxford, Blackwell, 2005)

Naughtie, James, *The Making of Music* (London, John Murray, 2007)

Origo, Iris, *The Merchant of Prato* (London, Penguin, 1992)

Origo, Iris, *War in the Val d'Orcia* (London, Allison & Busby, 2001)

Parker, Geoffrey, *The Military Revolution: Military Innovation and the Rise of the West, 1500–1800* (Cambridge, Cambridge University Press, 1988)

Riley-Smith, Jonathan, *The Crusades* (London, Continuum, 1990)

Strathern, Paul, *The Medici: Godfathers of the Renaissance* (London, Pimlico, 2003)

Romer, Elizabeth, *The Tuscan Year: Life and Food in an Italian Valley* (London, Weidenfeld & Nicolson, 1984)

Rosie, George, *Curious Scotland: Tales from a Hidden History* (London, Granta, 2004)

Shearman, John, *Mannerism* (London, Pelican, 1967)

Vasari, Giorgio, *Lives of the Artists* (London, Penguin edition, 1965)

Whitrow, G.J., *Time in History: Views of Time from Prehistory to the Present Day* (Oxford, Oxford University Press, 1988)

Yates, Frances A., *Giordano Bruno and the Hermetic Tradition* (London, Routledge & Kegan Paul, 1964)

Yates, Frances A., *The Art of Memory* (London, Penguin, 1966)

Index

Note: Throughout the index "K." and "Q." stand for "King" and "Queen" respectively and in long titles "GD." has been used to represent "Grand Duke".